THE EVERYTHING®

TROPICAL FISH BOOK

Carlo DeVito & Gregory Skomal

Adams Media Corporation
Avon, Massachusetts

An Everything® Series Book.
Everything® is a registered trademark of Adams Media Corporation.

Published by Adams Media Corporation
57 Littlefield Street, Avon, MA 02322. U.S.A
www.adamsmedia.com

ISBN: 1-58062-343-3

Printed in the United States of America.

J I H G F E D C B

Library of Congress Cataloging-in-Publication Data available
upon request from the Publisher

This publication is designed to provide accurate and authoritative information with regard
to the subject matter covered. It is sold with the understanding that the publisher is not
engaged in rendering legal, accounting, or other professional advice. If legal advice or other
expert assistance is required, the services of a competent professional person should be
sought.

> — From a *Declaration of Principles* jointly adopted
> by a Committee of the American Bar Association and a
> Committee of Publishers and Associations

Illustrations by Barry Littmann and Kathie Kelleher

This book is available at quantity discounts for bulk purchases.
For information, call 1-800-872-5627.

Table of Contents

CONTENTS

Introduction

You can't pet a fish. You can't take it for a ride in a car. You can't put a bandanna around its neck and call it Butch and bring it to college with you. Taco Bell and Red Dog Beer don't have catchy ads using fish as pitchmen. You can't teach it to repeat dirty words when your mother isn't around. When your boyfriend or girlfriend leaves you, your fish will never snuggle with you and make you feel better. Of course, fish don't shed on the couch or stain the carpet, either.

But in some respects, owning fish is about more than owning a dog or cat. I think it is important to understand that becoming an aquarist isn't really about keeping fish; it is about understanding and sustaining an ecosystem. It is about understanding the interaction of species and communities.

Like most people, I became fascinated with fish as a kid. In my case, it was when my parents brought home a goldfish that we had won at a local fair. After throwing a Ping-Pong ball into a crowded mountain of little goldfish bowls, we had brought home our smooth, flashy, golden trophy. I was thrilled. I was fascinated, and loved to watch it swim around and wait for food, or react when the bowl was moved or new things were placed near it on the counter. My mother was no fan of this new creature. It was yet another new pet she was responsible for, aside from the dog I had always promised to walk and feed, but never did, and the injured squirrel I had found and insisted we save.

Greg Skomal, my co-author, and I met when I was in fifth grade and he in sixth. Like other children our age, in the summers, bored with endless days of playing baseball, swimming, and capture the flag, we went to a small pond nearby. There with his brother Burt and another friend, Condo, we tried to catch frogs, turtles, and assorted wild fish, while avoiding snakes, water rats, and groundskeepers. This pond was on a golf course, and we knew for a fact that they were none too fond of their new "environmentalists." This, of course, made it all the more fun. We had in fact discovered a new world, far more fascinating than *Marlon Perkins' Wild Kingdom* ever showed us. It was real and up close, if not just a little less dangerous.

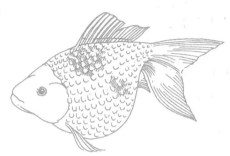

While we had already started to keep community tropical fish tanks, this gave us a fun new way of exploring the world. We brought home a huge array of sunnys, minnows, perches, and other wild fish and put them in the tank. There we watched them interact with the other fish. It was fascinating. While they were not nearly as pretty as some of the other fish, they were all the more intensely watched, because they were "real" fish, not purchased from pet stores, but daringly captured from the dangerous wilds of Connecticut golf courses.

Such was our introduction into the hobby of fishkeeping. Each of us moved forward, one ahead of the other, keeping more and more interesting fish. We all had community tanks, housing schools of neons, angelfish, swordtails, and various odd catfish. Then Greg moved up, as we perceived it, keeping wild fish in his tank. We all followed suit. Then he went on to some of the more incompatible fish, like oscars, Jack Dempseys, firemouths, and other cichlids. Then it was on to the mother of all fish tanks—saltwater.

It seems mean now, but I remember watching angelfish gang up on a group of other fish, and then watch a Siamese fighting fish chase the angelfish. We stood in horror as we watched the oscars dine first on food pellets, then on feeder goldfish. We experimented with tubifex worms and earthworms. We learned about chemistry, biology, and, in the long term, I think, learned many valuable lessons that went beyond the scope of just a hobbyist.

I had never enjoyed science in school, and didn't think of myself as a scientist. But, in setting up filters, learning how water is purified, learning about plants and how they are valuable to fish life, why algae is both good and bad, what nitrates are, and how babies are born to egg-layers and live-bearers, I became a participant in a mesmerizing show of nature's force and vibrancy. Fishkeeping was a crash course in how life works and an interesting one at that.

Understanding these elements meant the difference between being able to keep first goldfish and then more interesting species. And in the end, I realized that many of us understood a lot more science than we thought we did.

As we became more involved, we learned more about the different species and interacted with those who bred and raised tropical fish and exchanged tips and information. And we felt proud whenever someone came to our house and marveled at our aquariums.

Today, Greg is a marine biologist, enjoying to this day a calling that started out as just a hobby. And for me, as my wife and I plan a new water garden, complete with goldfish, those lessons are still invaluable. And fishkeeping is still just as fun.

Who Is This Book For?

The breadth of this book alone will make you a well-respected—and well-rounded—aquarist. Few hobbyists have this much interest in every type of fishkeeping. However, it is not uncommon for hobbyists to want to try something else after they have set up their first tank. Sometimes people want to spend more time raising fancy goldfish. Others start a perfectly nice community tank and then move into the world of more aggressive families of fish or to marine tanks. In any event, there is no book on the market more geared toward helping you understand the many types of ecosystems you can create, and the transitions you can make among them, than this book.

Each section of this book is designed for the beginner to the intermediate. Within these pages, we have tackled many different topics and hope that we have anticipated all the different questions that might arise for those hobbyists. Once you've mastered the basics, you'll be ready to explore the many resources available for experts in a particular area of interest—such as books specializing in your favorite exotic fish and their care.

How This Book Is Organized

This book looks at three different categories of fish: cold freshwater fish (goldfish and koi); tropical freshwater fish; and marine (or saltwater) fish. The difference between cold freshwater fish and tropical fish is that tropical fish need a warmer water temperature to thrive, while koi and goldfish need colder temperatures. Community fish found in a common tropical fish tank usually require temperatures of 75° to 82°F. Goldfish and koi require waters generally 10 to 15 degrees colder. Though it is possible for goldfish and koi to survive in warmer water, they tend to be sluggish and more prone to diseases. In short, it would be inhumane to keep them at warmer temperatures. Marine fish can only survive in salt water, and therefore bring with them their own unique issues.

The essentials of fishkeeping—setup, care, and feeding—appear in each of the three sections both for your convenience's sake and because the specifics vary from species to species. What aquarist wants to keep searching from one section to another, looking for important information in far-flung sections of the book? The idea is that for the hobbyist only interested in freshwater tropical fish, he or she does not have to go flipping all over the book, but can stay within the section of their interest. Where things are common to most species, we have grouped them together—such as certain common information about feeding (or to be more specific, growing these foods), diseases among freshwater fish, and breeding.

Definition Please: Ichthyology

(Pronounced: ick—thee—olo—gee) The word ichthylogy means the study of fish. Ichthyology is a branch of zoology.

CHAPTER ONE

The Freshwater Tropical Aquarium

About Fish and Aquariums

The Fish

There are more than 200,000 species of fish inhabiting many different waters. New species of fish are discovered every year. From the deepest part of the seas thousands of feet down in total darkness, to the beautiful aqua-blue waters of the coral reefs, to the streams, lakes, and ponds of freshwater found throughout the world, fish have adapted an incredible variety of life-forms, styles, and behaviors. The group of aquatic animals we call fishes has evolved for over 400 million years to be the most numerous and diverse of the major vertebrate groups.

Forty-one percent of the world's fish species inhabit only fresh water. This is pretty amazing considering that fresh water covers only 1 percent of the world's surface. As you probably already know, salt water covers 70 percent of the earth's surface. So the number and variety of fresh water species to marine or saltwater species is all the more mind-boggling. While they inhabit the smallest amount of water, they have, in fact, adapted to a much wider range of habitats and to a greater variety of water conditions. Let's take a closer look at the unique adaptations of fish that have allowed them to live so successfully in the medium we call water.

Water is a denser medium than air. In fact, it is 800 times denser than air. That being the case, fish have needed to adapt themselves to their environment in many fascinating ways. Their bodies, fins, scales, and swim bladder have all evolved so that they can move, eat, and breathe in this denser medium.

There really is no such thing as a "typical fish." There are over 8000 different varieties! Here we will discuss their similarities and common attributes.

Body Form

You can learn a lot about a species of fish by looking at its body form or shape. Many fish that live near the bottom of a body of water tend to be either flat or stocky, while those that live in open waters tend to be bullet-shaped or more streamlined, where speed is at a premium.

Fins

Fins are common to almost all species of fish. Whether to propel, stabilize, stop, or maneuver, the fins are critically important appendages.

Definition Please: Aquarist

An aquarist is someone who keeps fish either as a hobby or as an occupation. Just because you own a tank doesn't make you an aquarist. A real aquarist maintains a vibrant, healthy environment where fish can live and thrive. An aquarist understands the many nuances of tank maintenance and fish husbandry.

Again, depending on the habitat the fish lives in, the fins may take on different shapes or functions. Faster, open-water fishes generally have pointed and longer fins, while slower-moving, bottom feeders or more sedentary fishes sometimes possess rounded fins.

Fins can come in pairs or may appear as a single fin, depending on species and function. The forwardmost paired fins are the pectoral fins. These fins act to help the fish stabilize, turn, maneuver, hover, and swim backwards. Generally found just behind or below the gills on each side of the fish, the pectoral fins can be found under the midline of the body. The most variable paired fins in positioning are the pelvic fins. For the most part, the pelvic fins act as brakes while aiding in stabilizing and turning the fish. In some fishes, the pelvics lie under the fish toward the rear. In others, like many tropical fishes, the pelvics are closer to the head under the pectorals.

The dorsal and anal fins are unpaired fins which are found protruding from the top of the fish and from the bottom of the fish behind the genital and anal openings, respectively. Dorsal fins may be elongated or short, elaborate or simple, singular or multiple. In some species of fish, the dorsal or anal fin may be completely lacking. Both fins help stabilize the fish and keep it moving straight. The caudal or tail fin is a generally unpaired fin, which is largely responsible for propelling the fish forward. Some species have paired caudal fins, such as can be found in "fancy" goldfish. This fin is the source of forward

Fins

There are many different types of fins. Different species use some of the same fins in different ways. Some species are actually missing some fins. The Meteor goldfish doesn't have a tail fin!

Fins help steer and move a fish. They are also an excellent indicator of a fish's health!

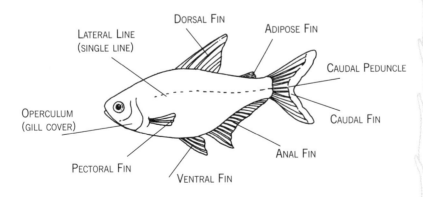

Characin (Tetra) Anatomy

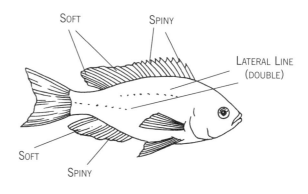

Chiclid Anatomy

**What Color
Are Scales?**

Scales are actually transparent!
The skin underneath dictates the
color of the scale!

momentum for most fishes and can also assist in turning and braking. Tail shape will tell much about the lifestyle of a fish. Faster fishes have deeply forked caudal fins while many deep-bodied and bottom fishes have square or rounded tails.

In general, the main supporting structures of fish fins are soft supports called rays, which can be compared to cartilage. However, anyone who has handled a fish knows that the dorsal, anal, or pectoral fins of many species also have spines. These sharp bony structures provide protection against predators.

Scales

The bodies of most tropical fish are covered with scales. Scales serve many purposes. What many people don't know is that fish scales are actually translucent and lack color. The source of the vibrant colors of tropical fishes comes from specialized pigment cells called chromatophores in the dermal layer of the skin! Some fish that actually appear clear, like the glassfish, lack these pigments. The color of the fish depends on the types of chromatophores present. There are generally three types of chromatophores in fish: melanophores, xanthophores, and iridophores. Melanophores give fish the darker colors of black, brown, and blue xanthophores produce the colors of red, yellow, and orange; and iridophores reflect light, producing a silvery shine common to many fish.

The scales are composed of a hard bony substance and serve to protect the fish, reducing the chance of injuries and infection. Covering the scales is a very thin layer of epidermal tissue that contains mucous cells. These cells produce the slimy texture that we normally attribute to fish. The mucous coating on fish not only protects the fish against injury and infection but helps the fish swim more easily in the water, reducing the friction between the body and the denser water.

Swim Bladder

The swim bladder has one important function—to keep the fish floating right-side up with as little effort as possible.

As mentioned earlier, living in the dense medium of water presents a few problems for fish, one of which is buoyancy. Maintaining a certain level in the water column without having to expend a lot of energy is very important to fish. Therefore, most species have special organs called swim bladders. This gas-filled sac located in the abdominal cavity of the fish acts as a life vest, keeping the fish at the correct level in the water column. There are many types of swim bladders ranging from a simple single-chambered sac of the trout to the two-chambered type in the goldfish and the three-chambered bladder of the angelfish. Fish may also have mechanisms that fill the swim bladder with air. Some fish have direct connections between the esophagus and the bladder and simply swallow air to fill it. Others must rely on gas exchange from specialized blood vessels in the circulatory system to fill the bladder.

In addition to its role in buoyancy control, the swim bladder helps to mechanically amplify sound for better hearing in certain species of fish.

Feeding

The size of the fish's mouth is directly related to the size of the food it eats. (Like some people I know!) But seriously, it's important to know that all fish don't eat the same things, as you'll find out later. Just as the body form of a fish can tell you a lot about its swimming habits, the mouth can tell you something about its feeding habits. Bottom feeders have downward-pointing mouths while surface feeders have mouths that are upward-pointing. For most fish, however, the mouth is at the end of the snout. Large predatory fish like oscars have

Gluttony Is One of the Seven Deadly Sins

Some species of fish don't know this. Be careful when feeding your fish. Some species will eat to the point of bursting. Goldfish are especially prone to this, but they are not the only ones. Only feed them as much as they can eat in five minutes.

Definition
Please:
Taxonomy

Taxonomy is the science of
classification. All animal life in
taxonomy is broken down
into various groups, sub-
groups, etc.

larger oval mouths for consuming smaller fish. On the other hand, fish
that normally feed on small aquatic invertebrates, like neon tetras, have
smaller mouths. Some tropical freshwater fishes have specialized mouths
for specialized feeding strategies. Plecostomus fishes, for example, have
special sucking-type mouths for bottom feeding. The sharp "beak" of
the parrot fish is helpful for feeding on the coral reef. The basking
shark, which feeds on microscopic planktonic creatures, has a mouth
that opens very wide and specialized gills that allow it to sift the water.

Most tropical and marine fishes have a relatively straightforward
digestive system that varies from species to species. In general, food
passes from the mouth, down the esophagus to the stomach, to the
small and large intestines, and out the anus. Several species lack true
stomachs and have elongated, supercoiled intestines.

Breathing

Like many other vertebrates, the most primary of the basic needs
of fish is oxygen. If you ever see a fish in a bowl gulping for air at the
surface, this means it's probably suffocating and that there is probably
little oxygen left in the water. This is not the way the fish was meant
to breathe. Like land animals, fish are living creatures that require
oxygen to live. However, fish must derive oxygen from water, and they
have specialized organs called gills that allow them to do so. The gills
of a fish are analogous to our lungs; they provide oxygen to, and
remove carbon dioxide from, the blood of the fish. This oxygen is then
transported by the blood to the tissues of the fish where it is utilized to
produce energy. Although a few types of fish can breathe air from the
water's surface, without gills, fish would certainly die if they had to rely
on this as a way of life.

Compared to a human being, the lungs of fish are located very
near the exterior of their bodies in order to extract as much oxygen as
possible. Most fish have four gills on each side of the head. These are
protected by a single gill flap, or operculum. To breathe, fish take water
into the mouth, then pass it over the gills and out the operculum. As
water passes over the membranes and filaments of the gills, oxygen is
removed and carbon dioxide is excreted. To accomplish this, the gills
have a very high number of blood vessels that deliver the oxygen to
the rest of the fish.

Other Organs

Aside from the notable exceptions outlined above, fish typically possess general circulatory, digestive, respiratory, and nervous system features common to most vertebrates. Curious readers should examine the suggested reading list in the back of this book for more detailed descriptions of the unique anatomy of fish.

Senses

Like almost all species, with a few exceptions, fish have no fewer than five senses, which they use to feed, avoid predators, communicate, and reproduce. Sight, smell, taste, hearing, and touch are the hallmarks of the animal and fish world. Of course, there are exceptions. Just as there are mammals that have no eyes, such as the golden mole of the desert, there are a few fish that lack one of the five senses. In these species, nature has found a way for the other senses to compensate. Many fish that live in the deepest depths of the sea, for example, can live and feed with little or no sight, yet are excellent predators. These fish are known to either have illuminated body parts to aid in vision, or extra barbels with which to feel and thus seek prey.

Sight

Sight is extremely important, especially for fish that are predators. The eyes of most fishes are similar to our own, except that they lack eyelids and their irises work much more slowly. Rapid changes in light intensity tend to shock a fish, and this should be taken into account by the aquarist. Gradual changes in light allow the fish to accommodate and avoid temporary blindness. You should, for example, turn on the lights in the room first for five minutes, before turning on the light on top of the aquarium. Maybe open some drapes or shades five minutes before that. You should do as best you can to imitate the way nature gradually lightens up, as opposed to darkness one second, blinding light another. It is also important to know that fish generally have poor sight. The location of the spherical lenses of fish eyes renders most fish nearsighted. Also, while it varies from species to species, some fish can see in color. All this goes a long way to saying that sight is very important, and your taking these precautions should help to keep your fishes' eyes healthier longer.

The Five Senses

Just like humans, fish have five senses. Of course, they experience some of these senses differently than us. First, they have mouths and eyes, so they can taste and see. Obviously, they don't have hands. But they do have a line of nerves along their body that enables them to feel. And they have no ears that we can see. Yet, in fact they do have an ability to hear. Their ears are somewhat hidden. How about noses? They don't have traditional noses, but they certainly do have nostrils, so they can smell, too.

Hearing

Since fish have no distinguishable ears as so many other animals do, it would be easy to assume that hearing is not one of a fish's more important senses. But hearing is actually an integral part of fish life. Water is a much more efficient conductor of sound than air, and sound carries much farther and faster in water than in air. Most fish do not posses, external ears, but rather an inner ear structure not noticeable on the outside of the fish. The auditory component of the inner ear consists of the sacculus and the lagena, which house the sensory components of hearing, the otoliths. Sound vibrations pass through the water, through the fish's sacculus and lagena, and then reverberate the otoliths in the inner ear. As mentioned previously, in some cases, the swim bladder articulates with the ear to amplify sound.

Smell

Fish have a highly developed sense of smell. They use it to prey on other fish and to avoid their own predators. Smell is also important for fish in the breeding season. Fish have external nasal passages called nares which allow water to pass into and out of the olfactory organ located above the mouth and below the eyes. Water flows through the nares and into the olfactory pits where odors are perceived and communicated to the brain via a large nerve. The olfactory system of the fish is not attached to the respiratory system as it is in humans, but remains isolated from the mouth and gills.

Taste

We're not talking about wearing black socks with sandals and shorts, or wearing a pink satin top that just doesn't go with that brown suede miniskirt. Fish use taste much more than humans do. This is generally a close range sense in fishes and is especially helpful in the identification of both food and noxious substances. The taste buds of fish are located in the mouth and on several external surfaces, like their skin, lips, and fins. Catfish have specialized barbels that possess taste buds and help the fish detect food items in murky waters.

Cloudy Eyes

If a fish's eyes are cloudy, it is usually a sign that the fish is blind.

Touch

It's very rare to see a fish trip and fall. It just doesn't happen. They rarely just bump into things by accident. Fish have very specialized organs comprising the lateral line system that allows them to detect water movements. Sensory receptors lying along the surface of the fish's body in low pits or grooves detect water displacement and therefore give the fish a sensation of touch. The lateral line is easily visible along the sides of most fish. This unique system helps the fish detect other fishes and avoid obstacles.

The Aquarium

Whether fishing or exploring, humans have always been fascinated with water. The sea and the creatures that inhabit its murky depths have always held a fascination for us. From streams, rivers, and lakes to small seas to the oceans of the world, we have attempted to understand and hold dear those few things we have gleaned over the centuries about our fellow creatures.

The first civilization to keep fish as pets were the Chinese. Among the first fishes to be kept in captivity were the common goldfish, which dates back to AD. 265 in China. Care and husbandry of fishes have come a long way over the centuries, and in recent years there has been an incredible explosion in fish culture for aquarium hobbyists.

Originally, Chinese fishkeepers kept their fish in large, ornately decorated pots, first outside in gardens and then inside the house. The keeping of goldfish was a mark of one's status in the community and became something of a fashion in Europe during the late Victorian era, tropical fish were all the rage. Most tropical freshwater fish kept in captivity were taken from their native rivers, streams, and lakes. This practice contributed to the degradation of tropical habitats and the local depletion of many species. Fortunately, modern husbandry techniques have taken tremendous pressure off natural stocks, and many of the common aquarium species are bred in captivity. Over the years, selective breeding has also allowed for fish to be better able to thrive and to adapt to the varying water conditions and changing technologies of the aquarium.

Another Definition of Fish

In a wide sense a fish may be regarded as an aquatic, cold-blooded, gill-breathing, chordate animal in which fins and not limbs are developed.
—*Encyclopedia Americana*

Freshwater, Saltwater, and Salt-Tolerant

When broken down by water type, there are actually three groups of fish: freshwater, saltwater, and those that can go back and forth. There are many more freshwater fish that go back and forth between the two than saltwater-based fish. Many of these fish live in the deltas of rivers where freshwater meets the sea. Few of these fish are kept by hobbyists. Carp, perches, catfish, salmon, pikes, and sunfish are some of the fishes from the last group. In some scientific communities these fish are called salt-tolerant fishes.

Being a fish in the wild is difficult enough. Fish in their natural environment are subjected to many challenges in order to survive. Most of these involve natural processes of predation, feeding, reproduction, and disease. Natural catastrophic events that alter water quality are rare, and fish can generally avoid them by moving to other areas. Basically, if they don't like where they are living, they can move on. In many ways, these outdoor fish are very much responsible for themselves. A possible exception to this would be fish that are living in areas assaulted by man-made pollution.

In an aquarium, however, fish can't move on. If they don't like it, there's no downstream to move on to. Fish that are maintained in an artificial environment like an aquarium are also faced with several challenges in order to survive. Most of these challenges cannot be met by the fish alone and must be met by the aquarist, the fishkeeper. When you decide to set up an aquarium, it's extremely important that you realize you are taking on the responsibility of many lives, and are not only responsible for the fishes' food, but are responsible for a whole ecosystem, however artificially it is maintained. This entails maintaining high water quality, proper feeding, correct water temperature, a balanced fish community of the proper density, appropriate habitat and shelter, and sufficient lighting. The fish are totally dependent upon you to meet their everyday needs. If they get sick or diseased, you must treat them. As you gain experience as a fishkeeper, you may go beyond the basic needs and start trying to breed your fish or establish specialty tanks. But first, it's important to start slow with your aquarium and develop your talents as an aquarist; you will learn a tremendous amount through your own experiences.

Meeting the Needs of Your Fish

Before purchasing your aquarium supplies and fish, it is very important to visit several local pet shops and tropical fish aquarium stores and understand which establishments will provide you with the best service and the most knowledgeable salespeople. Your local pet professional will be the most important aid in setting up your aquarium, especially in times of emergency. A reliable and experienced aquarist is essential and will serve you well in the years to come, during the setup and throughout the maintenance of your aquarium.

You want someone who maintains a good clean business, has healthy fish in their aquariums, and is always willing to answer your questions and spend time with you. The good dealer will give you valuable information on new products and reliable products. He or she will be motivated by the desire to help you maintain your system correctly and not solely by money. Choose someone with the right attitude, who will be consistently available to help. Try to avoid dealers who will not take the time to explain things to you or catch and sell you the specific fish you desire. Larger dealers (despite low prices or great combination packages) with many employees may not meet your needs as a beginner. I've always preferred the smaller pet shops that cater to the needs of all levels, are willing to special order supplies, and would rather send you elsewhere than sell you an improper choice. If you've found a dealer you are confident can answer your questions and who is willing to take the time to answer your questions, then you are ready to become an aquarist yourself. You are now ready to move on to the next vital and important steps.

The Fish Tank

Before you purchase or choose any equipment, take the time to plan your new aquarium in every possible way. Carefully think through where you are going to place the fish tank. To avoid excessive algae growth, do not place the aquarium in direct sunlight. Be sure that the area where you will place the aquarium can support the weight of a filled aquarium. Water weighs about 8.4 pounds per gallon, so a 30-gallon tank will weigh at least 250 pounds. Choose a location that is not too far from a source of water (you don't want to carry water too far—unless you want a real workout) and make sure that there is an adequate electrical supply close by. If you want your fish to be active and unintimidated by you when you enter the room, put them in well-used living areas. You want the fish to acclimate to people entering and leaving the room. If you don't, you'll end up with skittish and anxious fish when people enter the room or approach the tank.

Make sure that you place the tank in an area where no one will be upset if some water hits the floor. In dealing with a fish tank, you deal with lots of water. Even the most careful of hobbyists will splash water around a tank and in many cases water will escape from the

Fishkeeping in History

The Chinese were the first to keep fish. They didn't have glass, as we know it today. So they kept their fish in large beautiful bowls. This pottery today is greatly prized.

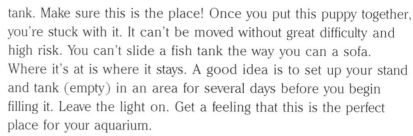

Before You Buy Anything!

Plan out what you're going to buy and how you're going to set up your tank. Begin by reading starting with the section, *Meeting the Needs of Your Fish* and those sections that follow before you buy anything. You don't want to come home thrilled with all your new equipment and then read that it's not right for your situation. Read and think it through carefully.

tank. Make sure this is the place! Once you put this puppy together, you're stuck with it. It can't be moved without great difficulty and high risk. You can't slide a fish tank the way you can a sofa. Where it's at is where it stays. A good idea is to set up your stand and tank (empty) in an area for several days before you begin filling it. Leave the light on. Get a feeling that this is the perfect place for your aquarium.

This may sound funny, but we've found that you are better off buying the biggest and best aquarium you can afford right up front. You don't want something that's going to dominate a room, unless that's part of your decorator's goal. But if you want healthy fish, you're going to need a tank that provides a large enough space to swim and a good air-to-water-surface ratio. The size of the tank directly affects both. The temperature of the water and the surface area of the tank dictate how much oxygen is in the water. Colder water has less oxygen than warmer water. Different fish require different temperatures for their comfort, but a good average is 75°F, a temperature where oxygen may be limited.

Since fish, like us, breathe oxygen, you need to make sure there is always oxygen in the tank, and that negative gases can be easily exchanged. The larger water surface area has a larger area for toxic gases to escape the water and be exchanged for oxygen. The larger the surface area, the better the tank is able to handle a larger number of fish.

The first question you want to ask yourself is this: How many fish do I want in my tank? The answer is not how many do you want; the answer is how many will your tank hold? How do you calculate this? Easy! By multiplying the width times the length, you can calculate the surface area. This is then used to determine the maximum number of inches of fish that the aquarium can hold. Most fish experts generally agree that one inch of cold-water fish requires 30 square inches of surface area and that one inch of warm-water fish requires 12 square inches of surface area. Because cold-water fish are used to breathing more oxygen, they generally have higher oxygen requirements than tropical fishes. So cold-water fish require differing amounts of space.

You still don't understand? How about an example? If you have space in your living room for a 30-gallon aquarium with a length and width of 32 and 14 inches, respectively, then you will have a surface area of 448 square inches (32x14). This tank has the capacity for 15 inches of cold-water fish (448/30) or 37 inches of warm-water fish (448/12). So, in reality, you could have seven two-inch goldfish, which are considered cold-water fish, or 37 one-inch neon tetras, which are warm-water fish, in this tank. This is just an example, of course. Very few aquarists want an aquarium solely occupied by one variety.

Therefore, choose tanks that are longer than they are tall because surface area is so important to the capacity and health of your aquarium. Are you still not understanding the difference? Let's say you are looking at two 30-gallon tanks. Even though both tanks may hold the same volume of water, a tall, thin tank will have a much lower carrying capacity of fish than a long, wide tank will, because of its smaller surface area. While many beginner kits are 10-gallon kits, we recommend your starter tank should be 20 gallons. In the end, it will allow you much more growing room as you become more interested in your hobby.

Once you've made up your mind on the right size aquarium for your needs, choosing the tank itself is very easily done. The most popular home aquariums today are constructed of glass plates sealed with a silicone rubber cement in a rectangular shape. These are by far the most common and practical aquarium to buy; I recommend one for the beginner. The most important thing to remember is that these products are non-toxic, because they have been built for the sole purpose of housing live animals. While glass may seem like a chancy substance, because we think of it as being fragile, it is the best of all possible choices. Glass does not scratch as easily or yellow as acrylic does. You may be worried that these tanks seem to lack a framework, but they are strong and sturdy and have been tested to withstand the rigors of the hobbyists' use. They are much stronger than they look. Aquariums with plastic or metal frames are sometimes available, but we've found that this design is not as aesthetically pleasing and that the frames are unnecessary.

Definition Please: Tropical Fish

Tropical fish is a general term for any number of fishes that may be kept in small, standing aquariums, usually in homes. They may either be freshwater or saltwater fish. Many of the most popular tropical fish come from the Amazon, India and the East Indian Archipelago, the Malay Peninsula, Africa, and Asia.

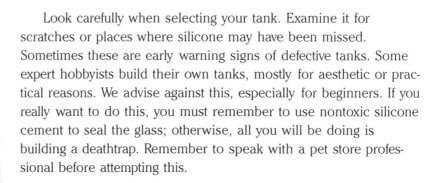

Fishbowls

Recently, some manufacturers have been making larger and larger bowls, holding up to 10 or 20 gallons. And some filtration manufacturers have created special underground filters for just such containers. Again, because of the water-surface-to-air-ratio, we would strongly caution against using these. But if you do insist on buying one, you must have a working filter and plenty of aeration.

Look carefully when selecting your tank. Examine it for scratches or places where silicone may have been missed. Sometimes these are early warning signs of defective tanks. Some expert hobbyists build their own tanks, mostly for aesthetic or practical reasons. We advise against this, especially for beginners. If you really want to do this, you must remember to use nontoxic silicone cement to seal the glass; otherwise, all you will be doing is building a deathtrap. Remember to speak with a pet store professional before attempting this.

Fishbowls

Certainly one of the most enduring images is that of the fishbowl. No matter the type or size, or the kind of fish in it, the fishbowl is a relic of our hobby's history—much like the tenement is to housing. In an earlier, more unsophisticated age, fishbowls were acceptable. But we simply know more now. Our recommendation is to stay away from them. The bowl is a confining and inhumane environment for a fish. Yes, they can survive in them. But it's like keeping a dog in a kennel its whole life, or a man or woman living their whole life in one very small room.

They have a very small water-surface-to-air ratio, which makes breathing difficult. That's why you always see fish gulping for air at the surface in a bowl. Since there is no filtration, the water is unfiltered, not properly aerated, and, as a result, very poorly maintained. While daily water changes may provide better oxygenated water, the constant changing environment would be a cruel treatment of your fish. A fishbowl is no more an aquarium than a closet is a house. Therefore, the unfiltered fishbowl will not be examined as such in this book.

The Stand

Hands down, the best way to support the heavy weight of a fully filled tank and all its components is the commercially manufactured aquarium stand. While it may seem like an added expense (who doesn't have an extra table sitting in the garage or attic?) this strongly built stand is especially made to hold the full aquarium. There are countless stories of TV stands, homemade tables, and

ACRYLIC VS. GLASS

We like glass better than acrylic, but there is a case to be made for acrylic. Acrylic is usually molded or welded at the seams. This makes acrylic tanks structurally better and stronger than glass tanks. Acrylic tanks also tend to have fewer defects.

Acrylic tanks are also less likely to shatter (although to shatter any kind of tank takes quite a lot of pressure—usually from an outside force). The other thing to be said of acrylic is that when it's empty, it's easier to move. Glass is heavier.

All that said, acrylic tends to yellow faster and more easily than glass, and it tends to scratch a lot more easily as well. This becomes very important over the years, as you want to see your fish—and you can't, because the acrylic has scuffed. Also, it's more difficult to clean algae effectively. You can't scrub it real hard because it will mar the viewing surface.

folding tables that didn't make the grade, and eventually collapsed under the pressure of supporting such a heavy load.

If and when the stand fails, it can be mighty costly. You may end up with a ruined rug or damaged house. It can cost you home repairs as well as the loss of tank, fish, and other equipment. You're spending some solid money up front, and a stand is a good way to protect that investment.

If you are sure that a commercially made stand is not for you, you need to place something under the tank to keep it from ruining your furniture. Place a 5/8" sheet of plywood and a 1/2" sheet of polystyrene cut to the dimensions of the tank under the tank. This will distribute the load of the aquarium more evenly and will help ensure that any imperfections in the support surface are properly leveled.

The Hood

While it may seem silly to inexperienced aquarists, the hood or cover is an essential item for any aquarium. First, it prevents fish who want to move on upstream from exiting the tank via the top. Fish can't survive without water, and there is nothing worse than noticing that a fish is missing only to find it dead, stuck to the rug or fallen behind the stand and critically injured. Second, it keeps items from falling into the tank and possibly injuring or killing your fish. When we were young, someone once threw a wad of bubble gum into a tank of large oscars. We sat there amazed as one of the oscars immediately attacked and ate the bubble gum, chewing it and spitting it out, chewing it and spitting it out. We were very lucky that nothing bad happened.

The hood also slows down the process of water evaporation, and therefore cuts down on the number of times you have to refill the tank. It prevents water from splashing around, which will protect your walls, especially if you have wallpaper. Hoods allow for an overhead light properly focused on the water,

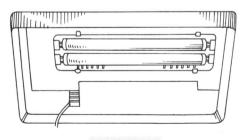

Hood

providing maximum viewing pleasure. It also keeps the water far enough from the light so as not to cause an electrical problem. We've seen cases where a light fell in and then there was fish stew. Not pretty. And finally, a hood helps the water retain its warmth by putting a cap on the tank and not allowing heat to escape too easily.

Usually, the hood or cover (sometimes called a canopy) is fitted to the size of your tank and has sections in it that allow for such things as a heater, filter, and aeration tubes. It's always a good idea to make sure that it is composed of thick (1/8") glass or plastic so that it can support the weight of other aquarium components if needed. It should never be a one-piece item, but should be segmented so that the entire assembly need not be removed in order for you to feed the fish or work in the tank. Especially for the beginner, we strongly suggest the use of a single unit that also contains a housing for an aquarium light.

The Water

You want healthy fish? OK, listen up. There is nothing more important to the health and well-being of your fish than clean water. Fish in the wild have it good (as long as they live in unpolluted streams, rivers, or lakes) because they have a continuous constant supply of fresh water. The excretions of the body, mostly toxic gases and waste, are whisked away by currents and naturally filtered out by the environment. However, fish that live in an aquarium live in a world where there is not a constant supply of fresh water, but recycled and treated water. The gases and wastes must be removed somehow or eventually your fish will die. That makes the filter, the device that removes all those things, the most important piece of equipment you will buy. Before we get into all the different types of filtration processes and the different types of filtering systems available to you through your local pet professional, it's important to discuss the different attributes of water quality and understand the natural cycles created in this artificial world.

Freshwater fish live all over the world, but the water in all these areas is not the same. Its chemical attributes vary. Therefore, we know that fish have adapted to various kinds of waters. How does water vary? We've already discussed oxygen content. Water also

Buying a Package from the Same Manufacturer Makes Sense

We've always found that the tank, stand, and hood are best purchased as a complete package built by the same manufacturer. The best reasons we can cite are those of common sense and safety. It ensures against the mismatching of aquarium components and may be less expensive to the beginner.

varies in temperature, hardness, and pH. We know that fish that have adapted to certain climates and pH don't survive well in different temperatures or pH levels.

pH refers to the amount of acidity of the water. The pH scale ranges from 0 to 14 with a pH of 7 being neutral, a pH of 1 being very acidic, and a pH of 14 being very alkaline. This scale is logarithmic, meaning that each number is ten times stronger than the preceding number. For example, a pH of 2 is 10 times more acidic than a pH of 3 and 100 times more acidic than a pH of 4.

The amount of carbon dioxide and fish wastes in the water, as well as a variety of other factors, greatly influence the pH levels of any water. For most freshwater fish, cold or tropical, the beginner's aquarium pH should be between 6.5 and 7.5. How does one achieve this very specific pH level? There are many commercial test kits available that are easy to use and that can be found in almost all pet shops dealing in tropical fish. You should monitor your fish tank regularly—every week to two weeks. An abrupt drop in pH may be indicative of an increase of carbon dioxide or fish wastes. An increase in aeration or partial water change can sometimes alleviate the problem.

There are chemical methods available to alter pH in the aquarium. However, unless you are attempting to attain specific pH levels as dictated by the special needs of certain species of fish, we generally don't recommend that you use them.

Water Hardness

Calcium and magnesium are mineral salts. Their presence, in varying amounts, along with some others, largely contribute to what is called water hardness. You've probably heard the term before. It's easy to spot because there are white calcium and salt deposits near sinks and washing machines—anywhere there's water. The more salts and minerals in the water, the harder it is. Low levels of these same materials result in soft water. The degree of hardness scale (dH) ranges from 0 to over 30 degrees with 4 to 8 degrees being soft water and 18 to 30 degrees being hard water. Most freshwater fish do best in water between 3 and 14 degrees of hardness. The beginner generally does not need to alter water hardness unless the local tap water is excessively hard or soft. Commercial kits are now available to test the degree of hardness and alter water hardness. These, too, can be purchased from your pet professional.

The Nitrogen Cycle

In short, this is Biology 101 for people who don't otherwise care for science class. We think it's much more interesting than science class, though. And if you're going to keep fish, you just have to know it. So stop rolling your eyes and follow along.

Fish are like human beings in that they need oxygen to breathe and need fuel to burn. In short, they breathe in oxygen and exhale what to them are toxic gases, or deposit solid waste. These wastes are returned to the environment via the gills and the anus. These wastes are primarily carbon dioxide and nitrogenous compounds, like ammonia. In the aquarium, these wastes must be removed. Would you want to live in that stuff? Carbon dioxide generally leaves the water through aeration at the surface or through photosynthesis by aquarium plants. Toxic nitrogenous compounds are converted to less toxic compounds via the nitrogen cycle.

What's the nitrogen cycle? In streams, ponds, and lakes, the fish's natural habitat, the nitrogen cycle involves the conversion of toxic nitrogenous wastes and ammonia into harmless products by bacterial colonies. In short, different species of bacteria convert solid wastes excreted by fish into ammonia, ammonia into nitrite, and nitrite into nitrate. Nitrate is then utilized by plants as fertilizer and removed from the water. A healthy aquarium depends greatly on the nitrogen cycle to reduce toxic ammonia into less toxic nitrogen compounds.

In nature, nitrogen compounds are readily removed from the fish's habitat. But in the aquarium, nature needs a little help. The filtration system is the cavalry. There are three basic types of filtration: mechanical, chemical, and biological.

Definition Please: Nitrogenous

Nitrogenous means that a substance such as the nitrogen compound ammonia, contains nitrogen.

The Filter

Mechanical filters sift particles though a fine filter medium, sifting out particles that are suspended in the water. Mechanical filters provide rapid mechanical filtration by using external power filters and canister filters.

Chemical filtration involves the chemical treatment of water to remove toxic substances. You are providing chemical filtration when you add activated carbon to an external power filter.

Biological filtration is probably the best kind of filtration. Although it is easy to set up, it sometimes takes a while to work properly. It is the best system because it establishes natural orders of bacteria and creates the nitrogen cycle, using natural methods. This system utilizes the nitrogen cycle to remove toxic compounds from the water. An excellent example of a biofilter is the under-gravel filter that draws water through the aquarium substrate. This substrate contains the necessary bacteria to convert nitrogenous wastes to nitrate. What takes the filter a while to establish itself is waiting for the bacteria to establish working colonies in the substrate. It may sound incredibly gross, and will probably look like gross muck at the bottom of your tank underneath the gravel, but it really is a very good way to filter your tank in the most natural way possible.

However, it is important to know that all three kinds of filtration take place no matter how you try to do it. In most commercially manufactured filters of any kind, you can find all three systems at work. For example, the external power filter will mechanically remove particles, chemically remove toxins if the filter contains activated carbon, and biologically convert nitrogenous wastes via the nitrogen cycle in its filter media.

The most common types of filters available to the beginner include the internal box filter, the external power filter, the external canister filter, and the under-gravel filter. Are these the only types available? Certainly not. However, they are the most common. There are others that are better suited to those setting up high-level, exotic aquariums. For the most part, the filters we'll discuss are the ones you want to use. But which one should you choose? There are many different kinds and configurations by many different manufacturers. Here, you'll find a description of the most common with their good and bad points. You need to pick the one that sounds like the right fit for you.

FILTERS 101

Different types of filters for beginners:

Box filter—the easiest
Under-gravel filter—easy
External power filter—moderate

The under-gravel filter takes longer to establish but it really is the best, provided you don't overload your aquarium with too many fish and plants. If you have fish that are going to grow quite large, such as goldfish in a large tank, or oscars, you probably should use an external power filter.

Power Heads

Make sure not to turn the pressure up on your power heads too much, as it may agitate your aquarium environment instead of keeping it healthy. You want some aeration . . . not a jet stream.

The Box Filter

The box filter is the simplest and most obvious of all the filters. It is also the most popular of all the filters for starters. It is inexpensive and easy to use. Shaped just like its namesake, the box filter sits inside the aquarium. It is driven by an external air pump. As air is pumped into a chamber where it mixes with water, the air eventually fights its way up through the filtering medium, and forces the water up through with it. It draws the water through a fibrous filter material and activated charcoal. Layers of filter media provide mechanical and chemical filtration as well as adequate substrate for biological filtration. Because it is driven by air, this filter circulates and aerates the water. This type of filter is fine for a lightly populated 10-gallon starter set. But any serious aquarist worth his or her salt doesn't use one of these. In our opinion the box filter does not provide adequate levels of filtration for the average aquarium. Aquarists who start with a tank of 20 gallons or more should not use this type of filter system to provide filtration. It won't aerate your water properly and is simply too small to handle the wastes and debris that accumulate in the tank. For the 20-gallon tank we recommend you start with, the water filtered by a box filter would have to be changed frequently and the aquarium would require too much maintenance. The tank would not be crystal clear and would provide for a bad habitat as well as for poor viewing.

The External Power Filter

While it looks intimidating to the beginner, and costs more than a box filter, the external power filter is the best filter for the beginner aquarist to use. Specifically designed to turn over large amounts of water, these filters, as described in the nitrogen cycle section, provide all three kinds of filtration. The external power filter hangs onto the side of a tank and is driven by its own electric motor. Via two siphon tubes, one for incoming water and one for outgoing water, the power filter draws water in through a medium of fibrous filter material and activated carbon. The water is then pumped back into the tank. Some

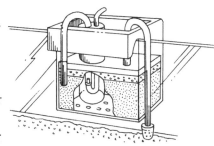

External Power Filter

filters have a system where the water trickles back into the tank rather than flowing back in through a tube.

Though similar in some respects to the box filter, the power external filter is much more efficient and will keep your water much cleaner. The external filters are generally bigger and can go for longer periods without needing to be cleaned. They remove particles and debris better and aerate the water better. Newer models have specialized filter cartridges that make cleaning these filters extremely easy. In addition, various types of cartridges can now be purchased that chemically alter water quality and correct water chemistry problems.

The External Canister Filter

The external canister filter is often used by more experienced aquarists. However, the canister filter isn't about experience—it's about size. This is a larger filter and is meant to be a filter for tanks of 50 gallons or more. A large, jar-shaped canister, this filter generally sits somewhere not far from the tank. Like the other filters, it passes water over filter media and activated carbon, but the motor is much more powerful and can manage cycling through a large tank quite easily. Water is drawn by an intake suction tube and sent back to the aquarium through a return tube. These are powerful filters and are not recommended for smaller tanks. Use this with a big tank only.

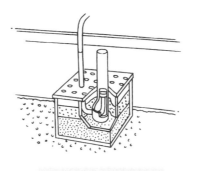

Canister Filter

The Under-Gravel Filter

The true aquarium aficionados prefer the under-gravel filter. It is considered to be the best because it provides biological filtration. However, it is deceptively simple. The filter consists of a large plastic plate that is placed underneath the bed of gravel in the tank. The filter pumps air through an external air pump into this bottom plate, mixing the air with water. Bubbles rising through the exit tube trap water, drawing it up through the gravel and through the substrate. Some under-gravel filters are driven by power heads mounted on the intake

I'm Suffocating in Here!

Despite the fact that fish live in water, one of the most important elements to their survival and health is fresh air. Aeration is the act of infusing their water with air. This happens in nature naturally. Streams and rivers have tremendous air to surface ratios, as well as rapids and waterfalls. Your aquarium does not. You should at least have one aeration device in a 10- or 20-gallon tank. In a 30-or more gallon tank (and larger), you should have at least two.

tubes. Power heads add extra aeration and move the water more quickly through the filter. Whether a powerhead is used or not, under-gravel filters provide excellent water circulation and aeration. It's so simple, and effective. This filter uses the aquarium gravel itself as the filter media! Thus, very little mechanical filtration, and no chemical filtration, is involved. And there's no acti-

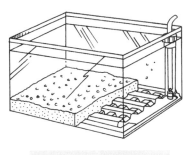

Undergravel Filter

vated carbon! The under-gravel filter relies chiefly on the establishment of a healthy bacterial colony in the gravel. This filter requires a lot less maintenance than the others and is wonderfully efficient.

However, this type of filter has several drawbacks. First, you need to use a certain size of gravel, which limits your aquascaping (aquarium landscaping) choices. Second, this type of filter takes a long time to set up, because it doesn't work immediately. You need to allow the colonies sufficient time to establish themselves. It may be two to three weeks before you can even think of adding fish to your lovely habitat.

There are more pitfalls. If there is excessive debris in your aquarium, these particles can eventually clog the filter bed. They need to be removed often. Some fish, especially goldfish and some catfish, as well as nest-builders, will push the gravel around and upset the substrate. And if you like to keep live plants, say goodbye to your green thumbs, because these filters will play havoc with your plants' root systems. All these things make this a difficult system for the beginner. We strongly recommend that you start with an external power filter, and leave the under-gravel filter system for the next stage in your development as an aquarist.

Power Heads

Power heads—you either love them or hate them. Generally they are used to power up under-gravel filters. They do not operate in the same way, however. Instead of forcing air through the under-gravel filter, they force water through the under-gravel filter. They suck water from the top of the tank though the feeding tubes, which causes the same effect in the aquarium's water circulation. These are small water pumps but they are very powerful, and again, we would only recommend them for experienced aquarists. Many inexperienced hobbyists turn their powerheads up too high, causing too much disruption and making the tank uninhabitable.

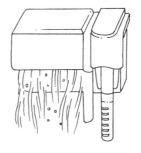

Power Head Air Pump

Aeration

As we have discussed previously, oxygen is a very important element in the husbandry of fish. While most manufacturers of filters will tell you that their filters clean and purify the water as well as aerate it (and they wouldn't be lying), filters don't nearly supply all the oxygen that fish need. Certainly filters provide circulation, and that's important. But fish need lots of oxygen available for respiration, and this is especially true of large tanks holding numerous fish. An aeration device will increase the circulation in your tank, and promote the oxygen level in the water, by increasing the amount of water exposed to oxygen. Also, it will help promote oxygen exchange at the surface, and increase the escape of carbon dioxide, carbon monoxide, and free ammonia from the tank. In addition, this increase in circulation will act to mix all the aquarium levels so that a uniform temperature is maintained throughout the tank.

There are two types of air pumps: the diaphragm and the piston. The size and power output of air pumps varies. Consult your local dealer to match your aquarium with the proper air pump. It's important to remember what you're going to use it for. A cheap diaphragm pump is fine for running a little bubbling shipwreck on your tank's floor, but it wouldn't be enough to power a 20-gallon underwater filter. Consult your pet professional to discuss the size of your tank, the use of the pump, and the number of

Air Pump

Mixing Species and Temperature

Make sure that you do not mix species that have very different temperature preferences. This could cause some to be fine while others languish or die. Be sure to consult your pet professional before choosing a new species for your tank. You might unintentionally do something inhumane.

fish you have. All these variables will play a part in deciding what's right for you.

The Diaphragm Pump

Diaphragm pumps are more prevalent than piston pumps. They tend to be less expensive and work fine. They are good to operate one airstone or maybe two, depending on the power of the pump you are buying. They will last a long time, but don't last as long as piston pumps and are not quite as efficient. These pumps have a small rubber diaphragm that is vibrated by a small electric motor. The vibrations cause the burping of the diaphragm which sends out jets of air.

The Piston Pump

Powered by a small electric motor, the piston pump pumps air via a piston through a small hole. The advantage of the piston pump is power. It is an excellent pump to operate an under-gravel filter or for operating several airstones in a large tank. These pumps are generally more expensive than diaphragm pumps. They will last a long time, withstand many repairs, and just keep on going.

Airstones

The most popular tank aeration items are airstones. These are simply porous stones that have a nozzle attached to them. By forcing air through them, the stones let the air bleed out in different places, thereby sending a stream of fine bubbles up through the water. You don't want too fine a mist, or else those tiny little bubbles that Don Ho is so fond of will cling to everything, including your fish! Of course, there's the opposite problem, too. You don't want your bub-

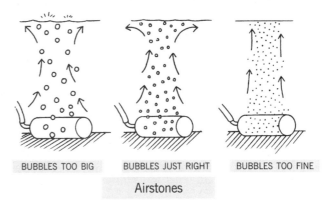

BUBBLES TOO BIG   BUBBLES JUST RIGHT   BUBBLES TOO FINE

Airstones

TEMPERATURE RANGES
FOR DIFFERENT
TYPES OF FISH

These are some very general temperature ranges for the following fish. Some goldfish and koi require much lower temperatures and can withstand a larger range of temperatures, cold as well as warm. This is merely meant as an example.

TYPE	TEMP
Goldfish and Koi	65-75°F (18-24°C)
Tropical Freshwater	75-79°F (24-26°C)
Marine Fishes	75-79°F (24-26°C)

While you may be sure that your heater is working, make sure to check your thermometer consistently, because something can go wrong at any time. This ounce of prevention is definitely worth a pound of cure.

Definition Please: Backdrop

Many hobbyists use a backdrop on their aquariums. A backdrop is a scene or solid color which you adhere to the outside back of your tank, so as to block the view of the outside filter and other equipment. It's also to try and establish an effect of sorts, whether a very naturalistic look or something much more stylized. Several different types of backdrops: a very natural-looking brook scene with rocks and plant life, a shipwreck, or a coral reef. There are a few backdrops that are created for the interior of the tank. Many hobbyists tend to not use these, as they tend to draw dirt quickly and are difficult to clean.

bles too big, either. Big bubbles are bad, because they race to the top too quickly and don't offer maximum aeration. They also race to the top and disturb the water instead of offering proper circulation. You want the bubbles, in small little groups, to slowly rise toward the surface and agitate the water.

Of course, there are the fun ones, too! Come on, admit it, you want one of those tacky bubbling treasure chests, shipwrecks, skeletons, or little divers. Or maybe you want the haunted castle. Commercially manufactured tank decorations, which act as airstones, can be purchased at almost any pet store. These are generally made of plastic or ceramic. They're goofy, fun, and practical. Whether you have an airstone or a sunken Titanic, aeration is very important.

Tubing

No, this isn't one of those beer commercials where everyone is twenty-something and laughing and flying downriver in an inner tube. We're talking about the tubing you use to bring the air from your pump to your filter or airstones. This tubing should fit snugly onto the outlets of the filter or airstones. It should be just a little tight and seem to take a little more muscle than you expected to connect the tubing. That's good, unless it's stretched too tight. There shouldn't be too much evidence of stretching. The idea is to avoid the possibility of air leaking. Air leaks will reduce the efficiency of the system (filter or airstone) and may ultimately burn out the pump. Make sure you buy your tubing at the pet store. Don't buy some cheap stuff your uncle got you a deal on at his auto body shop. It's not the same stuff. Some grades of plastic are toxic to fish! Make sure to use tubing that is manufactured for aquariums.

Air Valves

Some aquarists run several different airstones off a single pump. After all, there's no need to have a separate pump for each airstone. What you need is an air valve. This may be as close to plumbing and pipe fitting as some of you want to get. Air valves look like old-time spigots. You attach tubing in the fore and aft nozzles and then use the turnoff valve to regulate the flow of air through the tubes. Some can be turned down lower than others; not every-

Gang Valve

thing has to be on full blast. The other good thing is that if you need to, you can turn individual airstones off without disrupting the rest of the tank.

The Heater

As we discussed earlier, water temperature is one of the most important concerns of fishkeeping. Too warm or too cold could cause your fish to be sluggish, or it could kill them. Fish are sometimes grouped into categories based on their temperature preference. However, as far as the beginner aquarist is concerned, most freshwater tropical fish that he or she is going to see at their local pet emporium will probably require a similar temperature. Most of these are of the tropical species.

Tropical fish live in habitats where the waters are warm throughout the year. They don't know where you live and don't care. They need the water at *their* temperature—there really is no compromise. And thus was born the aquarium heater.

Regardless of the room temperature, the aquarium heater will maintain your fish tank temperature at appropriate levels. It is only natural that these temperatures fluctuate as the heaters react to changing temperatures outside of the tank, so it is important to note that you should be looking at a range. You don't have to keep the tank at one immovable temperature. This would be impossible. You should consult your local pet dealer or one of the many fish encyclopedias for specific temperature requirements.

The submersible glass tubular heater with a built-in thermostat is the most common of all the different kinds of heaters available to the aquarist. It has external controls so that it can be adjusted, and clips onto the side of the tank, with the glass tube submersed in the water. Generally speaking, the heater will automatically adjust to temperature changes once it has been set. Some manufacturers have preset temperature dials, which makes it that much easier for the beginning hobbyist to use. Regardless, the temperature gauge is easily set by the user. It is important to note that the use of a thermometer is the only good way to constantly monitor the heater's functionality and accuracy. We strongly urge you to always check a thermometer to measure your heater's success.

Thermostats

Almost all heaters come with automatic thermostats. These work very much like the ones in your own home. They will help you set a fairly consistent temperature range that will be comfortable for the fish in your tank. However, you need to remember to be careful that no outside forces, such as radiators or sunlight, will be able to heat the tank up too much. Heaters can warm the water, but they cannot cool it.

Sleeping with the Fishes

Shhhhh! Your fish is sleeping. You can tell when a fish is sleeping because it usually lies on or near the bottom, sometimes hidden behind plants. It moves just slightly, but it does not swim.

Do tropical fish close their eyes? No. They can't. Their eyelids are clear. So when they are asleep they may still look awake. It's also important to remember that in nature, fish usually sleep when it's dark. Sleep is just as important for tropical fish as it is for human beings. It helps them rejuvenate and remain healthy and vibrant. So let them sleep at night. And remember to turn out the light!

We have often found that one of the best areas to place your heater is near the filtering system or an airstone. The idea is to place the heater in an area of high water circulation, so that the heat can be evenly distributed throughout the tank. Some heaters are fully submersible. Generally, these are placed at the bottom of the tank, and allow for maximum penetration of heat. However, they are more expensive, and not always as reliable or as easily replaced as the submersible glass tubular heater.

Again, with heaters, size matters. The size of your aquarium dictates the size of your heater. The general rule of thumb is five watts of power for every gallon of water. Thus, a 20-gallon tank would require a 100-watt heater. A 30-gallon tank would require a 150-watt heater. If you have a tank of more than 50 gallons of water, you will need two heaters. It's not as important to be able to just heat the water as it is to heat it evenly. Especially if one heater fails, then you are covered. In such cases, you would want to evenly distribute the wattage. A 40-gallon tank would require two 100-watt heaters, placed at different spots in the tank.

The Thermometer

Here is one absolute rule: All aquarists need a reliable thermometer! We don't care how good your heater is, or how good your sense of approximating it yourself might be. In order to maintain your temperature at suitable levels, all aquarists need an accurate thermometer. There are two kinds of thermometers: the external stick-on kind and the internal floating or fixed kind. The internal type tends to be more accurate since the external type has a tendency to read a couple of degrees too low.

While it does not cost a lot of money, certainly the thermometer is one of the aquarist's most valuable tools. We recommend two thermometers. This will allow you to carefully monitor your aquarium temperature by letting you compare their reports as well as gauge them one against the other. When it comes to maintaining water quality and water temperature, don't be lazy or cheap. Buy these and it will stand you in good stead.

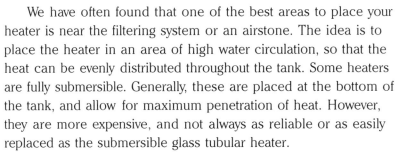

Thermometer

ELECTRICITY AND WATER— DON'T MIX 'EM!

Unless you want hair like the Bride of Frankenstein or really enjoy hospitals, we strongly suggest that you handle all electrical equipment with extreme care. The heaters are the most dangerous electrical components in your tank.

As with all electrical devices, please handle your heater with extreme care. Do not switch your submersible heater on until it is submersed in water. Keep all of your electrical components unplugged until the tank is completely set up and full. Heaters turned on before they are submerged may burn out or at worst explode. Also, you don't want to be handling live wires with wet hands.

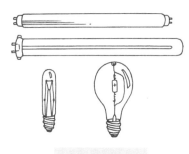

Tank Bulbs

The Light

Good lighting makes for a good tank. It promotes plant growth, which is very good if you have plants. But more important, it provides you and your fish with illumination so that they can see their way around and you can see them. Yes, the sun could easily provide you with plenty of natural, cheap light. But don't put your fish tank in front of a window. If you do, you'll be scraping algae off the insides of the tank for more days than you'll be able to see the fish. And they said nobody does windows anymore!

We recommend that the beginner buy a commercially manufactured light for the tank. Like many of the other items we've already talked about, these come in a variety of shapes and sizes. If they are not part of the hood, they should fit snugly on top of the hood. The one that most aquarists buy are fluorescent lights, because they don't heat the water, and they provide light evenly. The interesting thing about fluorescent lights is that they come in a variety of colors. These can be used to create special effects in your aquascape. There are red and blue bulbs that will enhance the reds and blues on your fish while also promoting plant growth. There are fluorescent bulbs that also cover the ideal spectral range that will ensure good plant growth. These bulbs are not uncommon and can be found at any well-stocked pet shop. If you bought a hood with a light as we suggested earlier, then that was almost certainly fluorescent as well. If you do not purchase a tank, cover, and light package, make sure that the light that you buy extends the entire length of the tank. This is by far the most efficient and economical form of lighting available for your tank, and we thoroughly recommend it for the beginning aquarist.

Are there other types of lights? What are they? Well, there are many other types. These include incandescent, sodium, mercury vapor, metal halide, and tungsten lights. They provide unique lighting opportunities, but tend to heat the water and are not as economical as fluorescent lights. We do not recommend any of these.

Full Spectrum Lights

Incandescent and fluorescent lights do not provide the full colors in the spectrum like natural light. Today many lights, which come close to recreating sunlight, are available on the market. These light bulbs are excellent, especially if you have live plants. Ask your pet store professional which ones he or she carries and ask for a recommendation from their selection.

DAYLIGHT SAVINGS?
ARE YOU KIDDING?

Most tropical freshwater fish come from regions where day-light lasts from 10 to 15 hours a day. That's a long time. To make sure you're giving your fish enough light, you need to make sure you leave the light on for those same hours so that they can be healthy and at their best. To ensure proper light hours for your fish, consider buying an automatic timer. That way you can set the timer so that your fish will get their 10 to 15 hours a day, and you won't always have to run over and remember to turn off the light.

An average of a 12-hour day is recommended by many experts. Another trick to keep from startling your fish is to turn off their light an hour before the rest of the lights are shut off around the house. This provides a simulation of sunset for the fish, so that they won't be startled when it's time for lights out.

There are several things to consider when you buy a light for your aquarium. Make sure that you take into consideration the depth of the tank, the number and kind of fish you intend to have, and the number and kind of plants you intend to place around the aquascape. If you don't have enough watts, it will be difficult to see some of your fish, and you won't be supplying enough light for your plants to grow. We generally go by a ratio of 2 to 2.5 watts per each gallon of water. More plants and fish might necessitate the need for more watts. Again, consulting your pet professional with the specifics will help you come to a good decision. Consult them before you buy your setup.

Inside the Tank

Many of the varieties of fish you are probably considering come from various spots around the world. Some come from rapidly moving bodies of water, while others come from small pools with rocky or murky bottoms. It takes both time and experience to move up to the level where you can recreate a particular fish's exact habitat. Especially for beginners, it's best to create an aquascape that is pleasing to you and your surroundings, since your fish will probably come from all over the world. Obviously, you also want to create a habitat that will keep your fish happy and healthy. To do this, you must consider what kind of fish you want and then choose your aquascaping materials carefully.

Gravel

Gravel is one of the most basic of all aquarium elements. This substance will make up the bottom substrate of your aquarium. It performs a great many tasks. First, it provides anchorage for plants, whether plastic or real, and for any other items such as airstones or other aerators. It also plays the important role of making a home for all kinds of useful bacteria that will assist in the nitrogen cycle, and helps rid your aquarium of toxic wastes. You need to be careful in deciding what kind of gravel you are going to choose.

First things first. Purchase coral sand only if you are planning on having a marine tank. If you are not planning a marine tank,

Definition, Please: Terrace

Terrace can be both a noun and a verb. The noun terrace means a ledge or flat surface on a hill or slope. Many aquarists provide a series of terraces or ledges from high to low. The higher terraces are usually in the back and the lower up front. You want the lower terrace in the front, because it allows for optimum viewing. Why terrace? Because it provides deeper gravel to anchor plants in and provides for some fish a territory similar to where they would normally reside in nature. When you use the word terrace as a verb, it's usually meant to address the setting up of your aquascape. You want to terrace the gravel into several layers or ledge on a slope of gravel.

GRAVEL BIG AND SMALL

Gravel comes in larger pebbles and smaller grades as well. Some advanced aquarists use different grades mixed together. Either they add the larger ones first, with the finer sand on top, or more normally use the larger pebbles up top while using the finer grades underneath. This is especially a good idea for under-gravel filters. It's almost like the setup in a traditional box filter, where the activated charcoal purifies and blocks large detritus, and the finer filter medium makes a home for working bacteria. The idea is that the larger pebbles will catch the larger detritus, while the finer gravel will make an excellent home for the bacteria so essential to the under-gravel filter's success.

If you are going to do this, it's important to note that you must take care during setup and cleanings, that the two gravels are kept apart as much as possible. You must keep them from mixing. This probably adds another 30 to 45 minutes in the yearly cleaning of the tank, but should reward you the rest of the year with a crystal clear aquarium. Some small amount of mixing, of course, is inevitable.

First
Things First!

Remember, if you are going to use an underground filter, make sure you place the filter in the tank first! And try to avoid any gravel under the filter's bottom. That should remain fairly free so that water can flow uninterrupted. Remember, the gravel bed is the filter in this setup.

then you don't want this stuff. It's going to turn your freshwater aquarium into a saltwater, slow-death chamber for your fish.

Gravel can be found in almost all pet stores. There is a wide variety of gravels, and the type you choose will depend on which fish you buy. Generally speaking, gravels are usually graded from coarse (or very coarse) to very fine. There are a number of things you need to know before picking any one of them. If you have any kind of bottom-feeding fish in mind, especially catfish or almost any type of goldfish, you'll want a coarse grade. However, don't get it too big, or some of the fish that like to root around in the gravel won't be able to. Smaller, finer gravel will certainly lead to choking deaths. Yes, a fish can die choking on a mouthful of gravel. Sometimes they'll manage to swallow a mouthful of fine gravel, and then they're in trouble. Their system can't pass such materials. Fine grain also tends to clog under-gravel filters. A good size for a beginner is pea-sized gravel.

One thing that's fun about gravel is that it comes in a great number of colors. Anything from almost fluorescent colors to neutral shades of grays and tans. Depending on your decision on how to decorate, you can go in any number of different directions. From Mod Squad to Jacques Cousteau, you can create the world you want your fish to inhabit. And, of course, remember, as we discussed earlier, your lighting decision will also have great bearing on how your aquascape will be viewed.

At minimum, you want to be able to cover the bottom with about 2 inches of the aquarium bottom. If you want to use an under-gravel filter, you'll want almost another inch of gravel, give or take. You might buy a little extra, in case you want to terrace your gravel at one point or another. If that's the case, you'll need more. You can always remove it if you feel you have too much.

Plants

All right, let's put this on the table fast and quick. There is no shame in using artificial plants! Purists will hate us. So be it. The decision between live and natural plants is a difficult one. Let us lay it out before you. First, real plants are a whole other realm of husbandry. Not only are you trying to keep your fish alive and

Let's Put On a Show!

Why do we use the word *foreground*? A foreground is usually what's referred to either in a painting or photograph, or on a stage. The foreground is the area closest to the viewer, in terms of depth. When you look at a fish tank, it's almost like watching television. Indeed, one of the main attractions of owning a fish tank is watching the fish interact. You want the foreground to be as open as possible, because that's where you want the fish to interact. Too many plants up front, and you won't be able to see the fish. The foreground usually is the lowest terrace and has few, if any, plants.

The middle ground is the area between the background and the foreground. It is usually the middle terrace, where the gravel is higher than the foreground, but not as high as the background. Intermittent plants and rocks, and maybe a broken clay pot or aeration device, are placed here.

The background is the highest terrace. Plant many plants here—where the gravel is the deepest. It gives an opportunity for fish to seek shelter or protection against aggressors or whenever they feel threatened. The background also helps hide unsightly wires and the filter.

**Definition Please:
Specimen Plants**

Specimen plants are also known as crown plants or majestic crown plants.

healthy, you're also trying to keep your plants alive and healthy. It's a lot of extra work. And for those who are new to the hobby, it may be dispiriting. Live plants, however, are an excellent source for oxygen exchange, and lend a natural beauty to your aquascape. They are a great way to utilize nitrates in your tank.

We recommend that beginners choose plastic plants for their first attempts at keeping a tank. Plants, in the beginning, are just another thing that can go wrong. They have their own needs, and if they are not met, they will die. Dead plants are even more worrisome than living plants. After they die they disintegrate and foul the water. They can cause new pH problems or even introduce new diseases or parasites.

Another thing to worry about is that some species of fish love to chew on plants. This is how herbivores eat in the wild. Goldfish are especially notorious for munching on plants. One of the other things to remember about plants is that fish love to swim through them and hide in them. Despite the fact that you want to see your fish, they aren't always so excited about you being in their face. Plants, whether artificial or real, give the fish an opportunity to hide when they want, and so provide them with some basic cover.

Plastic plants today are much better than they were years ago. Many are very lifelike and will add beauty and depth to your space without causing endless worry. You local pet emporium will be flooded with all types and varieties, including colorful variations to create a different, more stylized setting. Of course, the other positive is that your fish will have something to swim in and out of, and you won't have to worry about it being a detriment to the safety of the tank.

Real Plants

Okay, okay, we weren't able to dissuade you, and you feel you must conquer it all. In that case, it's important to have a basic understanding of plants and their needs. It's also a good idea to familiarize yourself with the most common tropical plants available to the freshwater aquarist.

While real plants do utilize nitrates, and they do give off oxygen and remove carbon dioxide, it is important to remember that they also need sufficient amounts of light. None of the above happens if there's no light, because all of this takes place during photosynthesis, and the plants use the light to function. As plants get less and less light, instead of taking in carbon dioxide, they release it. All this can have a negative affect on your tank's pH level. So, if you've really committed yourself to keeping live plants in your tank, it's imperative to provide adequate filtration and light. You want to make sure your plants are healthy and are an added feature of your aquarium, not a drain on your efforts.

One of the interesting things about live plants is that they are an excellent indicator of your aquarium's health. If anything goes wrong—pH, disease, anything—the plants are the first to die, giving you an important warning sign of where your fish tank is headed.

There are many different kinds of plants. Barry James, an aquatic plant expert, has stated that aquatic plants can be divided into several groups. Many of these groups are based on plant form, size, and growing characteristics.

- **Bunch plants.** Bunch plants are good because they tend to be inexpensive and fairly hardy. *Egeria densa* is a bunch plant that is great for beginners. It cleans the water, produces lots of oxygen, and grows fast. Bunch plants reproduce off a single stem and may quickly envelop a tank if not pruned. Arranged in groups or in lines, these plants are great for planting in the background of your aquascape, as they have long stems and leaves. Another plant that spreads rapidly is *Vallisneria spiralis*. It is very hardy and grows to about 15 inches.

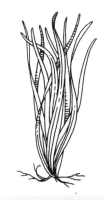

Twisted Vallisneria

- **Floating plants.** A common species of floating plant is *Riccia fluitans*. This plant provides an ideal spawning habitat and is fast growing. Floating plants float on or just below the surface; their root system dangles in the water. These plants provide shade to other fishes and plants in the aquarium or in a pond.

Water Sprite

- **Specimen plants.** These are also known as majestic crown plants. One of the most popular species of specimen plants is the amazon sword plant, *Echinodorus* species, which are extremely tolerant plants with leaves that are broad in the middle and tapered at the each end. These tend not to grow too high but can grow quite large. These plants should be planted in the middle ground to create a striking design. Another such plant is the *Saggittaria*.

- **Deep marginal plants.** These plants are good for a great many places in your aquascape, including the middle ground, background, or back corners of the tank. Generally, these plants grow from bulbs or tubers and produce long stems. Two types of these plants that have modest care needs are *Nymphaea* and *Aponogeton*. They are ideal deep marginal plants. The *Aponogeton* are also known as water lilies. When allowed to grow unchecked these plants can block out light from other plants. Pruning is necessary.

- **Middle ground plants.** These are plants that tend not to grow too tall. They are smaller than specimen plants, for example, and tend to have plants in the form of rosettes. These plants include *Cryptocoryne affinis*, which grows to only 12 inches and is very suitable for grouping. But we think these plants are better suited for a slightly more accomplished aquarist. *Cryptocoryne* species are slow growers and take time to establish themselves. They are also easily affected by disease and sometimes require iron supplements, which is why they are not recommended for beginners.

- **Foreground plants.** These plants are small, and are therefore ideally suited to the foreground of the tank. One group that is quite attractive with their bunched grass-like appearances includes the *Eleocharis* species.

This isn't everything! There are many plants in each category. Your local pet store will have a wide variety in each section. Plants take as much time and consideration as fish, and you would do well to spend some time speaking with your pet store professional, discussing just what kind of fish you have and what kind of plants you should have.

Just like the fish you put into the tank, the plants you choose also require specific temperatures to survive and thrive. Would you put a palm tree in Anchorage, Alaska, and expect it to thrive? Well, aquatic plants are the same way. It's important to remember, when you bring in plants, that you need to think like a gardener. The plants we have indicated above are those that are the most hardy in each type. Also, it's important to remember that most plants will do better in a finer size substrate than in a larger pebble-sized gravel. Again, when considering real plants, you need to take into account exactly what kind of fish you want, because that will dictate the plants and the kinds of gravel you will need. It's all very interconnected.

Select your plants carefully—just as carefully as you would select your fish. Avoid plants with brown leaves, or that have large areas of brown. Make sure the root system looks healthy. Any kind of decay will cause you incredible amounts of grief. Learn as much as you can about the various plants that appeal to you. How high will they grow? How wide? How hardy are they? Do any kind of fish in particular like to eat them? How much light do they require? Do you need to reconsider the bulb you bought for your

hood? These are the questions you need to ask. And don't buy plants that are too big for your aquascape. You don't want to add a plant that will outgrow or overly shade your aquarium. Remember, your fish want plants to swim through. They don't want to fight with the plants for space.

Once you've decided to put real plants in your tank, you've added another live thing you are responsible for. They, like the fish, require tender loving care. For example, some plants require routine fertilization. Fertilizers come in different forms. Commercially made fertilizers include liquid, tablet, and substrate fertilizer forms. Read the instructions carefully! The frequency and amount of fertilization depends on which product you purchase.

Now, here's something we know you weren't anticipating. Not only do you have to fertilize these things, you need to clean them, too! Are you sure this is a hobby? Since when is household cleaning a part of any hobby? About once a week you need to remove dead leaves from plants. This can easily be done by hand. This prevents debris from degrading water quality in the tank and from inhibiting photosynthesis on the plant. If you are successful, trimming and pruning will become an absolute necessity. There is nothing worse than an overgrown aquarium.

Decorations

Let's dish! Maybe you want the fabulous magical castle with bubbles (you know, the kind Ivana Trump might choose) and the treasure chest filled with finery, or you want the psychedelic fluorescent palate (you've never really gotten over the Grateful Dead), or maybe you want to go au naturel (ooo-la-la). Decorating is a purely personal thing.

All right, this is important, but brief. Who are you decorating this space for? You or the fish? It can be for you. Your fish need space to hide and relax. A fish with no place to hide is a fish that's headed for a nervous breakdown. In nature, fish have nooks and crannies where they can hide when they are intimidated by other fish as well as you, you big lummox! It's important to provide equal space where the fish can swim and hide, and you can view them and watch them interact.

Pet stores sell all kinds of wacky tank decorations that enhance the habitat you are providing your fish. When you get to the pet store, you'll see that a number of these fantastical creations are usually made of plastic or some ceramic material. They also have some simpler things, too, like large rocks or stones. Another fun thing are the huge clumps of colored glass that look like rocks. Don't pick this stuff up off the street or from the ocean, river, or woods. It's unsafe for your fish. Purchase tank decorations from the dealer. That way, you avoid the addition of toxic substances and water chemistry modifying agents to your tank. Don't pick up rocks and try to place them in your tank. However, slate and granite are excellent natural additions to the tank. Wood is an attractive addition to any tank, but this, too, should be purchased by the beginner from a pet store. Before buying any decorations for your aquarium, take the time to design the kind of setting you want for your fish.

An Aquarium Backdrop

Although they seem kind of corny, over the years the backdrop has become a more and more interesting part of the aquascape. More often than not, these are made of paper or plastic. The nicest part of the backdrop is that it will hide unsightly hoses, wires, filters, and other aquarium accessories from view. They do this by being affixed to the back of the tank, providing an added touch to your aquascape. They are more attractive than your living room wallpaper or anything else that's sitting behind your tank. Whether a solid color, a wild pattern or a scene of some kind, the backdrop is the final touch to the picture and creates something more pleasing to the eye.

Don't Buy Anything!

It's important to sketch out on paper what you're trying to achieve before you run down to the pet store and just start buying things. Don't be a shopaholic. Take some time, see what's available, and start putting it together in your head. Then write it down. Include the gravel, plants, decorations, and backdrop when you do so. Keep in mind that fish require shelters as well as

Vacuuming Tip

Vacuuming is an important part of aquarium maintenance. However, if you have small fish, such as fry or neon tetras, make sure you don't accidentally suck one of them up into the vacuum. Try to steer clear of the fish, to chase them away as you clean.

swimming space. The worst thing you can do to your fish is to constantly change the environment. It makes them skittish and unsure. They won't be happy with you and you won't be happy with them. Therefore, visualize your aquarium with rocks, caves, and areas of refuge. After you've taken the time to think it through and commit it to paper, you'll be surprised how easy it will be to arrange and create, and how much happier you'll be with it when it's done.

Other Accessories

After you set up your aquarium, you'll start advancing your knowledge of the hobby. You'll begin to accumulate various things that will make keeping your aquarium easier. Some of the following items will give you a head start in making your aquarium a healthier environment and easier to keep.

Water Quality Test Kits

We've already discussed the absolute necessity of water quality test kits. When you buy any prefab kit or purchase your aquarium materials, don't forget this important accessory. Test kits that measure pH, hardness, and nitrogen compounds are a must. Remember, the latter should test for ammonia, nitrite, and nitrate.

Algal Sponge

One of the best things that will keep your aquarium user friendly is the algal sponge. You'll use this more often than you think, so you'll want to keep it handy. Why an algal sponge? Even if you keep your tank out of direct sunlight, it's important to know that algae will form. Any light whatsoever will lead to this green monster, the moss of the deep. A quick cleaning of the inside of the aquarium with an algal sponge will improve visibility immediately—even when you didn't realize that there was a problem. The algae can form a slight film.

There are many kinds of algal sponges. The most typical algal sponge or aquarium cleaner is a sponge attached to a long handle, which is used for scraping down the inside of the tank without

Gravel Vacuum

having to empty the aquarium out. It will not scrape or leave scratches on the glass, but it will easily scrape off algae. Another, and more preferable algal sponge is the magnetized cleaner. This involves the use of two magnets with cleaning surfaces. One magnet is kept outside the tank and the other is driven on the inside walls of the tank by the outside magnet. These generally allow you to get into corners or behind plants more easily than the sponge on a handle might allow.

A Vacuum

Yes, there's vacuuming too. As if it's not bad enough that you have to clean the plants and do the windows, now you have to vacuum. It's like having a second house! Whatever your distaste for vacuuming or at least the idea of it, an aquarium vacuum is a must for the beginner. Vacuums range from the inexpensive to the very expensive. The vacuum is used to clean up any kind of debris that may be floating around in your tank, especially the kind that settles to the bottom and moves around the substrate. The less expensive ones operate via a hand pump siphon. The more expensive ones use a small battery-powered motor like a real vacuum. The hand pump is fine for the beginner, but as you move to larger and more complex aquariums, you may want to consider buying a more substantial vacuum.

Fish Nets

What's the most important reason to have a fish net? So that you can handle your fish properly. To do the job right, you'll need two. Make sure that you get a net that will fit your fish properly. It should be roomy. The idea is not to injure the fish. You don't want a fish that's too big for the net, flopping around or trying to fight its way out. You also want something that's long enough, so that you can dip deep into your tank when you have to. However, you don't want something too large, or it will be too difficult to maneuver inside the aquascape. Nets will come in more handy than you think. You'll use it to remove dead fish, to remove your

Casting a Wide Net

You should always have at least two good nets and should probably be smaller than the other. The small net is good for getting into tight corners where fish will go to avoid just such an intruder. The large one should be large, but not so large as to make it unwieldy in the tank. The larger one is usually good for the quick grab. Many experienced aquarists use two nets when trying to corner a fish. They use the smaller one to chase the fish, driving it into the larger net.

live fish when you're going to do a full cleaning, or to rescue an injured or diseased fish.

A Five-Gallon Bucket and a Siphon Hose

One of the most often used items during the year-long maintenance schedule is the five-gallon bucket and siphon hose. You'll also want to keep this in a place where it's easy to reach. This bucket and siphon hose should not be used for anything else. Buy the hose or tubing from a pet store. Don't wash the car with the bucket, think you're going to clean it out, and then fill it up with water for your aquarium. There are always residual chemicals that you can't see. Your fish can't see them either, but they will feel them. Many fish have been accidentally killed by people's carelessness with residual chemicals. Use the bucket and siphon hose only for your aquarium. You'll be glad you did.

CHAPTER TWO

Setting Up the Aquarium

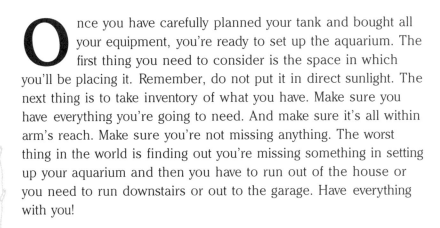

Once you have carefully planned your tank and bought all your equipment, you're ready to set up the aquarium. The first thing you need to consider is the space in which you'll be placing it. Remember, do not put it in direct sunlight. The next thing is to take inventory of what you have. Make sure you have everything you're going to need. And make sure it's all within arm's reach. Make sure you're not missing anything. The worst thing in the world is finding out you're missing something in setting up your aquarium and then you have to run out of the house or you need to run downstairs or out to the garage. Have everything with you!

Set Up Your Aquarium

If you have taken inventory and are convinced you are ready to begin, then it truly is time to start. Carefully follow these steps and your life will be much easier:

1. Everything must be clean! Thoroughly rinse the gravel, tank, filter, heater, aquarium decorations, artificial plants, and anything else you expect to put in the tank. Do this with warm tap water only. Never use any kind of chemical cleaner with these items. Never use soap or detergent, or anything similar. A thorough rinsing with clean warm water is perfect. Why, you may ask, do you need to wash off perfectly fine, brand new gravel? Residues, dirt, and other toxic agents can accumulate on your equipment between the time it is manufactured and the time it gets to your home. When it comes to cleaning aquarium decorations such as rocks and wood, use a new scrubbing brush to remove dirt. Again, don't ever use any kind of soap when cleaning your aquarium components; this can cause water quality problems as well as immediate health problems for your fish.

No Soap Allowed!

Note: Never use soap to clean anything in your tank. Water and elbow grease are always the best weapons against dirt and algae. Detergents or other chemicals can leave residue, which could be fatal to your fish.

THE "WHERE DO I PLACE MY AQUARIUM?" CHECKLIST

❏ Is it near an electrical outlet?

❏ Is it near a convenient source of water?

❏ Is there a fair amount of sunlight? Not too much, not too little?

❏ Is it in a place where I don't care if I spill a little water from time to time? (A bare floor is usually preferable.)

❏ Is the tank in an area where there will be traffic daily?

❏ Is the tank out of the way?

❏ Is the tank away from a heater that would adversely affect the water temperature?

Algae

Depending on which part of the scientific community you are talking to, algae are either simple-celled plants or simple-celled animals. Regardless, what plaque is to your teeth, algae is to your aquarium. Be careful to keep your tank clear of most algae, though a little is a good thing.

One of the most important parts of starting a new tank is cleaning the gravel. The biggest problem with new gravel is dust. This is a residue that is on your gravel, no matter how natural looking it is. If you don't clean the gravel, your aquarium will be cloudy and will need a cleaning almost immediately. This fine soot will get on everything. And it's unhealthy for the fish!

Another method of rinsing gravel

This is where your five-gallon bucket comes in handy. Empty all your gravel into the bucket. Then fill the rest with water. Now, roll up your sleeves, stick your hands into the bucket, and move that water around. Knead the gravel as you would dough if you were making bread or washing clothes the old-fashioned way. Really move that gravel around. Let the gravel settle and pour out as much water as you can. Now repeat the process all over again. Do this several times until the water that you pour off is clear. Brand new gravel can have a lot of dust. It might take as many as four to five rinsings before you are done. Sometimes it takes more. Be prepared.

2. If you haven't already done so, place the tank on the stand. Make sure it matches up perfectly. You can't make any mistakes here or you might ruin the tank and the rest of your house when you finally do fill it up. Make sure you're happy with where the tank is. Don't think you're going to move it once it's filled. As we said before, this is an aquarium, with lots of splashing water and a very heavy, unstable element and structure. It's staying where you put it.

OK, now it's time to aquascape! Where's Martha Stewart when you need her? And what do we start with first? That's right, the gravel. Not just any old gravel, but your fabulous, and now cleaner and heavier, gravel. Carefully put it into the tank, making sure not to pour the gravel straight from the bucket all in one shot. We've

SETTING UP AN AQUARIUM
EQUIPMENT CHECKLIST

Needed for the first day:

- ❏ Glass aquarium
- ❏ Fish tank stand or furniture with support board
- ❏ Electrical outlet or extension cord
- ❏ Five-gallon bucket (never been used)
- ❏ Hood with light or hood and light
- ❏ Gravel

- ❏ Filter
- ❏ Filter medium
- ❏ pH kit
- ❏ Aeration devices
- ❏ Heater
- ❏ Algae sponge
- ❏ Backdrop (optional)

Needed after establishment of working environment to maintain a healthy aquarium (2 days to 3 weeks later):

- ❏ Plants (real or artificial)
- ❏ Decorations
- ❏ Five-gallon bucket and siphon hose

- ❏ Vacuum
- ❏ Two nets
- ❏ A much smaller second tank for emergency situations

For Under-Gravel Filter Users

Remember, if you're going to have an under-gravel filter, be sure and put that in before you pour your gravel.

Designer Water

Never use any mineral waters! Never add Evian, Poland Spring, or any other mineral water to your aquarium. These waters are not designed for fish use. The minerals in them may be too much for them and cause illness.

seen gravel poured like that go right through the bottom of the tank straight onto the living room carpet. Be careful!

Now you need to start landscaping it. Create some terraces and some different grades.

The usual way to terrace is to make the gravel higher in the back than in the front. This will also be important when you're placing your plants, which will need a little extra depth so that you can anchor them properly. This also adds an extra depth of field to the aquascape.

3. Here's where planning comes in handy. At this point you want to add the largest pieces of your aquascape, such as wood, rocks, or the large ceramic castle. This is not the time to add plants! Don't add plants, artificial or real, until we tell you. The problem with plants is that they will move easily when you pour in the water. And don't put in the filter or water heater yet, either, but remember to leave room for them.

4. Now is an excellent time to place your airstones, because they'll probably be hidden, at least in part, beneath some of your larger objects. You want to do as much as you can to hide the tubing that goes along with the airstones, so you'll need to consider this when you place them. The larger objects are usually a great way to hide some of these things.

5. Now is the time to add the water. You want to avoid disturbing the portion of the aquascape you've already laid out. In order to do this, you need to place a clean plate or bowl on the substrate and carefully pour the water onto it, letting the water gently fill the tank as it spills off the sides of the plate or bowl. Once the tank is full, remove the plate or bowl. In most households, tap water will be the appropriate water source. The aquarium aging process combined with

filtration will in most cases alleviate minor tap water problems. If you suspect that your tap water is excessively hard or soft or contains high levels of chloramine, check with your local water company. In some cases, you may need to purchase water or chemically treat your tap water. Most hobbyists chemically treat their tap water and let it sit an extra few days to a week to complete the maturation process.

6. You are going to place the heater and filter next. Make absolutely sure neither is plugged in. Now, place the filter in the space you've planned for it. Make sure that the exiting water isn't going to disrupt your aquascape. Follow the manufacturer's instructions regarding filter media before setting it on or in the tank. Next, you need to position the heater. Remember, you need to do this in such a way as to maximize its output, so that the warm water is evenly distributed throughout the tank. Don't place it in a corner; place it somewhere near the filter output, so that the warm water is carried out into the tank's circulation. The airstone is also a good place for positioning the heater.

7. Now add some of the smaller things. If you're using artificial plants, you can add them now. If you are using real plants, you need to wait until the aquarium has matured before planting them. The temperatures must be adjusted and the water has to be treated. You can also add your thermometer now. Place the smaller decorations in the tank, like a bubbling treasure chest or diver. This is the time to fine-tune your aquascape.

8. Fit the hood, making sure that the external components and electrical equipment are properly placed. Again, nothing should be plugged in yet. Add the light on top of the canopy and make sure it is correctly hooked up.

9. If possible, use an extension cord with multiple outlets. You'll probably have the pump or filter to plug in, as well as a heater and maybe another pump for the airstone. You don't want to plug in too many things, but most of

Distilled Water

Distilled water? What's this gourmet stuff all about! *Distilled water is much different than mineral water.* Tropical fish hobbyists make distilled water storing tap water over a span of 3 days to a week. Usually this is done in 1-to-5 gallon jugs, with the cap on tight. This period of time gives the minerals present in tap water time to break down, so that they are not harmful to the fish.

Another thing to do is to test the water you have stored after 3 days to make sure it's the right pH. Wait a couple more days. Then you have water that is ready. If you have two or three containers of water available, and you'll be able to add water or make water changes without the fear the fish won't survive.

these are low-voltage electrical motors that won't cause a power overload. When you are confident that the electrical wiring is safely insulated from sources of water, plug the aquarium units in and turn on the system. Make sure the heater is properly adjusted; this may take a day or two. Check the operation of the filter, air pumps, and light.

10. Now you can add the final and most important ingredient—patience! You can't just add the fish now. First, you must let the tank water mature.

Aquarium Maturation

When you have completed the previous steps, you will have a tank filled with water, but you will not have the working, well-balanced artificial habitat for fish that we call an aquarium. This is just untested water in a tank. The filter hasn't had time to work through the cycling of the water. The heater hasn't been adjusted, which may take a few days. In short, while there's lots of cool stuff in your tank, it's not ready as an inhabitable place for your fish to live.

To achieve all of this, you need to let the tank mature. As you read in Chapter 1, fish require suitable water quality that has appropriate levels of water pH and hardness. Your tap water may be hazardous to your fish by harboring unknown additives (many municipal water supplies have treated water). And lest you forget, your brand-new tank does not have a well-established nitrogen cycle. Safe water parameters need to be established before fish can be added to the tank. Temperature regulation, filtration, and water circulation will help your water to mature. It just needs a little time.

Experts disagree a bit on how long it takes water to mature. Size and water condition are both factors that lead to those types of discrepancies. For example, a new under-gravel filter may take between four and six weeks to fully establish itself. You should see what the filter's manufacturer's directions advise. However, if you don't have an under-gravel filter, most experts agree that you should probably wait a minimum of 10 to 14 days before introducing the first plants and fish into your aquarium. We have added

STAY, PLANT, STAY!

There are two things you can do to insure that your plants (whether artificial or real) will stay placed securely. Try doing both.

1. Plant your plants in the middle and background where the gravel is deepest and you can plant them deeper into the substrate. Many aquarists who don't want to see their plants uprooted bury them at least an 1½" deep. Sometimes you might end up with you plants being shorter than you like, but they won't move.
2. You can buy plant weights at most pet centers. These also make the plants more difficult to move.

How do we keep other things from moving?

Aerators: Usually it's best to either plant an aerator underneath something heavy or trap it underneath several heavy things. If you don't, it will always come up. Rocks are usually very good. Driftwood is also excellent. If you have one of those plastic shipwrecks, you might want to weigh down the plastic tubing leading into it with a rock or some other heavy object.

Decorations: Buy decorations that are fairly heavy. Decorations that are light are extremely difficult to keep anchored. I have seen people try to use drinking glasses, jars, and bottles as decorations. Unless they are made of a heavy gauge, it is not generally recommended. (And remember, it's best to use only those decorations bought at your pet store.)

fish and plants to a new tank in as little as two to three days. It depends on when your pH and hardness stabilize and on how well the nitrogen cycle is established. There are commercial treatments available that will accelerate the maturation process. Some of these actually come with your aquarium kits that are available at your local pet store. Check with your local dealer and read instructions carefully.

Before you can add fish, though, you will need to test the pH of the water. You'll probably need to do this once a day to gauge how your water is doing. You cannot add fish into a tank in which the pH is off. You'll only kill your fish or make life difficult for them. The pH and hardness should stabilize in two to four days. Then it is important to fuel the nitrogen cycle. This can be done by introducing a few very hardy inexpensive fish, like common goldfish, into the tank. You will need to produce the necessary ammonia that will help establish bacterial colonies that comprise the nitrogen cycle. To do this you need to add a few fish that can biologically and naturally add that ammonia.

Now that you have introduced fish, it's important to continue to monitor ammonia, nitrite, and nitrate levels. You want to be careful of "new tank syndrome." At first, within a few days, you will see ammonia and nitrite levels begin to climb rapidly and nitrate will remain low. If you have introduced the fish too soon, this can result in the poisoning of your fish. This especially happens with many beginners who rush the maturation process. This means that the bacterial colonies which convert these compounds into the less harmful nitrate are not yet established. In most cases, if you wait a few days before introducing your "starter" fish, this will not occur. That's why patience is so important.

Generally, in about one to two weeks, your ammonia levels will stabilize. In this case, nitrite will decrease, and nitrate will increase. This is the sun breaking through the clouds. You can now add fish to your exciting new habitat.

This needs to be done slowly. You should add a couple of fish every few days in batches. Remember to calculate the number of fish you think your tank can handle, and buy conservatively. You need to think this through. As you continue to add fish, you need to continue to monitor ammonia, nitrite, and nitrate levels. If a sudden peak occurs in any of these categories, stop adding fish. When that peak diminishes, you can continue to add fish.

How to Spot Healthy Tropical Fish

Since fish don't jog and they don't have test scores, there must be some easier way to judge fish when you are buying them. No matter what the variety, there are some general tell-tale signs you should look for when selecting fish. If you listen to us and follow these tips, we can assure you that you'll be bringing home the best of all healthy pets. Jot down these points so that you won't forget them in all the excitement of buying your fish. If you fail to observe the key details, you might end up with a diseased pet right from the start.

Unfortunately, what should ultimately be one of the most exciting days as a hobbyist should be marked by suspicion. It can't be stated enough that you must be keen in your awareness of what is going on in each tank as you choose your fish. These fish will dictate how your experience with this new hobby will go. You need to be on your guard, as well as excited by the prospect of choosing your new pets. Choose indiscriminately, and you'll regret it for months. Choose well, and you'll be on your way as an accomplished and happy aquarist, with years and years of enjoyment ahead of you.

Activity

Big hint right off the top. If you see a fish swimming upside down, don't buy it. It's not cool or charming. It's either malformed or dying. In fact, you should avoid all fish, without exception, that are not swimming smoothly like their counterparts. Be aware that some fish swim oddly, especially any species that doesn't have a dorsal fin (and there are several). But be sure that any fish you

Bunch Plants

Bunch plants are so called because they are sold in bunches, usually in groups of six or eight. They are usually inexpensive and fairly hardy.

choose is swimming like the other members of its species. Other things to avoid are fish that constantly stay at the top, gulping air, or those who remain listlessly at the bottom. (Again, many varieties of catfish do that naturally, so be aware of the characteristics of the fish you are planning to purchase.)

Now, if you were buying a dog, you wouldn't want one of those puppies in a litter that's always bouncing off the walls. However, you definitely want a fish that's very active. This is the number one attribute that's important to identifying a healthy fish. If you want something that just floats, you can get water lilies. And if you want something that's just going to sit there, you should get a turtle or frog. But if you want fish, you want fish that are going to swim around. They need to be able to swim smoothly. They should have quick reactions, and they should appear to be cognizant of what is going on around them.

Eyes

Here's another unbreakable commandment: Never let a pet shop owner talk you into buying a fish that has cloudy eyes, cataracts, or any other kind of mutation where the eyes are concerned, unless such characteristics are particular to that breed. For example, there are some breeds of fish, especially in the goldfish family, that have some pretty funky eyes. But you should be aware of those distinctive features before going to the store. Eyes should be bright, clear, and unclouded, and the fish should react to light.

Fins

Fins are a very good indicator of health. If a fish's dorsal fin is folded down, you should steer clear of the fish. A folded-down fin is a sign of an ailing fish. Make sure never to bring home a fish that has any frayed or split fins. The fins should be absolutely free of fungus, slime, and white spots. Refuse any fish offered to you with flawed fins, no matter the seller's reasoning.

All fins, including the tail fin, should almost always be fanned out. The display of the fins is the sign from the fish that it is healthy and vibrant.

Scales

Another commandment is that you shall never buy a fish that has any unnatural blemishes on its skin or scales. You must not buy any fish that's missing scales (or that has any other kind of wound) or shows any signs of fungus, such as white, cottony spots, or an excessive mucus-like coating.

Healthy fish are gleaming with their shiny scales or are almost velvety in their appearance (especially dark fish), and their bodies should be absolutely unblemished. Any hint of disease is reason to pass on a fish. Bringing in one diseased fish can kill off an entire tank and necessitate your having to dismantle the entire aquarium, disinfect it, and start over.

Environment

Always look at the tank from which you are selecting your fish. Is there a white fungus on anything, including the plants or other living things? Are any of the other fish diseased? Is the tank well kept or is it cloudy, dirty, and poorly maintained? Do you really want to take a chance on a fish selected from a tank that looks infected or ill-kept? Many diseases are highly contagious when it comes to fish, so you can't be too careful, no matter what your pet store professional tells you.

Most respectable pet shop salespeople and dealers won't sell you diseased fish. However, use a little common sense. Always beware. Look at these people the same way people joke about used car salesmen. Do not buy a fish from someone who seems unsavory or whom you don't trust. The best way to ensure a good fishkeeping experience is to make sure you do it right the first time. Be wary, but have fun.

Placing Fish in the Tank

Okay, you've selected your fish. They are healthy, active, and free of blemishes. You are thrilled. Now, how do you get these fascinating creatures from their current home to their new home? In a plastic sandwich bag, of course. Only partly kidding. Most pet stores will put your fish in separate bags so that you can transport

**The First Fish
Is Very Important!**

When you chose a fish to bring home, try to buy the hardiest and the least territorial of fishes you are considering. Hat's usually the best fish to start with.

your fish home. Before he or she closes each bag, it's imperative that they leave a sizable amount of airspace in the bag when they tie it closed. This makes sure that the fish has a sufficient supply of air to make it home with you. Many stores will give you either an opaque plastic bag or a good old-fashioned grocery bag in which to place your fish, so that they will feel somewhat safe during transportation.

On the trip home, try to avoid sudden movements. You want the fish's ride home to be smooth and calm. Don't keep moving the fish in and out of strong light. Keep the fish in similar surroundings until you get home, and try to keep the temperature as constant as possible.

It's a good idea not to buy all your fish on your first trip, especially with a large tank. Buy only one or two species at first; that way you can introduce them to the tank and see how they react. If things go well, you can introduce a few more, and then a few more and be happy with your successes. Sometimes, however, things don't always go so well. Sometimes fish die. If this is the case, you'll be able to learn what's wrong without endangering too many healthy fish.

Introducing Your Pets to Their New Home

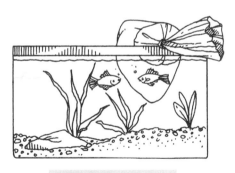

Introducing a New Fish into Your Tank

1. Take the hood and light off your aquarium. Place the clear plastic bags in the tank without opening them. They will float. Let them. You want to let them sit in the tank for approximately 10 to 15 minutes. The idea is to let the water temperature in the bag acclimate itself to the water temperature in your aquarium. You want this to happen slowly. Too great a shock can kill a fish instantly.

2. After the bags have been floating 10 or 15 minutes, it's OK to open them. But don't pour the contents out into the tank! Tear open the bag over the tank and place it in the aquarium. Just let the bag sit there another five minutes. Pour about one cup of water from the aquarium into the bag and let sit for another 10 to 15 minutes.

FISH-BUYING CHECKLIST:

- ❏ Is it a fish that will be compatible with my other fish?
- ❏ Is it a fish that needs the same temperature as my other fish?
- ❏ Where in the water column does it usually reside?
- ❏ Is it active and swimming around?
- ❏ Does it have anything wrong with it?
    - ❏ Scars?
    - ❏ Fungus?
    - ❏ Damaged fins?
- ❏ What does it eat?
- ❏ How big will it grow? Bigger than my other fish?

**Buon Giorno!
Mangia!**

Are you running an
aquarium or an Italian
restaurant? Don't try to
feed your fish just after
introducing them to
the new tank. Give
them a few hours.
They will be very
upset and probably
won't be ready to eat.
Some experts let them
wait a full 24 hours.
At least wait three or
four hours before
trying to ply your fish
with food. They need
time to get acclimated.

3. Now it's time to carry someone over the threshold.
Gently and slowly pour the contents of the bag into the
aquarium, or simply hold the bag in such a fashion that
the fish is able, under its own power and out of its own
sense of vitality, to swim into its new home.

Some more established aquarists, with more at stake than a
beginner, have established quarantine tanks. These are to fish what
Ellis Island was to America—a holding area to check out the newcomers. This gives the advanced aquarist an opportunity to inspect
the health and vitality of the fish in less hectic environs. Quarantine
tanks are usually smaller than the main tank, and are pretty simply
set up. They, of course, need to be properly filtered and monitored,
so that no fish will be put at risk. As a beginner, you shouldn't
need such a tank if you buy hardy fish from a reputable dealer.
For the advanced hobbyist, taking care of two tanks isn't a bad
thing. Many hobbyists who subscribe to this method are running
one or more than one tank that is extremely developed and they
don't want to risk years of work and development. For the
beginner, it's too much. One tank is enough to monitor for the
time being. Don't attempt monitoring two tanks until you have more
experience and a more elaborate setup.

Maintaining Your Aquarium

It seems like you've done everything. The aquarium was chosen
and set up. You checked the pH and let the water mature. Your
filter heater, and aeration equipment are running flawlessly. You've
introduced a fantastic array of new fish into their new aquatic
home and none of them have died. So far, you're a regular
Jacques Cousteau. However, this is where the work really begins.
What do we mean? Well, now it's about maintenance. In the world
of aquarists, maintenance is like clipping your dog's or cat's toe-
nails—it's not always inherently fun to do, but its necessary. You
and your pet will be better off and happier in the end.

Welcome to a set of new responsibilities. Maintaining a successful and healthy aquarium means that you'll be establishingsome

CALLING 911

Many things can go wrong when you introduce fish into a new tank. You should monitor your fish. Eating? Active? Alert? There have been cases where fish die instantly or within a week without warning. What to do?

Here's a list of things to check:

1. pH level
2. Temperature. Is it too cold, too warm? Is it consistent?
3. Did you use any commercial industrial cleansers?
4. Did you let the water mature long enough?
5. Water quality. Is it clear and well aerated?

Talk to your local pet professional and discuss with him or her what else may have gone wrong. It's important to let them know everything you did, to make sure you're not violating one of these fundamental steps.

new routines and getting to know how to provide for your fishes' basic needs. For example, you need to turn the light on and off regularly. You might want to regulate it by turning the light on an hour after sunrise and an hour before or after sunset. It's important to replicate the day for your aquatic pets.

One of the most important acts of maintenance is observation. Obviously, this is also the most fun. You need to get to know and understand your fish. You'll learn their behavior patterns and their activities. You'll learn how they interact. What's so important about this? The idea is to figure out what they normally do, so when they act unusually, you have a basis for comparison.

Consider this: Every morning, your neighbor gets up and takes a shower, plays his morning radio show too loudly, and leaves the house around the same time you do. One morning, your neighbor is walking the streets at daybreak in his underwear, reciting a Gregorian chant. Something odd? Now you get the picture. Is there one fish that's hanging out too much near the surface? Is there one that's hiding? Or getting picked on? Is there one that is having trouble swimming? Are their fins healthy and vibrant? Are their bodies clean and sleek? You need to observe your fish every day. This isn't a painting! It's a living, biological world that changes every day, sometimes for the better, sometimes for the worse.

For those of you who chose to install live plants, these are the smoke detectors of the aquatic world. If plants start to waver and decay, there's probably something wrong in your tank. With plants, you can cut off the offending branches or leaves. Pruning the affected parts is sometimes effective. Sometimes, you need to remove the whole plant.

The key word in aquarium success is stability. Stability is the key to maintaining healthy, vibrant fish. An aquarium wherein the conditions are always changing will put great stress on your fish. Fish don't react well to stress, as it makes them more prone to illness, disease, and death. If the quality of your water suddenly changes or the temperature suddenly rises or drops, this may cause stress and result in ill health for your fish. Rapid changes in water temperature are often the cause of stress and should be avoided at all costs. Is the heater working? How about your filter? Is your filter clogged? Does it need to be changed? Are your air pump, airstones, or other aerators working properly? You need to inspect, even if briefly, these things every day. Just a few moments of careful observation can mean the difference between a successful aquarium or a swamp. Most of this can be done while you are either feeding your fish or simply enjoying your new and exciting pets.

General Maintenance

Cleaning an aquarium involves an active, conscientious effort on your part. Maintaining a fish tank is not for the lazy at heart. Don't set up a tank if you don't intend to follow through and keep it clean and healthy. All too often, interest wanes after the first couple of months and the aquarium ultimately suffers the consequences. Realize that going into this hobby requires a real commitment on your part. Concern must be shown at every step and on every level. Your fishes' lives depend on your attention to detail.

Vacuuming

Vacuuming is one of the most important parts of maintaining your tank. You must prevent the accumulation of detritus in the gravel. Mulm is the combination of fish wastes, plant fragments, and uneaten food that settles and decays on the bottom of the aquarium. If not removed, this organic waste will ultimately break down into nitrites and nitrates via the nitrogen cycle. This will disturb your water chemistry, potentially harming your fish. If detritus is allowed to accumulate to excessive levels, your filter will clog and water quality will go downhill fast. If you have an undergravel filter, vacuuming is still very important because too much mulm will clog these filters as well, preventing water flow through the gravel.

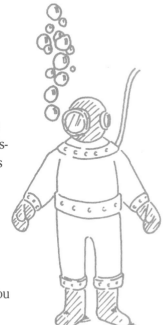

Aquarium vacuums are commercially available at your pet dealer. I recommend using a wide hose to siphon wastes while you are doing a water change. This accomplishes two goals at once: vacuuming mulm and removing water from the tank.

Check the Filter

Assuming you have an external filter or a box filter, it is very important to check the filter media. The top level matt gets dirty quickly and easily, as this is the level that collects the largest pieces of debris. An excessive buildup of detritus in your filter will inhibit flow and ultimately reduce the filter's effectiveness.

Rinse the filter mat under lukewarm water every three or four months until the water is clear. You should probably replace about 50 percent of the media every six months, making sure to reuse about half of the old filter material. You have established a viable working bacterial colony in your filter medium and you don't want to throw it out and start from square one. That's why some of the old media must be retained. One of the most common mistakes is the replacement of the entire filter contents every couple of months because it looks dirty. Some of that "dirt" is bacteria that are beneficial to the filtering process. For filters that utilize cartridges as media, check with the manufacturer for optimum maintenance and replacement rate.

Algae

Throughout this book we have intermittently referenced algae as an aquarium nuisance that should be controlled. What exactly is algae, and do all algae cause problems for your tank?

Algae are actually plants that belong to the class known as thallophyta with the fungi. They are relatively simple plants that range in size from the one-celled microscopic types to large sea-weeds that grow to over 230 feet. Algae are also very hardy plants that have a tremendous reproductive capacity. They can enter your aquarium as algal spores borne by the air or carried by new plants, snails, and tank furnishings from another aquarium.

Most species of algae occur in the waters and, like fish, have adapted to all kinds of water conditions. In your aquarium, they can be found on the surface, suspended in the water, or on the surfaces of rocks, gravel, and tank decorations. There are four groups of algae that are most troublesome to the aquarist:

VACUUMING! I HATE VACUUMING!

Vacuuming is easy to do, if not-a-little boring, whether we're talking about your living room or your aquarium. However, it's necessary. Imagine not vacuuming or washing your bathroom, kitchen, bedroom, or den floors for a whole year. Gross! It's the same for fish.

Vacuums can be manually operated, or you can buy battery-operated ones. Either are fine. The vacuum works like a small handheld filter. It sucks water up through a tube that looks like a wide-mouthed turkey baster. The water goes up the tube, is passed thorough a filter that traps the detritus, and then returns clean, to the tank.

Here are some quick, fast rules about vacuuming:

1. Remove the hood.
2. Vacuum slowly. Take the vacuum extension and place it over the gravel, but not into it. Watch it as the water swirls underneath it, and as the detritus flows up the tube. If you move too fast, you'll just stir everything up and you'll just make things messy.
3. Don't push things around. You'll only have to move everything back later.
4. Try to be as thorough as you can.
5. It shouldn't take more than 15 minutes.
6. Do it once every two weeks.

Magnetized
Algae Scraper

- **Green Algae.** These are the most common of the fresh-water algae. This group contains one-celled and multi-celled species. The one-celled green algae such as chlorella are not visible to the naked eye but appear as a green cloudiness in the water. These will sometimes form a green film on the aquarium glass. Multi-celled species including volvox also cause the water of your tank to look green. Green algae species like spirogyra form a filamentous mass in the aquarium while others form green threads attached to rocks and plants.
- **Diatoms.** These algae proliferate in aquariums with high nitrate levels. Diatoms form a brown slime on the gravel, rocks, decorations, and aquarium glass. Heavy concentrations of diatoms will discolor the water.
- **Whip Algae.** These single-celled species have tails or whips which they use to propel themselves through the water. These plants don't ordinarily affect the aquarium because they require such high nitrogen levels that the tank is usually dead by the time they proliferate. Water chemistry problems should be corrected before these species can take over.
- **Blue-green Algae.** These organisms are actually in a class of their own because they possess characteristics of both algae and bacteria. In your aquarium, blue-green algae form a dark green gelatinous mat on rocks, gravel, and plants. If allowed to proliferate, they will smother the tank. High nitrate levels and bright light feed these algae, which can survive in both acidic and alkaline water. They are also capable of producing toxins that will poison aquarium fish.

In low levels, algae can be somewhat beneficial to the aquarium, providing the same benefits as plants. But if algae is present, it will generally grow in excess if the right conditions exist. Excessive algal growth will overrun a tank unless water quality is properly maintained. High nitrate levels and sunlight will promote algal growth. Avoiding these conditions will minimize algae as a tank nuisance.

If you seem to have excessive algal growth, there are several other measures that you can employ to reduce the presence of algae in the aquarium:

- Introduce algae eaters, like flying foxes, black mollies, and Corydoras catfish, to keep algae in check on the gravel, rocks, and plants.
- Keep the aquarium well planted; nitrates will be consumed by healthy aquarium plants instead of being available for algae.
- Reduce the duration of light to 10 hours per day instead of 12 hours.
- Make sure that all rocks, plants, decorations, and gravel going into the tank are free of algae.
- Scrape algae from the aquarium walls with an algae scraper. These are usually sponges attached to a long stick, a razor blade attached to a stick, or magnetic scrapers.
- Remove excess nitrates that fuel algal growth by doing partial water changes regularly and in a timely fashion.

Don't become obsessed with algae to the point where you feel that all algae must be removed from the aquarium. I guarantee you that this is simply something that can't be effectively done. Expect to live with a little algae in your tank.

Test the Water

When you first set up the aquarium, testing the water every couple of days is critical to the water maturation process. When you begin to add fish, water chemistry changes radically, and water quality monitoring is critical to the survival of your fish. After this sensitive period of two to four weeks, it is still very important to test your water, and I recommend that you do so every week for the first two months. This will give you a good understanding of the mechanics of the nitrogen cycle and will indicate to you when nitrates are to the point where a water change is needed.

Algae—Friend and Foe!

Remember, algae does indeed have its useful side. Algae helps add oxygen to the water. And some species of fish love to munch on it. But too much algae can be harmful, and turn your water toxic as well as cut off light from the fish. It also obstructs your view.

After two months, your tank will certainly be well established and the need to test the water every week will diminish. At this point, a monthly water test will suffice unless you suspect that you might have tank problems. Sudden behavioral changes in your fish, fish disease, fish mortality, excessive algal growth, "smelly" water, and cloudy water all warrant an immediate water quality test and possible water change.

Water Changes

Water changes are one of the most important aspects of cleaning and maintaining your tank. And the nice part is you don't have to take the fish out. A water change is when you literally take out a percentage of the aquarium water and replace it with fresh or distilled water. The amount you change varies with the quality of your tank and with the frequency of water changes. Some experts feel that 10 percent water change is sufficient every week, while others feel that this volume should be closer to 30 percent. I recommend that you start with a water change of 10 to 20 percent every week and modify it either up or down, depending on your water quality.

Water changes help to maintain good water quality because you are diluting the amount of nitrogenous compounds, like nitrites and nitrates, harmful gases, and other toxic substances, each time you do one. The water you add, which should be pure distilled water if possible, will be more oxygen rich than the water that has been in your tank.

The best way to do a water change is to use a siphon and a large bucket. The siphon is basically just a three- or four-foot hose or tube that will transfer water from the tank to the bucket. Siphons are available at your local pet store. Be sure to use the siphon only for cleaning your tank.

How to Siphon

1. Fill the tube completely with water, making sure there is no trapped air or bubbles anywhere in the tube. Make

sure that the siphon is clean and that your hands are clean as well. You can fill the hose at the sink or by submerging it in the aquarium. Only do the latter if your aquarium is large enough to accommodate the hose without spooking the fish. Use your thumbs to block both ends of the siphon to keep the water in and air out.

2. Keeping your thumbs in place, place one end of the hose in the aquarium and the other in the bucket. Make sure that the bucket end is lower than the aquarium or siphoning will not work. If you filled your siphon in the aquarium, plug one end of the hose tightly, lift it from the aquarium, and bring it lower than the tank to the bucket.

3. Release your thumbs and the water will begin to flow rapidly from the aquarium into the bucket. Either squeeze the tube tightly or block with your thumb to stop the water.

Siphoning—Step 1

As I mentioned earlier, use the siphon to remove debris from the tank while you are making a water change. When it is time to add water and if distilled water is not available, use tap water that you have allowed to age for one or two days. Either keep a few one-gallon jugs stored in the house or keep a five-gallon bucket filled with water for a couple of days. Make sure that the water you add is close in temperature to that of your aquarium.

Siphoning—Step 2

There are now devices that can be attached to your tank that will change the water for you on a constant basis. Whether you have chlorinated water or not, your pet store will be able to equip you with one of these water changers. It makes life much easier but requires that you have a faucet constantly available somewhere near the aquarium. Water changers are labor-saving devices that make maintenance much easier and life better for your fish.

Feeding Your Fish

First, there's food. And who doesn't love food? And then there's nutrition. And who likes nutrition? Let's be honest, nobody likes nutrition. Funny how that works. But nature offers a balance to

MAINTENANCE CHECKLIST

DAILY
- Feed the fish twice a day.
- Turn the tank lights on and off.
- Check the water temperature.
- Make sure the filters are working properly and are not too dirty.
- Make sure the aerator is working properly. Are there the right amount of bubbles and are they getting too big?
- Study the fish closely, watching for behavioral changes and signs of disease.

WEEKLY
- Change approximately 10 to 20 percent of the aquarium water.
- Add distilled or aged water to compensate for water evaporation.
- Check the filter to see if the top mat needs to be replaced.
- Vacuum the tank thoroughly and attempt to clean up mulm and detritus.
- Test the water for pH, nitrates, softness (first two months).
- Trim and fertilize aquarium plants as needed.

MONTHLY
- Change 25 percent of the aquarium water.
- Clean the tank's inside glass with an algae scraper.
- Vacuum the tank thoroughly, stirring up the gravel and eliminating mulm.
- Test the water for pH, nitrates, and softness.
- Rinse any tank decorations that suffer from dirt buildup.
- Trim and fertilize plants; replace plants if necessary.

QUARTERLY (EVERY THREE MONTHS)

- Change 50 percent of the water; replace with distilled or aged water.
- Replace airstones.
- Rinse the filter materials completely and replace some of them if necessary.
- Clean the inside aquarium glass with an algae scraper.
- Vacuum the tank thoroughly, stirring up the gravel and eliminating mulm.
- Trim and fertilize plants as needed; replace if necessary.
- Test the water for pH, nitrates, and softness.
- Rinse any tank decorations that suffer from dirt buildup.

YEARLY

- Completely start over.
- Place fish in separate container with current water.
- Strip down the filter; replace at least 50 percent of the media with new matter and charcoal.
- Drain tank.
- Replace the airstones.
- Place live plants in container with some current water.
- Rinse the gravel thoroughly until most detritus is removed. (Do not use cleansers on anything!)
- Clean the inside of the tank thoroughly.
- Restart the aquarium all over again, but save some of the original aquarium water to help condition the tank. See the set-up process for areas you may have forgotten.

fish in the wild, and so must you. In this section, food, nutrition, diet, and eating habits will all be covered.

Fish don't eat like us. While you're sitting there contemplating a Big Mac or a sumptuous, steaming plate of vodka-penne pasta, your fish dream at night about blood worms, white worms, insects, algae, larvae, and a host of other things we would usually consider the stuff of nightmares. While you're sitting there wrinkling your nose, saying, "No way, pal. Not me," six months to a year from now you will have tried feeding your fish more than one of the above. And you will find it fascinating.

These things may be gross and slimy and crawly and gross, but they are nutritious. Your fish eat these things in the real world. These foods often offer more of the nutrients your fish need and crave than you can imagine. Look at it from their point of view. The fish must be sitting there saying, "Wait, let me get this straight. You get some root out of the dirt and submerge it in boiling animal or vegetable fats or oils, and then you sprinkle minerals on them and that's good? How about milk that's turned, gone solid, and turned blue with mold?" It's just a matter of perspective.

There are many things you need to take into consideration when you start thinking about feeding fish. In their natural habitat, fish have evolved various feeding strategies to optimize their ability to get nourishment. With all the different kinds of fish and habitats, you can imagine the many kinds of feeding strategies that exist. Fish can be divided into general groups based on the type of feeding strategy that they have evolved.

- **Carnivores.** These are basically the predators. They feed in nature mainly on smaller fishes or larger fishes that they incapacitate. When kept in the aquarium, many of these species (but not all) have been successfully fed prepared foods and commercially prepared pellets and flakes. Your carnivorous fish may eat pieces of fish, shrimp, and even bits of meat. Some species will simply not accept anything but live food. Common or feeder guppies and common or feeder goldfish are usually offered to these predators. None

Definition Please: Community Fish

Community fish are generally considered the most peaceful of all the fish groups. Many of the most popular breeds are found in this group. They tend to be the least aggressive and the least territorial. Some popular community fish are catfish, angelfish, neons, gouramis, swordtails, mollies, and guppies.

ACCEPTABLE HOUSEHOLD FOODS
FOR FISH TO EAT

FROZEN
clams, crabmeat, fish, lobster, mussels, oysters, and shrimp

CANNED
clams, crabmeat, fish, lobster, mussels, oysters, and shrimp
as well as beans and peas

RAW
clams, crabmeat, fish, lobster, mussels, oysters, and shrimp,
plus ground beef, spinach and lettuce

COOKED
beans, broccoli, cauliflower, chicken, egg yolk, peas, and potatoes

Rules of feeding these foods:

1. Never season any of these foods! No salad dressings, no salt or pepper. No hot sauce or barbecue sauce. Nothing!

2. Mince the foods. Make sure you don't feed a whole bean to a fish that might choke to death on it. Cut it up. Most fish don't chew like humans. You have to cut the foods into sizes they can swallow without choking.

3. No leftovers—of any kind!

of the recommended community fish require such measures. However, many of the fish noted in the predator section fall into this category.

- **Herbivores.** These are plant eaters. This seems nice, unless you suddenly realized that you wanted to have live plants and herbivorous fish. Oops! However, if you feed these fish correctly, they will not wreak that much havoc among your plant community. The one good thing is that these fish love to feed on algae. They're looking better, aren't they? Herbivorous fish will consume commercially prepared vegetable flakes. Nonetheless, their diet should be augmented with household vegetables, including peas, lettuce, potatoes, beans, and cauliflower.

- **Insectivores.** These fish eat insects. Like herbivores and many carnivores, these fish readily accept commercially prepared flakes and pellets. In addition to prepared foods, it's a good idea to include a variety of invertebrates, such as frozen brine shrimp and blood worms, in an insectivore's diet.

- **Omnivores.** Basically, these fish will eat anything and everything. It's like inviting a football team to your house for dinner. Is there anything they won't eat? These fish will feed on a variety of foods and have no specific dietary preferences. You have probably noticed that most of the recommended species outlined above are omnivorous. The beginner aquarist should not have to worry about special feeding strategies when setting up a tank for the first time. These fish will accept commercially prepared flake and pellet foods, but providing a good variety of foods is necessary to meet all the dietary requirements of these fish.

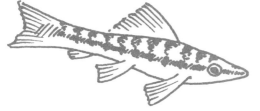

Nutrition

And you thought talking about worms and larvae was harsh. Now it's nutrition! Like all living animals, fish have dietary requirements for protein, fat, carbohydrate, vitamins, and minerals. In their natural environment, fish will meet their own needs by foraging as needed. In the home aquarium, fish rely entirely on you to provide their dietary needs. And that doesn't mean feeding them potato chips or corn flakes. You need to make sure that your fish are properly fed (that doesn't mean overfed) so that they are at their maximum strength and vitality. You want active and alert fish. They need consistent water conditions, good aeration, and proper nutrition.

Protein makes up a major part of all animal tissue. A constant amount of protein is needed in the diet to maintain normal growth. As with many animals, younger fish in particular require more protein in their diets than larger, older fish. Fats and carbohydrates are important sources of energy for fish. Vitamins and minerals fulfill the same important roles in fish as they do in mammals. They provide the necessary building blocks for proper metabolism and skeletal stability.

There are many different types of food for your tropical freshwater fish. Here are how the different categories break down (examples of each category follow in parentheses):

- *Insectivores* will eat flake food, red worms, white worms, earthworms, tubifex, brine shrimp, mosquito larvae, and fruit flies. (Jack Dempseys)
- *Carnivores* will consume almost any kind of seafood—crab, lobster, oysters, and clams. (oscars)
- *Herbivores* will eat canned vegetables, like beans, fresh spinach, broccoli, and cauliflower. (most community fish, i.e., angelfish, bettas, neon tetras)
- *Omnivores* will eat all of the above. (goldfish, catfish)

The Four Food Groups

Just like us, in the aquarium world, food is broken down into four major food groups. However, as you might have guessed from their gastronomic tastes, their food groups are somewhat different from ours.

The four different categories of food are flake or dried foods, frozen or freeze-dried foods, live foods, and household foods. Of these, the most harmful to your fish are the live foods. These can potentially carry diseases or parasites that can infect your fish. The following is a brief description of each category.

Flakes or Dried Foods

No, not corn flakes or frosted flakes! Fish flakes are commercially prepared foods that contain the three basic requirements of proteins, fats, and carbohydrates. Many are also supplemented with vitamins and minerals. These foods come in many varieties, depending on the type of fish (carnivore, insectivore, herbivore, omnivore). Many are aimed at specific species of fish, i.e., koi, goldfish, angelfish, oscars, etc.

They also come in many forms, depending on the size or feeding behavior of the fish. Flakes, tablets, pellets, and crumb forms are available. For example, koi, larger goldfish, and larger predatory fishes should be fed pellets as opposed to flakes because they prefer to consume a large quantity. In addition, fish that feed on the bottom may not venture to the surface for flakes, so they must be fed pellets or tablets that sink to the bottom.

All of the community fish reviewed in this book will survive on flake foods. However, if you want active, colorful, healthy fish, you should vary their diets. Flake is best as a staple (or basic) food, but you should make every effort to substitute other foods a couple of times a week to enrich your community fish.

Live! It's Food!

While live food may sound disgusting to you, it really is an excellent source of nutrition for the tropical aquarium. However, live food may carry a heavy price. Many experts feel that live foods may carry diseases that will infect your fish. To insure against this, live foods can easily be obtained from your pet store. You shouldn't ever collect foods from nearby ponds or lakes, no matter how harmless it may seem. The only two live foods that generally do not run the risk of carrying a disease are earthworms and brine shrimp. These are easily obtainable and will provide an excellent addition to your fishes' diet.

The following section is the *Joy of Cooking* of the tropical fish world. Here's how brine shrimp, white worms, larvae, and other creepy, slimy delicacies are grown or cultivated. These will come in handy as you become a more experienced aquarist.

Brine Shrimp

Mmmm! Shrimp! OK, so they don't take theirs with cocktail sauce. But shrimp are one of the best sources of nutrition available for fish of any type. Of all the live food available, they are the safest because they do not carry diseases. An added advantage to brine shrimp *(Artemia salina)* is that you can raise them yourself.

To raise brine shrimp, it is best to follow the instructions accompanying the eggs. If these are lacking, follow these simple steps:

1. In a plastic or glass container, add 12 ounces of iodized table salt per gallon of water.
2. Place an operating aerator at the bottom of the container and keep it from moving with a stone, most preferably a smooth one bought in a pet store.
3. Add 2 ounces of epsom salts and 1 ounce of sodium bicarbonate to the container per gallon of water.
4. Empty a container of brine eggs into the mixture. Pour them gently because they are small and delicate.
5. At a temperature of about 75°F, you should have brine shrimp in about two days. You can feed these to your fish as soon as they are hatched. Make sure to continue to feed the shrimp until they are entirely gone. The bigger the shrimp, the happier your fish will be.

Earthworms

Nothing like a nice big plate of oozing, squirming earthworms for dinner. Let's see, do you have chardonnay with that (it's white meat) or a nice Chianti?

These backyard occupants are rich in protein and are a readily available dietary change for your fish. You can search for them after rain showers on lawns, under stones, and around pools and lakes, or you can cultivate them in your backyard.

Gross as it may sound to some (the serious gardeners reading this won't be put off), cultivating earthworms is a really easy, reliable way of finding nutritious and fresh live food for your fish. To cultivate earthworms, dig up a couple of square yards of dirt in your backyard and throw burlap sacks over the tilled soil. Water the sacks until they are soaked every morning of the week. On the seventh day, lift the burlap sacks and you will find earthworms. The best time to harvest is early in the morning before the dew has evaporated.

Earthworms live in and consume dirt, so it is necessary to rinse them and clean them before feeding them to your fish. You don't want to introduce dirt into your tank if you can avoid it. After you get your worms, rinse them off, put them in a jar with holes in the lid, and let them sit for a day or two in a dark shaded area. Rinse them each day removing the dirt from their bodies. If you have small fish, you'll have to cut the worms up—just like cutting up spaghetti for a small child. For the larger fish, don't worry. They'll have a ball slurping those long, wiggly strands in one gulp!

Tubifex

These are long, thin red worms, also known as sludgeworms, that live in mud and are available from dealers. Live tubifex are an excellent addition to your fish's diet. Before feeding them to your fish, you must rinse them thoroughly in gently running water for at least one hour. If possible, rinse them for two additional hours. Tubifex require a lot of work and are very risky because their habitat makes them likely carriers of disease. We recommend that you feed them to your fish only once or twice a month.

Don't attempt to cultivate tubifex yourself! It is very difficult and not worth the risk, as it might cause serious illness if not done properly.

White Worms

These worms are the cheeseburgers of the fish world. They are filled with protein, but they are oh-so-fattening. These white or beige worms are also known as microworms. You can buy them from your dealer in serving size amounts or you can culture them at home. Starter sets are available from pet dealers or through mail order. It is best to feed these worms in small quantities to your fish. Some experts feel that they can be fattening and cause constipation.

To culture white worms follow these steps:

1. In a large tray or small shallow tub, place earth and mulched leaves.
2. Water the soil and place the worms on the dirt. Sprinkle bread crumbs or spread sliced bread on the dirt. Oatmeal has been recommended by some.
3. Place a sheet of glass over the tray and cover the entire unit with a sheet or blanket. Make sure that the glass is touching every part of the container.
4. Place the tray in a damp place at room temperature and leave it alone for two to three weeks. Varying temperatures will affect the maturation process.
5. When you unwrap the tray, the underside of the glass plate will be covered with white worms. Scrape them off and feed them to your fish.

These cultures last for about six weeks. If you suspect that the culture has gone bad, it is very important that you dispose of the entire batch and keep none of the worms. Lack of movement by the worms is a sure sign that things have gone wrong. If they start to smell even worse than they normally do, that's probably another sure sign that something is amiss.

Daphnia

No, this isn't the girl from *Scooby Doo*. Daphnia are water fleas. Believe it or not, these are another excellent live food for your fish. Daphnia should only be fed every now and then to your fish because they can act as a laxative, causing serious digestive problems in your fish. You can buy daphnia from your local pet store or easily culture them at home:

Free Range Earthworms

Make sure that no pesticides or weed killers were used in the area where you are cultivating or collecting your earthworms. Such chemicals will assuredly cause harm to your fish.

Some experts prefer to use organic topsoil procured from a local nursery. This is a good idea if you think your local environs have been sprayed with insecticides or other chemicals, especially household cleaners or disinfectants.

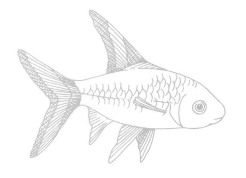

1. Fill a jar with an inch of topsoil and tamp it down, but don't pack it hard. Some suggest that you add manure or common baking yeast or brewer's yeast as well.
2. Carefully pour some water into the jar until it is three-quarters full.
3. Place the jar in the sun for a week until you get a full growth of algae. Wait another week if there is not good algal growth.
4. Add the daphnia culture and wait 10 to 14 days. After that time, water fleas are ready. To insure that the culture is maintained, never take more than one-fifth of the culture. You must feed the culture, so remember to add manure or yeast several times a week. This culture will only last two to three weeks, but will provide two to three feedings a week for your fish.

Drosophila

You may remember the drosophila from high school science class. These are the larvae of the wingless fruit fly. Like the other live foods, you can sometimes buy them from the pet store or you can culture them at home:

1. Add agar and some smashed banana to water that you have boiled.
2. Let the mixture stand for a few day to allow it to gel.
3. Add some fruit flies, let them sit for two weeks, and you will have a lot of drosophila.

Bloodworms

These worms are also known as two-winged fly larvae. These are usually in good supply year-round and can be purchased at your pet store. They are very difficult to cultivate at home, and, of course, we recommend you don't.

Feeder Fish

As discussed earlier, feeder fish are usually known as feeder or common guppies or goldfish. They are sold from large tanks teeming with these fish. They are sold by the dozens at an extremely cheap rate. These are used to feed large predatory fishes that will not be in the average community aquarium. These are the fish you would feed to the fish listed in the predator section. Before you buy these, discuss feeder fish with your local pet dealer. Many of the fish who eat feeder fish can thrive if fed pellet foods for a long time. However, many of these fish will eventually need real meat. Some substitutes can be found below.

Frozen or Freeze-Dried Foods

In this fast-paced world of ours, even poor, helpless fish are forced to eat frozen dinners. Frozen or freeze-dried foods offer the best of live food without the risk of disease and without the hassles of preparing cultures. No more scrubbing those pots and pans! Many of the live foods previously mentioned—brine shrimp, tubifex worms, daphnia, and bloodworms—as well as mosquito larvae and krill, are available to the aquarist frozen or freeze-dried. They are a great convenience to the hobbyist who wants to provide variety without having to purchase or grow live foods.

In truth, these are an aquarist's best friend. Convenience and safety for you, and maximum reward for your fish.

Finally—People Food!

OK, let's stop all the nonsense right here. No, they can't have nachos, beef jerky, caramel corn, fruit rolls, cheese puffs, chocolate, or even chicken wings. Some of these are trade names. We're talking about real food. Many household foods offer nutritional value and variety to the diet of your fish: fresh, frozen, or canned oysters, clams, mussels, crabmeat, lobster, or bits of raw fish. No canned tuna fish! Tuna is too hard to digest and leaves oil slicks. While the live and frozen foods are ideal for carnivores, insectivores, and omnivores, household foods are also available for the herbivores. Baked or boiled beans, steamed cauliflower or broccoli, and boiled or baked potatoes are excellent additions. Fresh spinach or lettuce is also good for your omnivorous and herbivorous fish.

That's a Spicy Meatball!

Make sure when you treat your fish to household foods that you are not offering table scraps that are covered in sauces: no barbecue or chili sauce, no tomato sauce, no honey sauces, nothing. Not only will they hurt your fish's digestive system (in most cases their stomachs can't handle such things), you'll also foul the water.

No spices either: no salt, pepper, curry, garlic, nothing. Serve it nice and plain, just the way nature intended it.

Carnivores, in particular, will especially enjoy small bits of ground beef or cooked chicken.

These foods must be given in moderation. Remember, you are augmenting your fish's diet with these foods, not creating a staple. Household foods must be diced or shredded so that your fish can eat them. Don't offer your fish table scraps unless they conform to what is listed above.

How To Feed Your Fish

Obviously, teaching your fish which fork to use when they sit at a formal dinner is the most difficult thing to train your fish to do. However, for the purposes of this book, that won't be necessary.

First, you need to determine how much and how often to feed your fish. Some fish are gluttons while others will stop when they are sated. In general, many feel that it is better to feed too little than too much to your fish. Follow the following guidelines when feeding your fish, and you will develop a working sense of how much and how often to feed your fish.

1. Offer as much food as your fish will eat in five minutes. Flakes should sink no deeper than one third the height of the tank. If most of it is falling before the fish can get to it, you're overfeeding them. You should provide one or two tablets or pellets for bottom fish.
2. Feed your fish in very small portions over the five-minute period.
3. If you are home during the day, feed your fish over the course of the day in small portions. If you are not home, feed your fish twice a day at the same times every day, once in the morning, once at night.
4. Always feed your fish at the same spot in the tank.
5. Don't overfeed the fish, no matter how much you think they need more food. Overeating will stress your fish and cause detritus to accumulate in the tank, degrading water quality.

Earlier in this chapter, you learned how to be mother nature. Now you get to be mother hen. You must watch all your fish during feeding. You need to make sure that each gets its share of food. Remember that fish have different mouth shapes that allow them to feed at different levels in the tank. Some species will not go to the surface to eat and will wait for food to disperse throughout the tank. Don't rely on surface feedings and the left-overs of others to feed bottom fish. Pellets that sink to the bottom should be provided to these fish. Remember, refusal to eat is one of the first signs of illness, so keep an eye out for fish that seem to have no interest in food.

Start with flake food as your staple and mix in a variety of foods as your fish acclimate to your aquarium. Try not to feed your fish right after turning on the light; they won't be fully alert until about 30 minutes later. In addition, don't crumble the flake food. This will add fine particles to the water that are not ingested, but degrade water quality. Your fish won't have any problems biting and grinding whole flake food.

If you are going to be away from your aquarium for a few days, the fish will be fine without food. For extended periods, make arrangements for someone to feed your fish or install an automatic food dispenser. Don't overload the dispenser and set a longer feeding interval so that fish will eat all that is offered.

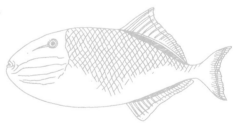

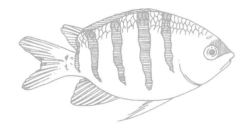

CHAPTER THREE

*Goldfish and Koi—
an Introduction*

T he goldfish and koi are practically cousins. They have many things in common. They are both cold freshwater fish. They share many of the same colorings. They both thrive on the same foods, more or less. They both gained fame in Asia, mainly in China and Japan. The koi is dramatically different from the goldfish in that the koi grow substantially larger on average, have fewer varieties (i.e., body shapes and tail finnage), and have tiny little barbels or whiskers that protrude just above their mouths, which goldfish do not. While koi are mainly identified by their markings, goldfish are defined by their bodies and finnage.

Are they any easier or more difficult to take care of than any other pet fish? No. Both fish are pretty hardy, which is why they are so popular as pond fish. That said, however, they have the same requirements as any other fish—clean, clear, aerated water, with the right pH, enough light, and enough room to roam freely.

Goldfish

The first pet fish adopted popularly by man was the goldfish. They are the most popular pet fish in the world, and have been the most commonly kept fish in history. Many famous people and families have kept fish or aquariums. Some of the most notable were the Chinese emperors, Winston Churchill, and President James Garfield.

The goldfish is a descendant of the crucian carp. These carp were found throughout Asia. They were very much like the common goldfish of today, except they were more brownish than gold. But something funny has happened over the years. From that one species, the family of the goldfish grew. Today, there are more than 125 varieties of this single species. That's got to make dating kind of fun, if you're a goldfish, no?

How did this happen? Well, the Chinese Emperors were very fond of goldfish. The Imperial Palace has recorded the keeping of fish as far back as A.D. 265, during the Tsin

Dynasty. In subsequent dynasties, goldfish became more and more popular, and more a symbol of the emperor's affluence. These were kept mostly in pools in courtyards. A thousand years later, a large pool was established to create a special breeding center where the husbanders of these creatures bred more and more exotic varieties. By this time, if you were a person of affluence in Chinese or Asian societies, it became fashionable to have goldfish. By the mid-14th century, fish had been brought into the house as pets. This was done as a means to show off your beautiful pottery, which had reached its zenith during the Ming Dynasty. And, of course, beautiful pottery had to be shown off with beautiful and exotic fish.

Established more than 500 years ago, one of the most famous goldfish breeding centers in the world is Koriyana, Japan. The breeding of goldfish, as an occupation, has been a growing business ever since. The most famous was established in 1704 by San Sanzaemon. Between them, China and Japan have bred some of the most famous and popular varieties of goldfish known today. Some of these include such variations as the fantail, the veiltailed, the globe-eyed, and the transparent-scaled varieties.

During the 18th century, the offering of goldfish became very popular in European society. These arrived on European shores as a result of the widespread trading of spices and other interesting Asian items during that time period. It wasn't until 1878, however, that the first goldfish reached American shores. This was 16 years after the first world goldfish show took place in Osaka, Japan. The first goldfish show in Europe didn't take place until 1926.

Only one variety of goldfish was ever developed in the United States. This was the comet goldfish. Despite this rather dubious contribution, the keeping of goldfish in the United States has been on an ever-upward growing curve.

The great thing about goldfish is that they are a fairly hardy species and are quite adaptable. They are excellent candidates for outdoor ponds or pools, in almost any climate. Given the wide range of colors, body shapes, and general disposition, there is, in fact, a goldfish for everybody.

Kissing Cousins?

Not really; however, goldfish and koi are related. As a matter of fact, some large common goldfish are often mistaken for koi. Koi and goldfish are both descendants of the carp.

What Is a Goldfish?

What's the difference between goldfish and tropical fish? There are many small differences that add up to big ones. Differences in the temperature of their habitat, their potential for size, and their temperament traits are all attributes which contribute to the differences between goldfish and the rest of the pet fish world.

Tropical fish require warmer temperatures than goldfish. Depending on where you live, you probably don't need a heater in the tank because goldfish are used to withstanding colder temperatures in the winter. It's actually good for them. Tropical fish tend to come from climates where the water temperature rarely changes.

This ability to withstand colder temperatures and greater variances in temperature make the goldfish hardier than many tropical fish. While a goldfish is likely to survive better in tropical conditions than a tropical fish would be in the opposite situation, the goldfish does become more susceptible to illness if left in warm waters for too long.

Goldfish are not enlightened. In other words, they don't get along extremely well with other fish. They might become aggressive in some cases. In other cases, the goldfish could be dinner. If you keep goldfish with community fish, you might find the goldfish too territorial. It is a fact that angelfish and goldfish do not get along. Whom is the aggressor depends on which camp you speak to.

Cichlids, on the other hand, will make a fabulous fish dinner of your new pet. And you won't need a detective when you come downstairs the next morning to find out why one of your goldfish is missing.

It's also well known by enthusiasts that some goldfish varieties should not be kept together. A comet should not be kept with a ranchu. The ranchu is too slow and not as aggressive. The comet would dominate the feeding times and would harass the ranchu. The ranchu, being a poor swimmer, would be no match for his faster, slimmer, more streamlined cousin.

And there is the size factor. Given a large enough tank, a goldfish would soon outgrow your angelfish or discus fish. Goldfish have been known to commonly grow larger than 10 inches, which would easily dwarf your other fish.

The Classification of the Goldfish

Today, in freshwater waterways throughout Asia, goldfish *(Carassius auratus)* can still be easily found. The wild goldfish are less colorful than their more carefully bred cousins and tend to be more brownish. The goldfish comes from the cyprinidae family, a classification of carp. They are descended from the crucian carp, also known as *Carassius carassius,* and are related to the common carp, which is known as *Cyprinus carpio.*

The best way to distinguish between a carp and a goldfish is to look at the dorsal fin. The goldfish's dorsal is usually straight up or is concave, while the carp's dorsal is generally convex. Of course, some goldfish don't have dorsal fins at all.

Body

The goldfish has much in common with the tropical fish, but there are some things that are different and important to note. The fins, gills, and other body parts are pretty much the same in terms of their function, but some of the parts are more extreme or slightly different than other fish. These characteristics are unique to the goldfish group.

Caudal fins vary when it comes to goldfish. It is sometimes difficult to identify what kind of caudal or tail fin your goldfish has. This happens because many goldfish have very fancy plumage. For example, the black moor's fins can sometimes be forked, while the veiltail's plumage can be wide and fan-shaped.

Goldfish have three distinct types of caudal fins: the single tail fin, the veiltail, and the fantail. Of course, nothing is simple. Each of these three main shapes has its own varieties. The common goldfish is the best example of the single fin. This is what we usually think of when we think of a tail fin. No frills, just the tail. Simple. The next is the fantail. Many goldfish varieties exhibit this trait. This is a pair of forked tails joined at the caudal peduncle. The most beautiful and elaborate is that of the veiltail. The veiltail is a beautiful large tail, which has no indentations (or forks) and is square finished. The tails are usually very long and elegant, like gossamer drapes being dragged by a beautiful fish.

Skin and Scales

The interesting thing about goldfish and koi is that some varieties are defined simply because of their markings, and not because of any other kind of physical makeup or difference. Taking that into account, the major factor is made up by the variety of scales to be found in the goldfish family. It's especially important to understand this when you delve into the numerous varieties.

Here's a shocker. The scale is actually transparent! The scale does not determine the color of the fish. The color of the goldfish usually comes from the dermis. This happens because the forward end of each scale is attached to the dermis. The dermis is the lower or inner layer of skin. The scales overlap each other like shingles on a house, providing a solid wall of protection as well as comfortable movement. For every variety of goldfish, the specific number of scales remains the same within that group, from fish to fish. That's the difference between breeding and claiming a mutated fish as a new variety. Can it reproduce itself consistently?

How is the color determined? That's a good question. A variety of factors contribute to the coloration of goldfish: water temperature, composition, diet, and environment. These all affect what are called chromatophores, the pigment cells. These are important because they determine, in part, a color variation as well. For example, orange goldfish have an abundance of xanthophores and an absence of melanophores, while the blue or black varieties, such as a black moor, have an abundance of melanophores and they lack xanthophores.

There are four major scale groups that give goldfish their color:

- **Metallic.** Basically, this is the coloration of the shiny, famous, common goldfish. Their scales are shiny.
- **Matte.** Basically, these scales appear flat or dry. They have no reflective quality to them whatsoever. They have a skin-like look to them. What some fanciers call scaleless goldfish are not really scaleless. They are matte. Real matte goldfish are for experienced fanciers only and are usually not available commercially.

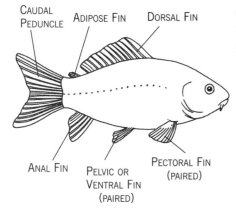

CAUDAL PEDUNCLE ADIPOSE FIN DORSAL FIN

ANAL FIN PELVIC OR VENTRAL FIN (PAIRED) PECTORAL FIN (PAIRED)

Goldfish Anatomy

- **Nacreous.** Some goldfish exhibit scales that are both metallic and matt. These goldfish are nacreous. The scales may appear evenly distributed throughout the body, or they may appear in patches.
- **Calico**. Goldfish fanciers will argue this category until the end of time. The easiest way to describe calico is to know that it really is part of the nacreous group, but that the fish display three colors in its markings. The three colors are usually gold, brown, and white. However, that is not always the case, and each color has its many variations and substitutes.

Swim Bladder

You read about the swim bladder in an earlier chapter. It's important to know that goldfish actually have two swim bladders. One is directly in front of the other. Like other fish, by inflating the swim bladder, the goldfish rises and, conversely, when the goldfish deflates the swim bladder, descent is easier. In the goldfish world, some of the more elaborate varieties are top heavy. These may seem odd when we first see them, especially since, as a result of their body shape, they will always swim at an angle. Some goldfish swim forward with their head at a downward angle, because it has a smaller forward sac. An excellent example of this is a lionhead.

Sociability

When kept with their own kind, goldfish tend to be peaceful fish. However, aggressive behavior can occur in any aquarium when too many fish of varying types are put together. The competition for food and territory may spark aggressive behavior. Great differences in size may also lead to the smaller fish being picked on. Ill fish will also be picked on. Some fish are more delicate than others and shouldn't be mixed. Veiltails and especially bubble-eyed goldfish should not be put in an aquarium with comet goldfish. Their water-filled sacs might be punctured by the hardier and more agile fish.

The only time goldfish will be truly aggressive toward one another is during breeding time. Unlike other species in the animal and aquatic world, no showdowns occur between male goldfish.

Head of the Class

The more goldfish you have, the more you notice that they travel in schools. There is never a lead fish. Schools may divide or unite without warning or meaning. They merely dart around following the whimsy of this fish and then that one. There is nothing learned about it.

Don't Mix and Match Goldfish?

Goldfish are generally broken down into three groups, which are distinguished by body types. It's important not to mix fast-swimming fish with the slower or more delicate ones. In the race for food or as a way to avoid aggressors, it's important to put like fish together. With goldfish, it's best to choose a group first, then the species from that group that you like best.

They will not fight to the death as Siamese fighting fish might. Basically, the male goldfish compete by chasing down the female goldfish. They will try to out-position each other, swimming farther and faster than the next as they chase the female. The male who can command the best position or who has the greatest stamina is nature's way of selecting.

Choosing Your Goldfish

Remember, all goldfish have basically been bred from the same fish. Therefore, they are never really more than a few genes away from each other. There are three basic body types, and each has a variety of colorations that define their varieties. For example, almost every new variety has several basic colorations, including orange metallic, a calico variety, and a tancho variety. In that way, you can choose one basic body type and still not be limited in the many variations that exist for that one group.

As a beginner, it is recommended that you not mix too many body types. For example, comets and lionheads should not be in the same tank. Again, the comets are excellent swimmers, while the slow, plodding, dorsalless lionheads are not. The comet would dominate the tank, especially being as aggressive as possible at feeding time, leaving little for the lionhead. This is not a good mixture.

On the other hand, ranchus and lionheads are similar and would be a good match. Or even ranchus and bubble-eyes. This is because they are all lack dorsals and neither would have an unfair advantage over the other.

Before you can finally mix, you need to learn about the body types and finnage that separate the numerous varieties. You need to understand their differences more clearly before you can mix your fish. When you choose your fish, be sure to talk with your pet professional. Explain to him or her your plans. Describe the tank size and the mixture you would like to put together. Good pet professionals will make a great difference between success and failure.

Mixing Goldfish with Other Species

Goldfish and koi can withstand a wide range of temperatures, which in the end makes them hardier fish than most. The common goldfish can live in water temperatures ranging from 40°F to 80°F. Most tropical fish prefer 72°F to 85°F.

However, compatibility is important. Goldfish and tropical fish do not mix well. One group or the other will become aggressive, and the result will be a badly injured or dead fish. The benefit of choosing goldfish is that there are more than 300 different varieties, providing a wide range of choice available in no other breed.

Avoid placing wild fish with your goldfish. In some cases, folks have dumped a large number of goldfish into a pond, and many have survived and even thrived. This has led a great many enthusiasts to find wildlife fish and mix them with goldfish. This really is not the thing to do. Perch, sunnys, and other fish from nature can be territorial and aggressive. Since they are hardier than goldfish in many ways, your goldfish will lose.

Packed Like Sardines

Remember these are goldfish, not sardines. They don't get packed in tins. Many varieties of goldfish can grow quite large. Goldfish can grow to at least one foot long. Think before you buy. If you've got a 10-gallon tank, you can buy 10 goldfish. But that's not going to work very well for long. Also, you can't put a 10-inch goldfish into a 10-gallon tank. You can, but it would be unhealthy for the fish!

It's important to avoid overcrowding. Doing this will result in bad water conditions, and it will be difficult for the aquarist to supply his or her tank with enough aerated water for the number of fish. The idea is to create an environment that fish will thrive in. Make sure you're not trying to pack too many into a small area. It's not rush hour. It's their living space. Fish live out in nature, where there's room to move on and not stay in crowded areas. They live in the country—they don't live in apartment buildings. Be thoughtful.

An Important Distinction

Goldfish are not tropical fish. Tropical fish come from warm, mostly equatorial countries. Goldfish come mostly from Asia, well above the equator.

Goldfish vs. the World

Goldfish are the pushy redheads of the aquarium fish world. While they are usually not aggressive, they are rough and tumble. They will pick on some species and be picked on by others

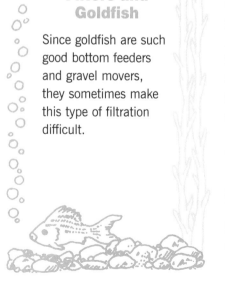

Avoiding overcrowding also brings another benefit. Your goldfish will grow larger. The more room they have to swim around in, the more likely your goldfish will grow larger. Environment plays a large part in how big your fish will grow. Give them room, and they will blossom and be the entertaining pets you envision them to be.

The Varieties

Zoologically speaking, there are no official divisions among the goldfish family. However, fanciers certainly have examined goldfish carefully and have broken them up into body types. Again, there is nothing official about these groupings, and no hard and fast rules. In fact, some fanciers regularly disobey them. But those are experts. It is important for the beginner to honor these well-acknowledged guidelines. Everyone from fanciers to pet store owners and professionals knows these guidelines and will help advise you based on them.

For example, the comet, the common goldfish, and both the Bristol and London shubunkin are all of the same type. These fish are long, sleek, fast swimmers, and they are very competitive. They are of the hardiest variety in the goldfish world. They should not be kept with lionheads or veiltails, which are extremely slow, and would not be able to compete for food at an adequate level.

What follows is only a partial listing of all the goldfish that exist. Still, the variety is wide ranging and offers the enthusiast many different types of fish to choose from. The fish listed here are also the ones that are most commonly available through the pet trade, and can be found by hobbyists fairly easily. Other types are available, but would have to be specially ordered, sometimes through special agents that can be found in the resources section of this book.

Classification by Body Type and Finnage

A combination of body type and finnage determine which groupings the fish fall into. Basically, there are two body types. There's the long, sleek body of the common goldfish, well known to many. There are the round, egg-shaped bodies, such as the orandas and veiltails. These fish have many of the same attributes

How Many Goldfish Will Fit in My Tank?

These are the general rules on the number of fish per gallons of water. These are the popular aquarium sizes:

1 gallon – one goldfish

5 gallon – two to three goldfish

10 gallon – three to four goldfish

20 gallon – six to eight goldfish

30 gallon – nine to twelve goldfish

of their flat-bodied cousins, but are placed in the context of the slower, heavier, round body.

It is within this second group that there is another grouping. Some prefer to think of it as a sub-grouping, as opposed to a distinct separate group. We break it into a separate group. The third group is the egg-shaped goldfish that lack dorsal fins. Why do we do this? There are a number of important reasons. The biggest difference is that fish lacking a dorsal fin do not swim half as well. These fish don't have the control in the water that fish with a dorsal fin have. A fantail is a better swimmer than a lionhead. Thus, the same advantage that a comet has over a fantail, the fantail has over the lionhead. Again, the better equipped fantail would get the lion(head's) share of the food.

Single Tail Flat-Bodies

This is the best known, and among the most popular variety, of the goldfish world. It is the best group for beginners. Why? They are among the hardiest in the entire tropical fish hobbyist world. They are fast swimmers, can withstand wide temperature ranges, and are more competitive and successful in feeding themselves and staying alive. They are relatively easy to care for, especially when compared to other goldfish, let alone tropical or marine fish. They are also popular because these are the fish most popularly found in outdoor water ponds and gardens. They also tend to live the longest and grow the largest. Some have grown up to 14 or 16 inches and have been known to live in excess of 24 years.

The Common Goldfish

Again, this is the hardiest of all pet fish. The average life expectancy is between five to ten years if properly maintained. They can withstand temperatures as low as 40°F and as high as 80°F. Some of the fancier breeds require only the higher temperatures. However, all goldfish should pretty much be kept in the 65°F to 75°F range. These are ideal candidates for outdoor ponds, as they are able to withstand great temperature changes.

This particular variety is the closest cousin to the carp in the goldfish family. The body is long and sleek. It is also flat bodied, meaning that is it substantially thinner in one dimension than it is the other. The side profile is quite handsome and detailed. The side profile displays the tapered head, the wider mid-section, and the tapered caudal area. But its head-on appearance is much diminished and easily passed over.

Goldfish tend not to exhibit their orange coloring until they get older. They are a bluish color when young. As they get older, provided they are well cared for, they will usually display a beautiful, deep metallic gold.

The fins of a common goldfish are not unique to the goldfish. They possess the classic lines of most fish. Common goldfish have an erect dorsal fin, a single-forked tail, and well-proportioned pectoral and ventral fins. They are not overly large fins and are more utilitarian than ornamental.

Because they are competitive and hardy, they are a popular choice for most ponds and water gardens. They are strong enough to withstand rapid temperature changes, and they survive aerial attacks from most local birds of prey. In a pond they can grow as large as 12 to 14 inches, and in a large aquarium, 6 to 9 inches, depending on the size of the tank.

The Comet Goldfish

At a quick glance, the uneducated eye sees little difference between the comet and the common goldfish. However, a closer examination will yield the obvious differences. The common goldfish has less pronounced colors and smaller fins. The comet is sleeker and its fins are more exaggerated. The tail fin on a comet is twice the size of that on a common goldfish. On some fish, the tail can be as large, if not larger, than the body and, when fully displayed, is quite beautiful.

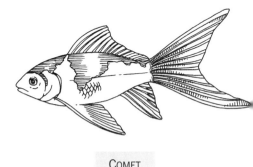

COMET

Of course, there are nacreous comets, too. This is the only goldfish developed in the United States. They were developed by the U.S. Fisheries Department and a hobbyist named Hugo Mulrett around the 1880s. In Japan, the fish is known as tetsugyo.

Other than these slight differences, the common goldfish and the comet have much in common. The comet is smaller than the common goldfish and will only grow 7 to 10 inches. Because they, too, can withstand great temperature swings, from as low as 40°F to as high as 80°F, these are excellent pond or water garden fish.

Shubunkin

The shubunkin is very similar to the common goldfish in body type, although it tends to be slightly thicker through the middle. There are two types of shubunkins—the London and the Bristol. Although they are named for two cities in England, they were originally bred in Japan almost a century ago. What separates the shubunkin from the common goldfish is its colorings. The shubunkin is calico. In some circles, these fish are also known as harlequins.

Calico, as we discussed earlier, includes a variety of shadings. The most common colors include deep red, yellows, whites, and dark blues, violets, or black. Fanciers favor the darker hues. The more dominated by violets, blues, and blacks, the more valuable the fish is in the marketplace.

So, what's the difference between the London and Bristol shubunkin? The difference is the tail. The Bristol has a much larger tail than the London shubunkin. Also, the Bristol's tail is of a forked variety. The London variety, which is more common (and, some fanciers might argue, more popular), has a tail that is rather blunt or squared off.

These fish don't grow nearly as large as the common or comet goldfish. They tend to grow no longer than 6 inches. They are excellent swimmers and require room to grow. Like the comet and the common goldfish, they, too, can withstand wide temperature swings, which also makes them excellent candidates for ponds or water gardens. Their average life span is quite a bit longer than their two aforementioned cousins. Shubunkins, with proper and consistent care, can live 10 to 20 years!

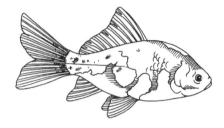

SHUBUNKIN

Do I Need a Catfish or Snails to Keep the Bottom of the Tank Clean?

The short answer is no. Goldfish are excellent bottom feeders, constantly scouting the aquarium floor for available food. In the end, goldfish will do the job themselves. Also, many tropical catfish are not able to withstand the cold temperatures that goldfish can survive. Cold, freshwater catfish are not a good idea since some have actually been known to suck the eyes out of the fancier goldfish varieties. Why they have done this is not known.

Having snails in your aquarium can bring on more problems than anything else. You don't need anything other than goldfish. Snails and catfish are highly advised against.

The Wakin

The wakin is also known as the common goldfish of Japan. What the comet is to America, the wakin is to Japan. Wakin actually means fish in Japanese. This is a bit of a joke, since the wakin was originally bred in China. A newborn or young wakin is bluish in color, but as it ages, most wakin will develop a beautiful, rich vermilion red. Some other strains develop red and white patches.

Despite the double tail, the wakin is an excellent swimmer and can hold its own in the company of the other fish in this category. In all other respects, the wakin is very much a cousin of the common goldfish, in body type and other finnage.

The Jikin Goldfish

Among aquarists, the jikin goldfish is known more commonly as the butterfly-tail goldfish. In some circles they are referred to as peacock-tailed goldfish. It is thought that this fish was bred from the wakin. In many respects, it mirrors the wakin, except in the tail. The tail is what separates the wakin from the jikin. The tail, when displayed, opens like a butterfly and forms a large X.

While it is not as easily found as some of the others in this category, it is hardy and long lived. It is another good candidate for ponds or water gardens, as it is hardy and can withstand similar temperature changes in the water.

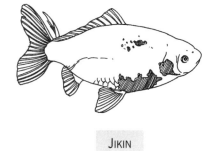

JIKIN

The Tancho Single Tail

Tancho is more a coloring than a variety by body type or finnage. Tancho is a highly regarded and specific coloration that is highly prized. The name tancho is Japanese for crane. Generally, this variation exhibits a red cap on the head, contrasted against a white or silver body. Sometimes, pink can mark the fins or shade slight portions of the body. Many different goldfish varieties have a tancho coloration. Tancho is even a popular type of koi.

The tancho goldfish's forked tail is smaller than that of the comet's, but larger than the common goldfish's. In all other aspects it is more similar to the comet than the common goldfish and has many of the same tendencies and physical hardiness.

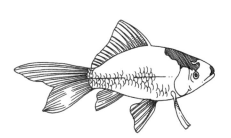

TANCHO SINGLE TAIL

Egg-Shaped Goldfish with Dorsal Fins

Here's where it starts to get interesting. In this next group you will see some of the most exotic fish in all of the fish hobbyist world. There are a mind-boggling variety of tails, body shapes, eye shapes, head shapes, etc. After viewing this next group, one can easily understand why the goldfish has held man's fascination for almost a millennia, and how it can easily last one lifetime.

EGG SHAPED

These fish are almost comical because the body shape literally looks like an egg with fins. Imagine an egg swimming around an aquarium. That's what these fish look like. Some tend to be more oblong than egg-like, but nonetheless, these are some fascinating creatures. Many have short, rounded bodies, and it is difficult to distinguish the head from the rest of the body in some cases.

In terms of physical abilities to compete for food and withstand wide swings in temperature, this is the middle group. Some tend to be hardier than others, but they are all of a moderate ability when compared with their faster, sleeker relatives. However, what they lack in speed and stamina, they make up for in extravagance, plumage, and coloration. These are some of the most exotic fish in the fish world. It's also important to remember that they are not the slowest nor the least hardy of the goldfish family. That group lies just after these.

There are only two fish that are good for outdoor ponds in this section: the fantail and the black moor. Both of these are less hardy than the fish in the previous group, and require mild climates to compete and survive in water gardens or ponds. If you live in warm weather, the ryukin is also a possibility. The rest of this group are strictly for the aquarium.

Fantails

This is the most common of all the fancy breeds, and the most popular. The fantail is one of the oldest varieties of goldfish known to man, and can be found in recorded history as far back as 1500 years ago. This egg-shaped fish should develop a color of deep, bright, shiny metallic gold. Its claim to fame is its large, double caudal or tail fin. The larger and more exaggerated the tail is, the more highly prized the fish will be. Fanciers are very particular about the tail: it should not be joined anywhere but at the base, and should mirror its opposite member as exactly as possible. While it is egg-shaped, it can look more like a fat comet or common goldfish than any of the following fish.

The most popular and plentiful of all these fish are the solid orange metallic. They are also the hardiest. With good care, a fantail will grow from 3 to 6 inches, and has a life expectancy of between five and ten years. This is an excellent transition fish for the hobbyist who would like to start keeping the more exotic breeds. It's not as difficult as some, but certainly easier than others. And it certainly is hardier than others.

The Nymph Goldfish

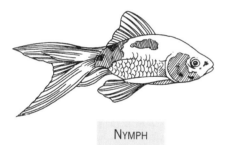

NYMPH

The nymph goldfish has long been thought to be a cross between a comet and a fantail. It has the short, round body of the fantail, with a short head and a large mouth. Its belly is deep and round. Its dorsal fin sits very far back on the spine. All of its fins are extremely long. The finnage is thought to be the contribution of the comet. There are three varieties, each of which have all the popular color markings found in the other breeds. Nymphs are available in single-tail, fan-tail, and fringe-tail varieties.

Ryukin

Fanciers argue over which is older—the fantail or the ryukin. What they don't argue over is that the ryukin was bred in Japan. The easiest way to see the difference between a fantail and a ryukin is to see their high, arching back and deep belly. They have a distinct profile. The ryukin's back almost looks like it has a hump behind its head. The dorsal fin sits high atop the spine, not far back as in a fantail. The ryukin's tail is also larger and more exaggerated.

A full-grown ryukin can grow up to 6 inches. All the color variations available in other varieties can be found here, too. Ryukins are hardier than some of the other exotic breeds and they're also good for those looking to make the transition, eventually, to fish that require a bit more experience.

The Veiltail

It is not known from what breed of goldfish the veiltail origi-nates. Regardless of this debate, the veiltail looks a lot like a fantail, with one key difference: the veiltail's finnage is extraordinary. Its fins unwind in long, flowing ribbons. The paired anal fins are so long, they usually come out to the middle of the veiltail's extremely long caudal fin. The caudal fin is a paired tail, but not forked. It is extremely long, graceful, and exaggerated. There is even a globe-eyed or telescoped-eyed version of this fish.

The veiltail is neither the hardest nor the easiest goldfish to keep. Because of their finnage, they need more room than most to swim around a tank, and for that reason, you should have fewer in your tank than you might of other fish. You also need to avoid overcrowding the tank with too many plants or too much bric-a-brac. Veiltails tend to lose their color if the water temperature is not consistently maintained; also, the water must be kept as clean and clear as possible, and algae should be kept to a minimum. The veiltail's fins are extremely susceptible to rot or other fungal dis-eases. They are also easily damaged. It's extremely important to do everything necessary to keep these fish from ruining their exotic and beautiful plumage. Because of this, they should really only be kept with other veiltails.

Veiltails can grow to be 5 inches in length (not including the tail) and may live as long as six years. They require warmer tem-peratures than other goldfish; the water should be maintained con-sistently between 65°F and 75°F.

Veiltails are for a more experienced hobbyist. They are not for pond or outdoor use at all. Veiltails are not very hardy or competi-tive when compared to any of the previously mentioned fish.

The Oranda

Some people call this breed a fantailed lionhead, but this is incorrect. The oranda is certainly among some of the most beau-tiful and strangest goldfish that are popularly kept. The oranda is an egg-shaped fish that has a cap of hard, bumpy growth on top of its head. The growth looks like a small gourd. This growth should

Beginner's Luck!

These are the goldfish that are recommended for beginners:

- Common goldfish
- Comet goldfish
- Shubunkin (either type)
- Fantail
- Black moor
- Jikin

cover only the top of the head and not any of the facial features, such as eyes, nose, or mouth. An oranda takes two to three years before it begins to display this growth. It has dual fins along the bottom of its body and flowing dual caudal fins. Its dorsal fin is similar to that of the veiltail.

They are most readily available in gold or orange, where the cap takes on a deep, vibrant orange color. They are also available in calico. There is even a red cap or tancho variety oranda, which is very striking and among the most highly prized, as their white bodies provide stark contrast to the bright cherry red cap or hood that covers their heads.

The oranda may grow to a length of 4 inches (tail not included), and can be expected to live as long as approximately five to ten years. To accomplish these things, you need to keep them in a roomy tank with consistently good water quality. The temperature needs to be maintained consistently, too, at somewhere around 65°F. Given enough room, an oranda will grow somewhere between 3 and 4 inches, not including the length of the tail.

Like the veiltail, the oranda's cap sometimes poses a health problem, as it is susceptible to various infections, fungi, and diseases. To reduce the chances of this, the tank must be kept sparkling clean. Orandas should only be kept by someone who has experience with goldfish. These fish are definitely not for the beginner, nor should they be included in an outdoor pond.

The Pearl-Scaled Goldfish

The pearl-scaled goldfish gets its name from its oddly shaped scales. Usually, scales are flat and flexible, like a soft contact lens. The pearl-scaled goldfish features scales that are raised in the middle, so that they are not flat, but almost round. These scales are usually tinged with white. Fanciers consider larger scales more desirable. The more these scales encompass the body, the better. It's important to know that if these scales come off, through fighting or rubbing up against something, they are replaced by the body with the more normal, flat variations. However, these should be considered scars, and will not be passed on to offspring.

Pearl-scaled goldfish are becoming more popular. It looks like a ryunkin, but with less exaggerated finnage. It has the same high arching, hump-like back, but the abdomen protrudes much deeper.

Disease and fungus are sometimes a problem, as these tend to ferment in the folds and crevices of the skin. Again, like the veiltail and the oranda, you need to have consistent, high-quality water. It must be well filtered and aerated. The temperature should be kept between 55°F and 65°F for better success. If they are in an environment that encourages their growth, the pearl-scaled goldfish will grow to the size of a regulation baseball. These are not pond fish.

Telescope-Eyed or Globe-Eyed Goldfish

This odd fish is known by many names. You know what they say: as long as they're talking about you, that's all that matters. These fish are also known as dragon fish, dragon-eyed goldfish, and, in England, they are known as the pop-eyed goldfish. As you might have guessed by now, these goldfish are known for their eyes, which protrude in almost tube-like fashion, sometimes up to 3/4" long in adults. The term telescope is misleading since these fish have limited vision to begin with. There are four different eye shapes in the globe- or telescope-eye varieties.

Their eyes don't begin to protrude until they are about six months old. Until then, they are able to compete for food quite easily. Later on, though, as their eyes begin to protrude, their sight lines become limited. This puts them at a disadvantage. It must be recommended that this type of fish be kept with its own kind or with other similarly handicapped fish.

They have the body and finnage of a fantail. And their markings include all the popular variations. You should probably keep this fish between 55°F and 65°F. They may grow up to 6 inches long and live approximately five to ten years. Disease and fungus are sometimes a problem, as the eyes are very delicate and sensitive. These fish are only for the experienced aquarist, and are not for the beginner. They are not to be kept in pond or water gardens.

The Heimlich for Goldfish

Goldfish sometimes get bits of gravel caught in their mouths. Usually this will dislodge itself over the course of several hours without damage to the fish. However, in those cases where the gravel does not dislodge, attempt the following tip recommended by the Goldfish Society of America in their Official Guide to the Goldfish:

1. Capture the fish with a fish net.
2. Hold the fish head down and press against both sides of the lips, opening the mouth.
3. With your other hand, press the throat behind the stone. Relief is usually immediate.

Experts Only

Sorry, rookie—these goldfish are for advanced aquarists only:

Bubble-eyed goldfish
Veiltailed goldfish
Pearl-scaled goldfish
Celestial goldfish

The Black Moor

The black moor is a telescope- or globe-eyed goldfish, but it is solely known for its color, which appears as a velvet-like black coat. Black moors are hardier than globe-eyed goldfish, and less prone to disease. The black moor is a popular fish and is often used as a starter fish. Because it is so hardy, it is a great starter fish for those who really want to eventually house exotics.

With enough room, a black moor can grow as large as 6 inches (tail not included) and may be expected to live as long as five to ten years. It should be kept at a relatively constant temperature somewhere between 49°F and 65°F. You should err toward the cooler. This is very important. As black moors get older they develop a velvety texture. However, if the water is consistently too warm, orange will sometimes begin to show through. Once this occurs it usually cannot be reversed. Keep them at their appropriate temperature and they'll be fine.

The Exotics

These goldfish are all grouped together because of two things. First, they all lack dorsal fins, which makes them extremely poor swimmers. A dorsal fin allows the fish to swim steady and straight and, therefore, faster. It also allows for better maneuverability, giving many fish the ability to turn on a dime when necessary. The exotic fish lack these abilities. Therefore, they lack the ability to compete for food against better-equipped competitors.

Second, this group tends to have some of the most exotic of all the goldfishes and, as a result, many of these are not recommended for beginners. If you really feel the need to mix varieties of fish, you should only mix these fish with one another, and not with any fish from the two preceding groups. Many of these fish require the care and maintenance that are only part of the experienced hobbyist's knowledge. None of this final group are for outdoor ponds or pools.

Once you have mastered the care of some of the goldfish in the first two categories, you will be able to move bravely into the world of the exotics.

The Ranchu

There are a great number of the lionhead varieties. The ranchu is Japanese in origin. These fish are known for the hard growth that encapsulates the head. This growth looks similar to the one we talked about in the oranda, but now the whole head is enveloped. The growth should not obscure the eyes, mouth, or nostrils of the fish. Again, as in the oranda, the bumpy, wart-like growth is usually very deeply colored.

RANCHU

The ranchu is a round fish, and its back is a graceful arch all the way to the caudal peduncle, which is pointed downward. This arch results in a tail that is also pointed downward at approximately a 45° angle. The finnage is usually short and has a dual caudal or tail fin.

It isn't until the second year that the cap begins to appear in most fish. The cap or hood may grow until the fish is a little over three years old. This fish is available in all the most popular markings and color variations. As in some of the other, more complicated breeds, disease and fungus are sometimes a problem, as these tend to ferment in the folds and crevices of the cap. Maintenance and vigilance will be the key to keeping this variety successfully.

Ranchus should be kept at a relatively constant temperature somewhere around 55°F and 65°F. This fish will only grow to 3 inches at best (not including the tail). Ranchus have a life expectancy of approximately five to ten years. This fish should only be kept by someone who has experience with goldfish and is definitely not for the beginner.

The Lionhead

These fish are also known as brambleheads, the buffalo-head, and tomato-head. The lionhead was developed in China and is more popular in America than the ranchu. The head growth is much more pronounced and all-encompassing around the head than the ranchu. The ranchu is smaller and more streamlined than the lionhead. The lionhead grows on average about 1 inch longer and is broader around the back and wider across the mid-section.

While its head markings are more pronounced, its fins are also larger and more exaggerated. The fish was given its name because its hard, fleshy hood was so large, it gave one the impression of a lion's mane.

Disease and fungus are sometimes a problem, as these tend to ferment in the folds and crevices of the cap. As with all exotics, it is especially important to maintain the water quality, temperature, and aeration as best as possible. They should be kept at a relatively constant temperature somewhere between 55°F and 65°F. In total length, the lionhead may grow up to 4 inches. It may live between five and ten years.

Because of their odd, heavy shape, these fish swim at a downward angle. They are also slow. These are not the kinds of fish you keep with a comet, for example. Lionheads should be kept only by an experienced hobbyist.

The Marigold Chinese Lionhead

These fish are sometimes called sunrises. Essentially just a variation of a lionhead, these fish are especially known for their brightly colored hoods.

The hood is extremely pronounced, so much so that the deep orange-yellow color of it looks very much like a marigold flower. The fish themselves are shiny, deep, yellow gold. The contrast is quite striking. They are not as rare as they used to be, and can be found in some commercial retail outlets. However, a majority of them are still special ordered.

As with all the fish in this section, these are difficult to keep and require incredible maintenance to keep them healthy and alive.

The Pompon

This variety is also known by the names "velvetball" and "velvetyball." The pompon is very much like a lionhead. However, the growth from the head is a little different. Instead of having a hood or a cap, the pompon has a hard, raspberry-like growth spiraling out of its nostrils. This gives the effect of the fish having two small pompons on either side of its head. Thus, the name pompon.

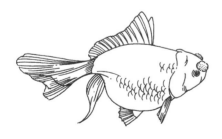

POMPON

These pompons are also known as nasal flaps. The nasal flaps are not as hard as the cap or hood of other fish, and the pompons tend to sway when the fish swims. These growths are very suceptible to disease and fungus, and are easily damaged. Sometimes, but not always, pompons do develop a cap of head growth as they get older.

These nasal features have been bred into other lines, including pompon orandas and lionhead pompons, as well as others. These are not normally available to the average consumer, and have to be specially ordered. Pompons come in a wide range of markings and colorations.

Pompons may live up to ten years, and should be kept at a relatively constant temperature somewhere between 55°F and 65°F. Given enough room, a pompon will grow to between 3 and 4 inches (tail not included). This fish should only be kept by someone who has experience with goldfish. It is definitely not for the beginner.

Brocaded Goldfish

First bred in Japan, the brocaded goldfish is known for its fine, mottled coloring. The body resembles that of the wakin, while the finnage, especially the lack of a dorsal fin, reminds one of a lionhead. Its mottling is a rich gold color, mixed with black, red, and white, which looks just like gold brocade.

The Celestial Goldfish

Celestial goldfish are also known as stargazers. They were named for the direction in which their eyes pointed. It was posited that they were always looking at the stars.

Unlike a globe-eyed goldfish, where the eyes are at the end of the protuberance, the celestial goldfish's eyes are positioned on top of their outgrowths.

The eyes are held in strong casings. This growth begins very early on. Since they are only able to see upward, their forward and lateral vision is poor. It is interesting to see how the fish make up for this anatomical difficulty. Celestials tend to feel their way around or position themselves in the direction they want to see. It is impor-

Oranda and Lionhead Tip

Note: Oranda and lionhead owners beware. In the spring or summer, a whitish film will cover the head of these fish. Be very discerning. More times than not this is new growth.

Rules for Feeding Goldfish

1. Only feed them what they can eat in five minutes.

2. Feed them at the same time every day, once in the morning, once at night.

3. Always feed them at the same spot in the tank.

4. Do not overfeed the fish, no matter how humane you think you are being. More goldfish die, especially older ones, from overeating than anything else.

tant to find a celestial where the fish's eyes point in the same direction as each other. Their pupils should be the same size also.

The celestial is somewhat more streamlined than most other dorsalless goldfish. As usual, they come in a great variety of colorations and markings. They can grow up to 6 inches long and can live up to 10 years. They should be kept at a relatively constant temperature somewhere between 55°F and 65°F. As with all the exotics, disease and fungus are sometimes a problem. The eyes of a celestial are very delicate and sensitive.

The Bubble-Eye

If you couldn't sleep or stayed up too late the night before, watching your favorite movie or sports team, you sometimes have puffy eyes. But once you look at these fish, you'll never feel so bad about staying up late again. The bubble-eyed goldfish has got to be one of the weirdest-looking fish you will ever see. These fish have large fluid-filled sacs that grow underneath each eye. The eye itself is quite normal. In most cases, though, the sacs grow so tight and large that the eyes begin to point upward, in some cases as badly as in a celestial. On a healthy, good representative of the species, the sacs should always be of the same size. The most scary thing about these sacs is that they sway when the fish swims, as if they could tear any second.

These sacs are very delicate, and hobbyists should know that they are prone to injury. However, they do repair themselves. You should avoid putting any kind of sharp objects in the tank with these fish, so as to avoid any unfortunate injury. Disease and fungus are sometimes a problem, as the eyes are very delicate and sensitive. Again, maintenance is the key to avoiding any problems later on.

The body of the bubble-eye is very much like that of a celestial, and they have a dual caudal fin. They develop no other head growth. They come in variety of colorations and markings. They can grow up to 5 inches long (tail not included). These fish are not for beginners. Experts only.

Snack Foods, or Your Goldfish Versus the Plants

Your goldfish look at plants the same way we look at potato chips and pretzels. Mmmmmmm! Yum. It's important to know, therefore, that goldfish are not especially respectful of your gardening abilities. Rather, they tend to view you as a farmer raising some very tasty foods. They don't give a hoot how long it's taken you to get to the plant level in your hobby. They only know what's sitting in front of them.

Of course, there are many goldfish hobbyists who keep live plants, but they will tell you they spend just as much time, if not more, with the plants as they do with the goldfish.

Another thing goldfish like to do is root around the tank, and they love to move plants. Many goldfish fanciers, even if they have kept living plants, have almost lost their patience with goldfish who keep rooting around in the gravel and uprooting their plants. Before investing in plants, you should consider how much time you want to spend with your aquarium plants.

BLACK BUBBLE-EYE

The Black Bubble-Eye

What the black moor is to the globe-eyed goldfish, the black bubble-eye is to the bubble-eye. It is covered in the same dark brown to black velvety coat as the black moor. However, while the black moor is a relatively hardy fish, this fish is delicate and needs to be handled as carefully as the bubble-eye. Read the bubble-eye description for all you need to know about this one. Also, remember that if you keep the tank too warm, the velvet sheen might begin to erode, and there's no going back. Shoot for 60°F.

Goldfish Feeding

A feeding section is included later in this book. Here we'll discuss a few topics specific to goldfish. For feeding instructions, see Section 3.

Basics

Goldfish are omnivores, which basically means they will eat anything. However, you can be sure that they will grow bored with flake food as their only source of nutrition. You can use it as their staple food, but you really should make an attempt to substitute other foods several times a week to insure the best possible results.

You may want to consider added nutritional needs if you are keeping fancier goldfish, especially orandas and pompons or any other kind of goldfish that has headgrowth. Proteins, vitamins, and minerals will insure better head growth and brighter coloration. Fats, carbohydrates, and oils are, of course, necessary for energy. Fat storage is important for fish who live outdoors so that they can sustain themselves through the winter months.

What Do I Feed My Goldfish?

They will eat red worms, white worms, earthworms, and tubifex; they also like brine shrimp, mosquito larvae, and fruit flies. They love almost any kind of seafood—crab, lobster, oysters, and clams, either fresh or canned. They can also be fed canned foods, such as canned vegetables; beans are especially good for them. Fresh spinach, broccoli, and cauliflower are also excellent additions.

Goldfish Feeding Kits and Foods

There are now many manufacturers that have begun marketing specialized foods for your fish. These kits promise to improve their growth and color. After speaking to a number of experts, we've learned that the results of these kits are mixed. However, for the beginner who is just starting out, and is just feeding flake foods, a combination of vitamin supplements and specialized food would be excellent additives to your goldfish's staple diet foods.

Make sure you only buy the products meant for goldfish, or even your particular breed of goldfish. Orandas and lionhead owners are definitely the target audience for some of these foods. Do not buy the ones that are aimed at general tropical fish. The nutritional needs of goldfish differ greatly from those of community or incompatible tropical fish.

Frozen or Freeze-Dried Foods

If you really want to give your goldfish a treat they will love without a lot of hassle, frozen or freeze-dried foods offer the best of the live world without any of the challenges of growing your own. Besides, the nice part is that the manufacturer has taken out all the worry of disease or fungus. Frozen or freeze-dried foods your goldfish will love include brine shrimp, krill, tubifex worms, mosquito larvae, daphnia, and bloodworms. These are a great convenience to the hobbyist who wants a quick, safe, and easy way to provide variety to his or her fish.

Koi

What Are Koi?

The history of koi is certainly even more fascinating than that of the goldfish. Koi is a short form of the Japanese word for "colorful carp." Koi, in fact, are actually just colorful mutations of the common carp, *Cyprinus carpio.* This is also the progenitor of the common goldfish. The first recorded mentioning of these color mutations dates back 2,500 years to both Persia and China. In

No Miss Manners Here

Let's be honest, so that we can get this out of the way. Goldfish are gluttons! They will literally eat to the point of bursting. All right, who hasn't had one extra piece of dessert too often. Sure we all have. But there are a lot of other fish (tropical and marine) that won't do that. Not so with goldfish. That's important.

Since they can't control themselves, you'll have to do it for them. It's best to feed goldfish no more than they can eat in five minutes. Twice a day, at the same time, and you'll be the Julia Child of your aquarium.

But don't expect them to say 'please.'

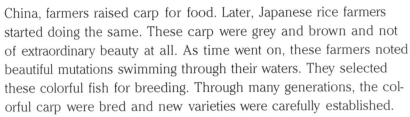

Vary Your Foods

While live foods and foods other than flakes are highly desirable, it is important to know that no one group supplies everything your goldfish needs. Food that always comes from one group or another will lead to overload. Too many live foods, and your goldfish may not have enough fats or carbohydrates in their diets. Too much of any one food may cause digestive problems too difficult to remedy.

China, farmers raised carp for food. Later, Japanese rice farmers started doing the same. These carp were grey and brown and not of extraordinary beauty at all. As time went on, these farmers noted beautiful mutations swimming through their waters. They selected these colorful fish for breeding. Through many generations, the colorful carp were bred and new varieties were carefully established.

It was not until a Tokyo exhibition around the turn of the century that a few varieties were exhibited. The fish was an oddity and an immediate hit. Suddenly, everyone had to have one of these fish. From a friendly farmer's hobby, koi have grown into a multimillion-dollar worldwide industry. Today, individual koi have sold for hundreds of thousands of dollars. Now, koi are bred all over the world, including the United States, western Europe, Israel, and Singapore. However, Japan remains the major origin of the finest koi in the world.

The problem for the tropical fish hobbyist is that koi are too big for the aquarium. The average koi grows at least 16 inches. Considered by many to be the most elegant and colorful of the freshwater fishes, koi have become popular inhabitants of domestic garden ponds. So, if you want to keep koi, you have to be ready to turn your backyard into an ornamental or garden pond in an area where you will be able to fully enjoy and maintain your pet koi.

Koi are part of the Cyprinidae family of fishes, which has the widest distribution of freshwater fishes in the world. Goldfish are part of this same family. Goldfish are smaller and lack the whiskers or barbels around the mouth that koi have. Koi are hardy fish and can survive in small ponds, moving streams, and rivers in a wide range of temperatures.

Though there are many different varieties of carp, they are still classified as a single species. This is a result of careful breeding by the Japanese farmers over the years. Thus, all koi have the same general anatomy. This anatomy exerts itself quickly, as carp will grow to 6 inches in the first year, and reach 16 inches in the third year. Koi have been recorded tipping the scales at over 45 pounds! And some have grown as large as 22 inches. They are also a long-lived species: some have been known to live as long as 50 to 70 years!

The Varieties

The names of most koi are in Japanese, since most were bred there. Sometimes it takes a while for a beginner to get the terminology down correctly. Differences and difficulties in translating information on koi from Japanese has led to even more confusion in trying to interpret all there is to know about koi. The important thing is to maintain a healthy and vibrant koi, and leave all the classification of koi to the experts. Have fun creating your pond and enjoy your new pets.

Classifications

It's helpful to know something about classification, though you need not memorize it. Several factors aid in classifying koi. Scale type and arrangement, patterns and markings, and color are all factors. Basically, there are three colors, and these colors are incorporated into the names of the koi. Single-color koi are named for their color. If the koi has more than one color, those colors are incorporated into the name. Patterns and marking come next.

A good example is hajiro. This means "crow" in Japanese. A crow is a black koi with white tips on its fins.

Four types of scales are recognized in koi:

- **Normal**: glossy metallic sheen scales
- **Doitsu**: large scales sparsely spaced
- **Leather**: no scales
- **Gin rin**: a matte or flat look; lacking sheen

There are 13 major varieties, and within each variety are many different types or variations. These varieties are used in judging during competitions. Each variety has its own Japanese name. For these, there are few translations. Several are just the Japanese word for a particular color. Others are the names of a Japanese emperor.

Listed here are the 13 recognized varieties of koi. Translations of these may vary from expert to expert and author to author, but many people can agree on these 13.

Koi Lingo

Beta-gin: uneven scales
Bu: size
Gaku: deformed koi
Kana: male
Mena: female
Pongoi: high-quality koi
Shitsu: quality koi
Dagoi: poor-quality koi

All three of the following phrases are used to describe wild koi:

Goior koi: wild koi
Ma: wild
Magoi: wild carp

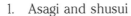

1. Asagi and shusui
2. Bekko
3. Hikarimoyo mono
4. Hikari utsuri mono
5. Kawari mono
6. Kinginrin
7. Kohaku
8. Koromo
9. Ogon
10. Showa sanke
11. Taisho sanke
12. Tancho
13. Utsuri mono

Obviously, these names mean nothing to those who don't know Japanese. Use the following explanations to help you identify the variety of your koi.

1. **Asagi and shusui**

These two koi are so similar, they are usually combined, especially at competitions. Asagi are scaled, light blue koi. They were developed more than 150 years ago. They have a reddish-orange belly and pectoral fins. The highest quality asagi have a pinecone reticulated pattern on their back and a consistent blue coloration throughout.

Some common varieties of asagi are:

- *Asagi sanke:* red head and sides, pale blue back
- *Hi asagi:* red on belly that extends above the lateral line
- *Konjo asagi:* dark grey to black asagi
- *Mizu asagi:* light patterned asagi
- *Taki asagi:* blue and red with pinecone pattern

Room to Grow

Remember, koi can grow rather large. If you're going to build a pond for koi, make sure they'll be enough room in the pond when your fish begin to grow. Many people don't plan properly and their ponds later suffer from over-crowding because they didn't take into account how crowded it would be after their fish had grown.

Shusui are doitsu asagi with large, dark blue scales along the back and lateral line. Doitsu scales are large scales sparsely spaced. Shusui are a descendant of the asagi variety and also have a blue back with orange-red below the lateral line and on the pectoral fins.

Some common varieties are:

- *Hana shusui:* red markings on both sides of the body and abdomen
- *Hi shusui:* red from abdomen to back
- *Ki shusui:* yellow and dark blue back shusui

2. Bekko

The patterns on these koi resemble those found on tortoise shells. They were developed in the 1800s. There are many different-colored bekko, but most are white. Some have colors with black patches. These are called sumi.

Some common varieties are:

- *Aka bekko:* red body with sumi
- *Ki bekko:* yellow body with sumi
- *Shiro bekko:* white body with sumi

3. Hikarimoyo mono

The name literally means "metallic pattern." While the heads of these koi remain largely unmarked, their bodies are usually multicolored. At least one of the colors is made up of normal scales, and the other is made up of gin rin scales.

Some common varieties are:

- *Hariwake*: platinum body with orange or gold pattern
- *Kinsui:* red metallic coloration
- *Kikisui:* platinum doitsu with yellow waves
- *Yamabuki:* metallic patterns over a platinum body
- *Yamatonishiki:* red and black patterns over a metallic white body

The Color of Koi

Below are the Japanese terms for the colorations that are used in classifying koi.

• Red	Aka
• Purple	Budo
• Scales	Doitsu
• Silver	Gin
• Five-colors	Go-shiki
• White	Haku
• Metallic	Hikari
• Fawn-dappled	Kanoko
• Yellow	Ki
• Gold	Kin
• Peacock	Kujaku
• Solid	Muji
• Gold	Ogon
• Scales	Rin
• Three colors	Sanke
• White	Shiro
• Black	Sumi
• Red spot on head	Tancho
	Utsuri
• Reflection	Yamabuki
• Yellow	

Sorry, These Guys Don't Come Inside

Remember, koi grow very large, and are not meant for aquariums . . . unless you're bent on opening your own version of Sea World! Make sure when you think about the pond you are building that it is heated (not too much) and that it is deep in an area where these fish can congregate in the winter.

Some people who do bring their fish inside, have large pools inside where their fish can spend the winter.

4. **Hikari utsuri mono**

All the koi in this variety have metallic scales and display two or three colors. The heads usually have black markings, while the bodies have bright metallic patterns.

Some common varieties are:

- *Kin ki utsuri:* golden metallic yellow pattern on black
- *Kin hi utsuri:* golden metallic red pattern on black
- *Gin showa:* black and red patterns on metallic silver body
- *Kin showa:* black and golden metallic red patterns on white body

5. **Kawari mono**

This is sort of a catch-all classification. The idea is that these koi don't fit into any other group. Some experts have literally translated this name as "unusual ones."

Some common varieties are:

- *Karasu goi:* black colored body
- *Ki goi:* yellow body with variable fin colors and normal or doitsu scales
- *Hajiro:* white tips on fins, black body
- *Goshiki:* multi-colored body, black with red, white, brown, blue
- *Kumonryu:* black body lined with white on back and sides

6. **Kinginrin**

This variety of koi has a very bright metallic sheen and numerous rows of silver body patterns. These silver markings differ in distribution and appearance, depending on the type of koi.

Common examples are:

- *Ginrin:* silver scales on white portions of the body
- *Kinginrin bekko:* black body with silver scales
- *Kinginrin kohaku:* a red and white body with silver markings
- *Kinginrin sanke:* a red, black, and white body with silver scales

7. **Kohaku**

This is one of the most popular koi in the world, and they are relatively easy to obtain. Kohaku have a white body with red markings. This variety was developed almost 200 years ago, and it's still the popular favorite among the Japanese. Kohaku generally lack black markings (also known as sumi) and may have doitsu or normal scales.

Some common varieties are:

- *Aka muji:* mostly red kohaku
- *Goten zakura:* red "cherry blossom" pattern
- *Shiro muji:* mostly white kohaku
- *Inazuma:* lightning-shaped pattern on back
- *Kuchibeni:* head and lips marked by red
- *Ippon:* one continuous pattern on body, red
- *Nidan:* two patterns on body, red
- *Sandan:* three patterns on body, red
- *Yodan:* four patterns on body, red
- *Godan:* five patterns on body, red
- *Omoyo:* wavy pattern on back, red

8. **Koromo**

This is not a very common variety. The translation for koromo is "robed." They are usually white or red, marked with black, silver, or blue.

Some common varieties are:

- *Ai goromo:* blue pinecone edging on red patterns, white body
- *Sumi goromo:* black pinecone edging on red patterns, white body
- *Budo sanskoku:* black scales on red scales, white body

Popular Beginner Koi

Most koi have the same requirements. Koi are mostly priced on the difficulty of obtaining them, i.e., the rarer they are, the more expensive they are.

Kohaku are certainly very popular and easily obtained. So are ogon, tancho, and butterfly.

Buying Koi

Where to buy your koi? Many garden centers are selling koi now. However, you would probably do better with a professional breeder, who has a reputation for breeding healthy, quality fish that will be able to last a winter and bring joy into your life for many years to come.

9. **Ogon**

This variety is also known as hikari muji mono. These are a popular variety of koi. They usually have metallic gold or metallic silver as one of the scale types on their body. They may also possess leather or doitsu.

Some common varieties are:

- *Ogon:* platinum scales, gold metallic, yellowish-gold scales
- *Kin matsuba:* pinecone pattern with gold metallic scales
- *Gin matsuba:* pinecone pattern with silver metallic scales

10. **Showa sanke**

Many of these fish are primarily made up of fish that are mostly black, with varying red and white markings.

Some common varieties are:

- *Boke showa:* light bluish color
- *Hi showa:* black and white dominated by red
- *Kage showa:* white scales edged thinly with black
- *Kindai showa:* red and black, dominated by black

11. **Sanke** or **taisho sanke**

While different authors can't agree on the correct name for this variety, they all agree on one thing—the fish are tri-colored. This fish dates to the turn of the century, sometime around 1900. All have red, white, and black colors.

Some common varieties are:

- *Fuji sanke:* head has metallic sheen
- *Aka sanke:* predominantly red
- *Kuchibeni:* snout and lips marked with red
- *Tsubaki sanke:* covered by black pattern

12. **Tancho**

Tancho is a popular coloration. The same as in goldfish, the white fish are white. They should have a bright red mark on it, and they are very easily spotted.

Some common varieties are:

- *Tancho kohaku:* white body with single red mark on head
- *Tancho showa:* a showa with single red pattern on top of head
- *Shinzo tancho:* heart-shaped pattern on top of head

13. **Utsuri mono**

Each fish is marked by two colors. The under color is black and is checked by a contrasting color. This is another variety over 100 years old.

Some common varieties are:

- *Hi utsuri:* red body markings, black body
- *Shiro utsuri:* white body markings, black body

The Fourteenth Variety: Butterfly Koi

In Japan, there is officially no fourteenth variety. But one of the most popular fish in the world today, especially for United States koi fans, is the butterfly koi. These fish were bred in the 1980s and are not officially recognized by the koi competitions. That's because they are technically not of the same species, but have been cross-bred with the Asian carp. However, this is the most popular koi on the market today. They are popular because their finnage, like those of several goldfish varieties, is long and exaggerated. It flows beautifully in the water. These can easily be distinguished from what are considered by aficionados to be the only true carp—the 13 recognized groups.

Butterfly koi are popular especially because they are quite hardy and are excellent for pond or water gardens. They can withstand great changes in temperatures and are excellent swimmers. They come in a variety of colors and patterns.

Thinking More About Your Koi

It's time to think about which koi you're going to choose. As far as your new water garden is concerned, this is one of the most important decisions you will make. The good thing about koi is that

Cinderella, Cinderella

The butterfly koi is an American phenomenon. The Japanese have not yet embraced this beautiful fish. Consequently, butterfly koi are not invited to compete at the biggest koi shows in Asia, which are certainly the most prestigious.

Koi and Biofiltration

A biofilter uses natural bacteria as an aid in filtering your aquarium water. Most filtration systems use at least a certain amount of biofiltration. But filters that maximize the space where these helpful bacteria reside are the best in keeping harmful toxins at a minimum.

For the koi owner the canister filter is the best filter, because you never really throw out the filter medium . . . you just rinse it off. Your pond doesn't have to re-adjust while your filter spends weeks re-building its bacteria base.

All three of the most popular filtration systems for ponds make use of a canister filter. Lateral-flow systems often work best.

they are extremely hardy fish. However, you really shouldn't rely on their stamina and hardiness as much as on your ability to create a good home where they will thrive. But it's nice to know that they can withstand a lot of stress. One of their most stressful moments occur when you are bringing them home. Transportation is a very stressful time for fish, especially koi.

Choosing Your Dealer

These days, with koi, water gardens, and ponds so popular, you can find koi in many retail outlets. Koi are available at pet stores, some garden centers, and through individual breeders and koi farms. Make sure you thoroughly check the place you're buying your koi from. Ask for references, ask a lot of questions, and try to visit the store or supplier before you buy.

The idea is to buy from someone reliable. That way, when you have questions, they'll help you out. If you can establish a relationship with a good dealer, you're halfway home, before you even look at a fish. If you've been referred by a happy customer, then you should be very happy. You need someone who's going to spend the time you need answering questions. If you can't get the dealer on the phone before you buy the fish, you're going to be out of luck after you buy it. Good dealers are worth their weight in gold to koi fanciers.

The worst thing you can do when you want to buy your koi is rush. The desire to find that fish and bring it home is strong. You can't think like that. You need to be as responsible as possible, because you will find that the really good dealers earn their money when you get home with your fish, not when you buy it. A good dealer will be with you a long time and will be both a fellow enthusiast and an advisor. Take the time to choose a dealer carefully.

Choosing Your Koi

By now, you must have a pretty good idea of the koi you are thinking of choosing. Try to choose the ones you like best, because koi live a long time, and you're going to have to take care of them

A Koi Checklist
When You Are Buying

Take care to look for or ask the following of your koi dealer:

❑ Are the display tanks clean? Are they bio-filtered? Does each tank have its own filter?

❑ Do they quarantine new fish for two weeks in separate tanks before dropping them into general distribution?

❑ Do they have background information on the koi? The origin of the koi is important because koi with good backgrounds command hefty fees. Don't fall for the sale come-on that these are "Japanese koi." Dealers can say it in this way, and yet the koi may not, in fact, be from Japan. If you have the money, you would prefer a koi bred in Japan. They are simply of higher quality and better breeding. Generally speaking, they cost a bit more.

❑ Breeders and dealers who care will supply you with additional oxygen for your fish. Between being netted and set into a confined place, the koi are stressing out. Just like you, when koi stress, they use more oxygen. Refilling your bags with oxygen will go a long way in making sure your koi makes it home in a healthy state.

❑ There are many pet-product manufacturers in the marketplace. Is your dealer dealing in the newest koi products? You don't want a dealer who's into all the latest fads, but you don't want one whose product line is hopelessly out of date. You want to make sure you're buying from a smart dealer who's in the know. These products range from certain chemical treatments, to food, vitamins, and minerals.

for a long time. Don't pick fish that are too exotic or that are very popular right now just to have something no one else has.

These fish live a long time, and you'll want to enjoy them for a long time. Make sure you get the fish *you* like.

Don't try to get a deal on your koi or buy one from a friend of a friend. These fish are going to be your pets, and you want to make sure you're not cutting corners that in the end may cost you. On the other hand, don't spend a lot of money on your first few koi, especially if you are establishing a new pond. If there are any problems in your systems, you don't want to find that out with fish you just bought at a well-known auction.

There is a debate on what age koi you should purchase. Many feel you should only buy mature koi. First, if you buy young ones, you're never sure whether or not their markings and colorings will fade or improve as they start to mature. Koi change drastically as they age. Some that had intense colors when they are young often fade as they mature. Those with pale or washed-out colors often have intense colors during their mature years. For example, fish that have black in them may go one way or another. Young fish might display black as gray when they are older, or they might grow into a deep, true black. However, those with intense colors, such as red, when they are young, often fade to orange-yellow-red when they get older.

Do you need to buy show grade quality koi? Yes, you can buy show grade, but should you? No. No doubt it's a great feeling to be able to say to friends and family that you have purchased a show quality koi. But these are expensive. However, if you are buying because you eventually want to show koi, then that is something else entirely.

Koi are judged on the following characteristics: color, pattern, and shape.

A competitive quality koi is symmetrical from the front and from above. The head and tail are tapered, while the middle is the thickest part. The dorsal should be closer to the tail than the head by a third. This is an important buying tip. If the dorsal is too close to the tail, the fish is considered unacceptable by breeders and is useless other than as a pet. The colors must be deep, strong, and bright. White should always be the whitest possible and lack any specks of another color completely. The edge of where color meets color should be clear and not blurry. Color lines must be sharp, as they separate one color field from another. The skin should be unblemished and appear vibrant.

Picking Out Healthy Koi

You need to be able to judge the health and quality of the fish when you go to buy it. You should be as selective as possible. Make no exceptions. Make sure there are no dead fish in the tanks. The fish you choose should have clear eyes. Do not buy fish with cloudy eyes, no matter what your dealer or pet professional tells you. Its skin should be completely unblemished. Look for any signs of damage or disease on the body and fins. Don't buy any fish with tattered or shredded fins.

Does the fish act healthy? Is it swimming throughout the area or is it sitting listlessly at the bottom? Is the fish you like gulping air from the surface? This tells you that the fish is stressed, since it's not getting enough oxygen from the water.

It's important to remember that a lot is riding on any koi you pick. Whether it's your first or your sixth, it doesn't matter. If you bring home a diseased fish, you may be placing your entire school of fish in danger, and may be ruining a perfectly good pond. Stories abound of people who've brought home diseased fish, only to find that they had to go through a lengthy cleaning process of their pond before they could bring home another fish. So, if the fish are not properly cared for at the establishment where you are shopping, then make the right choice. Go to another store.

Make sure to be there for the netting of your fish once you've made your selection. Professionals should be able to net the koi easily and safely. The net should be large and soft. Make sure they don't harm your fish as they are taking it out of the tank and placing it in a bag or tub to ready it for transportation.

If the fish is bagged (in a heavy-duty, heavy-milled plastic bag), as most of them are, it's important to make sure there's enough air

Pick Noticeable Fish

When you're picking out your koi, make sure to pick fish that will be easily spotted. It will make your pond-keeping experience much more enjoyable.

in the bag. You don't want your koi to die from suffocation on the way home. Make sure that the water in the bag is good, clean, aerated water, not cloudy or dirty.

The more time your koi spends in the bag, the more likely there could be a buildup of carbon dioxide and ammonia. However, the worst part is that the longer the fish stays in the bag, the more stressed the fish is going to be. To reduce the effects of stress, one of the tips we've found is to add some common non-iodized salt to the water. Two level tablespoons per gallon is recommended. This is only for fish that will be in a bag for more than a few hours. It will lessen the stress on your fish, and it won't hurt it, either. Longer term transportation will require additional handling, and your dealer should be able to help you figure out the best way to get your new pet home. Some experts have suggested ammonia detoxifier to remove the ammonia toxic to your fish. Others have suggested other medications. Ask your koi dealer for their recommendation. The best method is to keep them in a bag for the shortest amount of time possible.

The Pond

There is a separate section for your pond in this book. Koi and goldfish have many of the same requirements when it comes to pond life. Koi can really only be kept in large pools of water. While there are hobbyists who have spent large amounts of money on indoor pools for their koi, most keep them outside. Therefore, our pond section is about outdoor ponds. The size of the pool is directly related to the number and size of the fish.

Feeding Your Koi

We've included a separate section in this book about feeding. After reviewing the points here, you should read that section, as there are many things there that will help you. This section won't cover everything you need to know; only those things that differ between koi and other freshwater fish.

How does feeding koi differ from feeding freshwater fish? Not only are koi larger, they also have to deal with a wide range of

Puppy Chow

Like dogs, koi go through a major growth spurt in the first 12 to 24 months. Size and age will determine how much food each koi will eat. The one thing that's important to know, however, is that young fish eat more than adult fish. In order to sustain their incredible growth period, koi eat quite a lot. The larger adults don't need as much.

temperatures, which will, of course, add stress to their system. Many koi owners admit that one of their favorite things to do is feed their pets. Therefore, they must be careful to not overfeed. Like goldfish, koi are omnivorous. They are more than happy to eat whatever it is you give them. However, especially because they live outside and deal with seasonal changes, their dietary needs change.

Digestion for koi is an interesting and important thing to know. Koi are different from almost all the other fish in this book for one simple reason—koi don't have stomachs! They chew their food with their teeth. This is where digestion begins. They obviously digest food better than others. But there are outside forces, too, which will also go a long way in determining their rate of digestion. The season and temperature are some key factors. How much they metabolize also depends on their age. Older koi don't need as much food as younger ones.

Dietary Needs

Like other living creatures, koi have their own dietary needs. These needs include fats, carbohydrates, vitamins, and minerals. In the wild, fish scavenge and hunt, meeting their needs as they go. And while it is true that your koi will get a certain amount of food from nature, i.e., water bugs and other insects that live near still bodies of water, the fish will still rely on you to feed them.

Protein

Younger koi require more protein than older koi. Fry and fingerling koi should be fed diets that range from 37 to 42 percent protein while adults require a diet of 28 to 32 percent protein. Protein is more difficult to break down relative to other nutritional groups. So, most experts feel that less protein should be fed during the colder months of the year. Koi should never be fed a diet containing less than 28 percent protein because a deficiency will develop.

What's For Dinner?

There are many different types of food for your koi. Being omnivores, koi will eat processed foods, red worms, white worms, earthworms, tubifex, brine shrimp, mosquito larvae, fruit flies, crab, lobster, oysters, clams, canned vegetables like beans, fresh spinach, broccoli, and cauliflower. All of these are excellent foods for your koi.

Lipids

Lipids or fats provide energy and so are important to the internal organs and cells. A diet with too much saturated fat derived from pork, beef, or poultry is not beneficial to koi. A diet rich in unsaturated oils is preferable for koi. Most commercially prepared foods contain five to eight percent fat, which is suitable for koi. Too much fat will cause excessive weight and fat deposits, while a deficiency will cause heart problems and fin erosion.

If you plan to buy commercially prepared foods, make sure you buy the ones that have been especially prepared for koi only. There are other specialty foods that have been prepared for trout, salmon, and catfish. These contain fats that are not good for koi. Don't buy them as a substitute!

Carbohydrates

Carbohydrate is another important source of energy for koi. Most commercially prepared foods are high in carbohydrates. Sources of carbohydrates include wheat, corn, barley, and rice. Koi do not digest carbohydrates as efficiently as previously thought. Thus, foods very high in cereals should be avoided. So, while we will encourage you to feed your fish household foods, you should not feed them bread, dog biscuits, or breakfast cereals.

Vitamins

Vitamins provide the necessary building blocks for proper metabolism. Vitamins can be either water-soluble or fat-soluble. Vitamin deficiencies will cause a variety of disease symptoms, such as loss of appetite, reduced growth, eye protrusion (exophthalmus), and bone malformation. The richest source of vitamins is found in green plants, vegetables, fruit, and liver and fish oils. These foods should be used to supplement the diet of koi so that a vitamin deficiency does not develop.

Minerals

Minerals provide the important building blocks for tissue formation and metabolism. Two very important minerals are calcium and phosphorous. Calcium and phosphorous deficiencies cause poor bone formation, slow growth, and appetite depression. High sources of minerals include vegetables such as spinach, kale, and lettuce.

Food Categories

There are basically four different categories of food: commercially prepared foods, frozen or freeze-dried foods, live foods, and household foods. Of these, the most harmful to your fish are the live foods. These can potentially carry diseases or parasites that can infect your fish. Many of these are covered in the separate food section.

Prepared foods

Commercially prepared foods contain the three basic requirements of proteins, fats, and carbohydrates. They are also supplemented with vitamins and minerals. These foods come in a variety of forms, but are typically pelleted for koi. Commercial pellets are very popular for feeding koi. They can sink or float and come in a variety of sizes. Floating pellets are preferred by many koi owners because they can watch their fish feed at the surface, and they can more effectively monitor the amount that they are feeding. Sinking pellets draw the koi deeper, may result in overfeeding, and cause water quality degradation.

Care must be taken to scrutinize the ingredients of the commercially prepared koi foods to be sure that they are properly balanced. Use the information provided above to be sure that all the nutritional needs of your koi are being met. Commercial prepared foods provide a good foundation for your pet's diet, but it should be augmented with other supplements so that a balanced diet is maintained. As mentioned earlier, only use supplements specially prepared for koi and not those for other species of fish.

The Pros and Cons of Table Scraps

Fresh, frozen, or canned oysters, clams, mussels, crabmeat, lobster, or bits of raw fish are excellent. Baked or boiled beans, steamed cauliflower or broccoli, and boiled or baked potatoes are excellent additions. Fresh spinach or lettuce are also good for your koi.

Koi will eat almost anything that we eat, including beef, boneless chicken, and pasta, but don't let your pond become a place to dispose of leftovers. These foods must be given in moderation. Remember, you are augmenting your fish's diet with these foods, not creating a staple. Household foods must be diced or shredded so that your fish can eat them. Don't offer your koi table scraps unless they conform to what is listed above.

These supplements are readily available in great variety at most pet stores.

Care must be taken when storing dry commercial feeds to ensure that the quality of the product is maintained. Heat and moisture will degrade the product. Vitamins are very sensitive to high temperatures. Prepared foods should be stored in cool, dry areas for a maximum of 90 days. They should not be left open and exposed to the air while in storage.

Live Foods

Live food is an excellent source of nutrition for koi. However, many feel that live foods may carry diseases that will infect your fish. To insure against this, live foods can easily be obtained from your dealer or a pet store. This is much safer than collecting live foods from a pond or lake.

Color-Enhancing

The quality of your koi is largely determined by the quality of its coloration. The colors of your koi are dictated by the genetic potential of your fish, the quality of your pond water, and what your koi consumes. You can feed your koi specific color-enhancing ingredients to maximize its color.

Naturally occurring pigments like those found in shrimp, marigold petals, plankton, and the blue-green algae Spirulina have been added to commercial koi feeds to enhance coloration. Koi will also feed naturally on the Spirulina that grows in your pond. This will enhance the red, orange, and yellow colors in your koi. Many of the freeze-dried and live foods mentioned above, such as brine shrimp and daphnia, contain high concentrations of carotenoid pigments, which are major pigments of the koi's skin. Be aware that koi that feed on too much color-enhancing food may develop too much color. This is particularly true for koi that are predominantly white. If this happens, simply reduce the amount of color-enhancing food that you are feeding your koi.

How To Feed Your Fish

The biggest problem when feeding your koi is determining how much and how often to feed them. In general, many feel that it is better to feed too little than too much. Remember, koi are omnivorous and opportunistic. They will spend much of the day foraging, eating algae, plants, and insects that end up in the pond. Follow these guidelines when feeding your fish and you will develop a working sense of how much and how often to feed them.

1. Offer as much food as your koi will eat in five minutes.
2. Feed your fish in very small portions over the five-minute period.
3. If you are home during the day, feed your fish over the course of the day in small portions. If you are not home, feed your fish at least twice a day at the same times every day, once in the morning, then mid or late afternoon. Younger koi need to eat more frequently.
4. Always feed your fish in the same general area of the pond.
5. Don't overfeed the fish, no matter how much you think they need more food. Overfeeding will stress your fish and cause detritus to accumulate in the pond, degrading water quality.

Watch all your fish during feeding to make sure that each gets its share of food. Remember, refusal to eat is one of the first signs of illness, so keep an eye out for fish that seem to have no interest in food.

Start with commercially prepared food as your staple and mix in a variety of foods as your fish acclimate to the pond. Also, don't crumble the food. This will add fine particles to the water that are not ingested, but degrade water quality. Your fish won't have any problems biting and grinding whole pelleted food. Make every effort to remove uneaten food so that it is not left to decompose in the pond.

Seasonal Feeding

The quantity and type of food will change with the seasons. As the water temperature decreases in the autumn and winter you will need to pay attention to the amount of food that you give your koi. Remember that koi activity will decrease during this time and the food requirements of the fish will decrease as well. Feed your koi less and less as the temperature continues to decline. During the winter or when the water temperature is below 50°F, stop feeding your koi completely, regardless of how hungry you think they might be. Remember, they are scavenger fish, so they scavenge when they're hungry. Any uneaten food will accumulate in the pond and cloud the water.

In addition, the dietary requirements of your koi will change with the decrease in temperature. You should alter the dietary composition of your koi's diet in the fall to help your fish prepare for the winter season. Reduce the amount of protein and slightly increase the amount of carbohydrates and fat to promote fat storage for overwintering.

As the water warms again in the spring to about 60°F, begin feeding your koi in very low quantities once a day. As the weather continues to warm, slowly increase the food amount and frequency of feedings. Be aware that your bio-filter has most likely been shut down for the winter and must be re-established at this time as well. Therefore, don't overtax your filter with large amounts of koi waste; it may not be able to handle it.

In the active season of summer, a high-protein diet is important to keep your koi healthy. This is the time to feed your koi at levels that will sustain high activity, but still be careful and do not overfeed.

If you are going to be away from your pond for up to a few days, the koi will be fine without food. For extended periods, make arrangements for someone to feed your fish.

CHAPTER FOUR

Ponds and Water Gardens for Goldfish and Koi

This Ain't Ellie Mae's Cee-ment Pond!

There are a wide variety of ponds and styles to choose from. And at this stage, before you've read this section, you are not qualified to design one, let alone buy one. But whether you're one of the Clampetts (and can afford a big, expensive pond) or just a regular Joe (like many of us), this section will help you understand ponds and how to get the one you want.

It's important to note right off the top that you are better prepared to operate a pond if you have been a tropical fish hobbyist first, as opposed to having had a swimming pool. There is little similarity between having a pool and maintaining a habitat that replicates that of nature. One is a carefully created ecosystem, and the other is chemically treated water that bleaches your hair and hurts your eyes. A pond is a habitat and a place of natural beauty.

Ponds and water gardens have become quite popular in recent years. Many garden centers abound in the materials you'll need to create and enjoy a place of lasting beauty on your property. Whether creating a complex custom-designed pond, or buying a prefabricated one, having a pond filled with fish is a thing of lasting and long-term beauty and joy.

The Fish

The large size of koi does not allow for fish other than small juveniles to be kept in a home aquarium, and these fish outgrow their home quite rapidly. The preferred habitat for koi is the garden or ornamental pond. Both koi and goldfish are cold-water freshwater fish that are capable of surviving in conditions that are less favorable for many species of fish. Koi are temperate fish, which means that they can handle wide seasonal fluctuations in temperature. This hardiness, combined with their elegant beauty, have increased the popularity of keeping koi in backyard ponds. Some goldfish also share this hardiness.

Fish in their natural environment are subjected to many challenges in order to survive. Most of these involve natural processes of predation, feeding, reproduction, and disease. Natural catastrophic events that alter water quality are rare, and fish can generally avoid them by moving to other areas. In many ways, these fish are very much responsible for themselves.

Fish that are maintained in an artificial environment like an aquarium or pond are also faced with several challenges in order to survive. However, most of these challenges cannot be met by the fish and must be met by the aquarist and the pond keeper. When you take it upon yourself to set up a koi pond you are accepting the responsibility of meeting all of the needs of its inhabitants. This includes maintaining good water quality, proper feeding, a balanced fish community of the proper density, and the appropriate habitat and shelter, to name a few.

If you have maintained an aquarium in the past and are moving on to build a pond, you will see that there are many similarities and differences between the two. For example, in a pond there is usually not a heater. It is important that you read this section before going out in the yard and digging a hole!

Pond Design

So, you're no Frank Lloyd Wright. Well, who is? How are you going to plan a pond? We're going to take it step by step. The first and foremost step is planning. Planning and designing your pool is critical to the process of building a pond. Consideration must be given to the style of pond, placement of the pond, construction material, filtration, and ornamentation.

The style of pond that the enthusiast chooses is purely subjective, but must be considered at the start of the design process. It is generally recognized that there are two general types of ponds: formal and informal. Formal ponds follow geometric shapes and are generally inspired by the formal ponds built over the centuries in the gardens of Europe and the Near and Middle East. Japan is famous for its formal koi ponds.

A formal pond has a symmetrical shape, such as a circle, square, rectangle, oval, or octagon. They are often constructed of cement and don't contain many plants either in or around them. Instead, they generally have more visually formal settings like flower

Things to Consider When Deciding on a Pond

- Where are you going to place your pond?

- Is there enough shade?

- Is there enough light?

- Do you want koi or goldfish?

- How many fish do you want?

- Is the pond the right size for the number of fish that you want?

- Is it sufficiently deep to help your fish survive the winter?

- Are there ledges or plants for your fish to seek shelter under?

- What plants do you want in the pond?

- Is there an electrical outlet somewhere near?

- Where will you house the filter?

beds or green plants. They are generally placed close to the home where the fish are well attended and easy to see. These ponds are popular with some enthusiasts because they are simple to build and maintain. Others find formal ponds too stiff and conforming.

The other type of pond is informal or "free-form." This style was developed in China, Korea, and later in Japan. There is very little symmetry to an informal pond and the shape is more natural. The idea is to try to recreate a beautiful, ideal setting that might be found in nature. The informal pond can take the shape of a kidney or any other free-form object. Some are constructed with cement, but durable synthetic liners are the material of choice because they conform to the curves and angles of the pond. Typically, informal ponds are rich in beauty and garnished with waterfalls, fountains, elaborate plantings (both inside and outside the pond), wood structures, stones, and a variety of ornaments. The informal pond setting, coupled with the beauty of koi or goldfish, creates a symphony of natural elegance that enhances any home and enchants even the casual observer.

Be Practical

Whether you choose a formal or informal pond depends on your personal preference, but be sure to choose a shape that provides good water circulation and prevents the development of stagnant areas. Elaborate pond design is an art form in some respects. For those who are so inclined, there are companies that specialize in the design and construction of ponds. Reputable experts not only assist you with the development of your pond, but they also make sure that your pond is properly plumbed to maintain very high water quality.

However, there are fantasy ponds, and then there's reality. Reality is better. Make sure you're not fantasizing about something that's so complicated you won't be able to maintain it once it's established. There have been many instances where hobbyists have built elaborate ponds only to find that they'll have to quit their jobs to maintain them. Don't fall into the trap of creating something too complex. Remember the old maxim—Keep It Simple, Stupid.

Where to Place the Pond

Placement, or site selection, is the most important part of installing your pond. This is a critical decision. You need to take into account a number of factors relative to water quality, fish maintenance, and fish safety.

Sunlight is both a gift and a curse. It is one of the most important aspects of siting your pond. Direct exposure to sunlight will elevate water temperatures in the pond to levels higher than koi or goldfish prefer. Neither fish wants to take a warm bath. In addition, sunlight will create algae. Small amounts of algae are beneficial to the pond by consuming nitrogen and releasing oxygen. And your fish will like munching on it. Excessive amounts will cause water fouling and oxygen deprivation. You want your pond to be placed in partial light and partial shade. That way it will warm the water slightly and give some algal effect, but it won't turn your pond into a swamp.

While it's a good thing to have some shade near your pond, it's not so much fun digging through very large, established root systems. Care should be taken not to site the pond too close to trees because root systems will not only make it difficult to construct the pond, but will eventually do damage to the structure of the pond, especially those made of cement. In addition, overhanging trees leach toxins and shed leaves that acidify the pond water and make pond maintenance more difficult.

Be sure to take into consideration the grade or slope of the land when you are siting your pond. The pond must be level, so extensive grading and sculpturing of the land may be required to achieve this. Take precautions to be sure that the area does not funnel water into your pond. Run off will destroy water quality by adding organic materials and toxic chemicals, such as fertilizers and

I Fought the Law, and the Law Won

Wherever you site your pond, be sure that you conform with local zoning restrictions. Before you put one shovel into the earth, you should check with your local zoning board. Some towns or townships require permits before you add such an item to your property. Also, some require fencing, as they do for pools. So go to your local government seat, before they take you to one. Fines after the fact can be hefty, and some ponds have had to be filled in because they didn't adhere to local laws, especially in suburban neighborhoods.

pesticides to your pond. In some cases, heavily sloped land can be used to add a waterfall to the pond system.

There are many practical reasons to site your pond near your house. Your fish will get more attention if they are living close to where you are living. Logistically, if the pond is close to the home, it will be close to water and power sources as well. The closer the pond is to your house, the cheaper it will be to construct because it reduces the need to move water and electricity great distances. Having the pond close to your home may also deter common predators like raccoons and birds from consuming your fish.

Pond Size and Depth

The first question you have to answer is what kind of fish are you going to put in your pond? Goldfish or koi? The size of your pond will be directly related to the size of the fish. If you're thinking of a large pond, you probably want koi. If you're thinking of a small pond, then you probably want goldfish. Putting as large a fish as a koi in a small pond is like placing it in solitary confinement. The fish will go nuts.

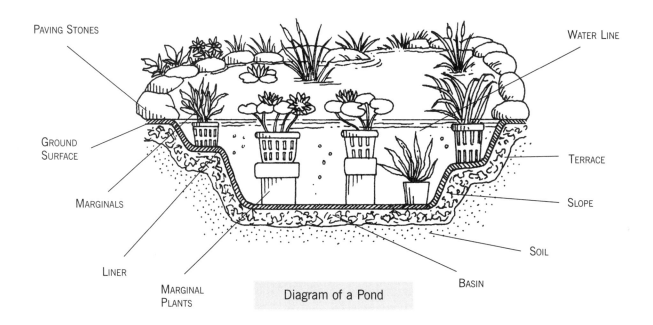

PAVING STONES

WATER LINE

GROUND SURFACE

TERRACE

MARGINALS

SLOPE

LINER

SOIL

MARGINAL PLANTS

BASIN

Diagram of a Pond

If you're going to choose koi, make sure you really think out the size of the pond you've envisioned. All too often, the first pond of the koi enthusiast is too small. That is why every effort should be made to build as large a pond as possible the first time. Pond expansions can be a difficult and expensive task. A small pond is more difficult to maintain, and you are restricted in the number of koi that can be kept. Small ponds are fine to maintain if you're going to fill them with goldfish. Koi are large and can foul a small area quite easily. Koi experts recommend that the minimum surface area for a koi pond be 150 square feet. That's about 15 feet by 10 feet. That's a big pond, and it will hold a good number of koi. If that sounds way too big for you, then you need to think about goldfish.

The number of fish that you will be able to maintain in your pond is directly related to the size of the pond and the surface area. Koi and goldfish require adequate space to swim and sufficient oxygen to live; both are dictated by the size of the pond. The oxygen content of water is related to the surface area of the pond and the temperature of the water. Warmer water has less oxygen than colder water. Since ponds are maintained outside and most do not have heaters, the amount of oxygen in the pond is dictated by the season and time of day. There are times when oxygen is limited in the pond. The more surface area a pond has, the more room for gas exchange at the surface, and the more oxygen entering the water and toxic gases leaving the water.

A general rule of thumb is 30 square inches of surface area per 1 inch of fish. Therefore, a 150-square-foot pond (21,600 square inches) can hold approximately thirty-six 20-inch koi. When making this calculation, always take into account the maximum size that your koi will attain and not the size that they are when you buy them.

Even though surface area is important, adequate depth is also a necessity. The depth of the pond required depends greatly on your local climate, but deep water is integral to maintaining healthy koi and goldfish. The depth of your pond should vary in a shelf-like fashion. Ponds with a uniform depth pose problems relative to temperature fluctuations and predation. Deeper ponds do not have as much temperature fluctuation as shallow ponds, which is often

Koi vs. Goldfish

Maybe you've been dreaming about koi for some time now. Koi can grow quite large, and they need lots of room to maneuver. They can foul small pools quite quickly and that makes maintenance difficult. It also makes for lethargic and unhappy fish. If you've got the room and the desire, by all means go for it. But if space is a concern, maybe you should reconsider.

Goldfish are just as colorful as koi, and only half the size. Still, goldfish can grow to be quite large. Large enough, maybe, for what you were envisioning. Read both sections if you are undecided.

more important than absolute water temperature. Deep ponds also provide better protection from predators such as herons, raccoons, and cats. Koi and goldfish are healthier if provided with vertical swimming activity as well as horizontal swimming area. Deeper ponds will not freeze in the winter, thereby allowing you to keep your fish outside throughout the year.

Some experts feel that a pond depth of 8 feet is ideal for fish, especially koi. However, since both fish are naturally bottom feeders, many feel that the enthusiast will rarely see the fish in a pond this deep. The shelf-style or terraced pond with gradually changing depth is a logical compromise to this dilemma. The shallow zone should not exceed 20 inches, sloping into water with a depth of five feet or more, depending on the severity of the winter. Shallow areas should slope at a steep angle into deeper pond zones. A deep central zone will accumulate debris which can easily be removed. The range of depths will serve multiple purposes. In the shallow zones, plants can be maintained and koi can be fed. In the deeper areas, the fish can seek refuge from predators and extreme heat, and they can hibernate below the ice during the winter months.

Pond Materials

Throughout the centuries koi and goldfish have been maintained in ponds. But over the years the materials used to build them have evolved. It seems now, more than ever, that new products are developed every day. For many years, the concrete pond was the only choice for pond keepers. These are expensive and unchangeable (except at great expense). However, recent technologies have produced new materials that are lighter, easier to install, and less likely to leak. These include the pre-molded and flexible liners.

Concrete

The concrete pond was the standard for many years. They can be custom built to fit any landscape, but the initial design and construction costs can be quite high.

While concrete is very strong and easily shaped, time may slowly take its toll on your pond. Climatic changes can eventually cause cracks to form, and your pond will develop leaks. Repairs will be costly, and it's very likely the problem will eventually return. If you are interested in building a concrete pond, you must make sure that the walls and bottom are thick and that the concrete used is not porous. The bottom should be up to 12 inches thick and the walls at least 4 inches thick. Any concrete pond that does not conform to a simple geometric shape should be constructed by a contractor who specializes in such work. In addition, you must be sure to condition the pond over a three- to five-day period so that the excessive amounts of lime associated with the concrete will be neutralized. This requires the addition of phosphoric acid and continuous pH monitoring.

Premolded or Rigid Liners

The premolded liner is considered by many to be the preferred starter pond for the novice because of their ease of installation. However, be mindful that most preformed ponds are relatively small. These are ideal for goldfish, but are questionable for koi. Think through the calculations. Once your koi is past two and a half years of age, your koi will be 12 inches long. Will it have enough room to turn around? And you certainly want more than one. In many cases these ponds are usually just too small for koi. Consult the supplier and your local pet retailer before making up your mind. Just remember, big fish need a big area to swim. The bigger the fish, the bigger the pool you need.

These ponds are available in a number of formal and informal shapes. Overall, this pond material has a long life expectancy. The current preference in preformed (or rigid) liners are those made of polyethylene. These black liners are lightweight, heavy duty, and can withstand wide seasonal fluctuations. They also come in a variety of sizes and shapes. Polyethylene preformed waterfalls are also available to complement the pond. One drawback to this pond material is that the edges can be difficult to camouflage; they're awkward to work with, and usually require some creative efforts to hide. As with any premolded pond, care must be taken to make

A Room of One's Own

Can you imagine living in one room the rest of your life? Neither can we. But your fish don't have a choice. They can't move on. They can't pick up and go. It would be mean spirited to confine large fish to a small area. Fish need to be able to swim, not sit there. Make sure you plan a pond big enough for the fish you are selecting.

sure that the hole you dig accommodates the form very snugly. It is a good idea to line the pit that you dig with 6 inches of sand. As you fill the pond and the form settles, there will be some play in the earth beneath it.

Flexible Liners

More and more water garden enthusiasts are building ponds using new flexible liners. These come in a variety of materials and have several advantages over preformed and concrete ponds. These liners can be adapted to any shape, and they come in a variety of sizes, colors, and thicknesses. Although they will tear on occasion, they can be repaired with a patch kit.

Beware, though: These ponds take a lot more work to set up by the owner than other forms. However, they do offer to the pond owner the ability to change the design of the pond more easily and more cheaply than any of the other methods.

PVC

Liners made of polyvinyl chloride (PVC) are inexpensive, but they are easily torn, and they do not hold up to colder climates. They just don't last very long. This is not the preferred material for a pond liner, and it is rarely used today for large outdoor ponds.

Rubber

New synthetic rubbers are the preferred materials for today's goldfish and especially koi ponds. The most common of these comes in rubber sheets constructed of a synthetic polymer called EPDM (ethylene, propylene, diene, monomer). This material is manufactured specifically for pond use and is, therefore, safe for your fish. Make sure the EPDM you buy says "fish friendly" on the packaging. Rubber liners are very flexible, mold easily to the form of your pond, and are not susceptible to UV light degradation. Most of these liners have a long term guarantee of 10 to 20 years and a projected life expectancy in excess of 40 years. If a tear should develop, patch kits are readily available. Another rubber is butyl rubber. It will last longer than EPDM, but is more expensive, more difficult to work with, and is not recommended for use with plants.

How Much Liner Should I Buy?

Here's a simple calculation to figure out how much liner you need. This calculation takes into account pond depth. Measure only after pond is dug.

1. Determine the length and width of your pond
2. Use the following formula:

   Liner length = pond length + 2' (depth) + 2' (overhang)
   Liner width = pond width + 2' (depth) + 2' (overhang)

3. Calculate the area by multiplying the new liner length by the new width length.

The extra two feet are added to account for an overhang of one foot around the perimeter of the pond. You will also need to add separate liners for your waterfalls and any other pond elements that contain water; these can be seamed to your main liner using adhesives available from your pond or pet supplier. Follow the manufacturer's instructions.

When installing liners, you must place a layer of sand on the bottom of the pond to help protect the liner from punctures by rock or stone. In extremely rocky areas, it is recommended that you use a strong fiber underlay for extra protection. Some pond keepers have reported good results with newspapers or old carpeting to accomplish this. Since these liners are a common component of your typical pond, some garden centers or distributors sell them with pumps and filters as a package.

Liner Size

Before you buy your liner material, make sure you have dug your hole and examined it many times. Most beginners make the mistake of purchasing a liner of a certain size and then digging a hole of that size and finding that the liner is too small for the pond hole. You must take into account the depth of the pond when calculating the size of the liner. You always need to think bigger when buying your liner. Remember this rule: You can always trim it, but you can't add to it.

Ornamentation and Decorations

As it is with aquariums, so it is with ponds. Either you want scene out of an Ansel Adams photo, or you want Phillippe Stark-esque post modernist experience. Or maybe you want something out of a John Waters film. Have at it, and enjoy.

There are a number of ways to make your pond and its surroundings very beautiful. Some elements, such as terraces and islands, have to do with the initial design of the pond. Others, like plants and ornaments, are simple additions to the pond.

Terraces and Islands

Terracing the pond from shallow to deep water in a shelf-like fashion is an excellent idea. In addition to providing a range of depths for your fish, this also provides areas for plants and other ornamentation. Terracing is done during the building phase when the pond is excavated. In other words, when you're digging, make sure you plan the terraces. Depending on which end you dig from, you're either going to have to dig deeper or shallower. It's all a matter of perspective.

ISLANDS IN THE STREAM

Some garden ponds are big enough to support an island in the middle. They are easy enough to construct and can sometimes be added later. There are many ways to add an island.

The Good Earth—The island can be part of the design from the very first, so that you leave the earth where it is as you are digging. However, that's not quite good enough. You'll probably want to put some wire mesh around it, depending on its size, with a layer of gravel underneath the net so that the structure remains over a period of time. Ask a local landscaper what he or she might recommend to shore this type of island up.

A Dock or Platform—What some inventive folks do is build a dock or platform that juts out over the water. I have seen some ponds where a narrow bridge or dock leads to a larger deck, maybe at mid pond. This lends shade to the fish as well as some place to hide from predators. The most important thing here is to use materials that won't affect your fish. Also, make sure to base the platform joints on broad pieces of thick slate that won't rip the lining. It's usually a good idea to put one or two pieces of lining underneath the slate, again, in an effort to avoid ripping.

Rock or Cement—Some folks use cement or a combination of cement and rock to create a small island in the middle of their pond. This of course is more expensive and time consuming, but it is also certainly more long lasting.

Lighting

Lighting is a good thing, but in moderation. Excessive lighting will disturb your fish and place terrible stress on them. Do you want a spotlight shining on you when you're trying to sleep? No. So don't use too much lighting on or in your pond. Low-voltage spotlights have dramatic effects and give you plenty of light to see your fish.

Lighting your pond can be a good thing. Some enthusiasts use lighting to showcase various features, like waterfalls or fountains. Exterior lights are easy to install and come in a variety of styles and sizes.

There is no real benefit to illuminating the interior of the pond. The fish will not enjoy it, and we strongly recommend against it. At best, it's not necessary, and at worst it is a safety hazard to your fish and to you. Never attempt to install internal lights yourself. Use a qualified electrician if you plan to install lights in or very close to the pond.

Waterfalls and Fountains

By installing waterfalls or fountains, you not only add very attractive features to your pond, you increase the health of your pond. Both additions move water and increase aeration, making the water quality better. Before building your pond, carefully design where you want a waterfall or fountain to be. It is best if these features are tied in with your filtration pump.

Aquatic Plants

A beautiful addition to any fish pond is the aquatic plant. Just as important, they help improve water quality and provide areas for fish to hide under and to spawn in. However, both koi and goldfish are notorious for consuming plants, eating shoots, and rooting around in soil containing plants. While considered by many to be incompatible, the fish and plants can be maintained together if care is taken to select and protect the proper plants. In addition, if your fish are well fed and their diets include greens, they may be less likely to feed on your pond plants.

Do not try to anchor plants in the bottom of the pond. The koi and goldfish will uproot them in about 10 minutes. The most pop-

Potted Pond Plant

ular method is potting them in containers specifically designed for pond use. This way, they can be readily moved for cleaning or overwintering. Potted plants can, however, present a few problems unless measures are taken to prevent koi and goldfish from rooting around in the soil. Some pond keepers employ plant protectors that screen the plants, keeping the fish away from the soil. Others place a heavy layer of small pea-sized gravel or lava rock on top of the soil to keep the fish from getting to the plant roots.

Another popular plan is to avoid plants that require soil by adding those that are grown hydroponically. Hydroponic plants float and can be grown in a plastic mesh basket with lava rock about the size of golf balls. In addition to protecting the plant, the lava rock provides substrate for beneficial nitrifying bacteria. Each plant basket can become a small biological filter that assists with water quality maintenance.

There is another section on plants in this book, but the plants featured in this section are geared especially for pond and water gardens. Aquatic plants can be divided into three general categories: floating plants, shallow plants, and submerged plants.

Floating Plants

Floating plants float in the water. That was tough to figure out, huh? They are administered to by either an anchored or a floating root system. These plants are relatively easy to care for and provide excellent filtration.

Floating plants that are recommended for koi and goldfish ponds include:

- **Water hyacinth** *(Eichornia crassipes):* This is a large flowering aquatic plant with intense lavender-blue flowers that stand in clusters well above its waxy green leaves. These are cold-sensitive plants. You must take these indoors for wintering in colder climates.
- **Fairy Moss** *(Azolla caroliniana):* An attractive floating fern. It is bright green in spring and summer and turns reddish during the fall. This plant is also sensitive to cold and must be moved inside during the winter or replaced in the spring.

- **Water lettuce** *(Pistia stratiotes)*: This rosette-shaped plant is medium green and has a somewhat compact mass of roots. It is a very hardy plant. You won't have to worry about its survival; you'll more often have to prune it.

- **Water lilies** *(Nymphaea spp.):* You were wondering when we were going to mention these. These are definitely the most popular aquatic plants in water gardens and fish ponds. They possess beautiful leaves and an abundance of flowers. There are two general types of water lilies: hardy and tropical. Both will do fine in your fish pond. Hardy varieties are the best choice. They are easy to grow and can overwinter in the pond itself. There are over 250 species of hardy water lilies in color choices of white, red, pink, yellow, cream, and peach.

Water Lilies and Pads

Tropical water lilies don't overwinter and should be treated as one would annuals. They also tend to be more expensive. These water lilies also come in a larger variety of colors: deep purple, lavender, magenta, deep red, burgundy, cream, white, peach, salmon, and green.

Water lilies can be planted in pots or placed in floating baskets. New plants should be anchored in pots and placed in shallow areas of the pond until they are established. They can then be moved into deeper areas as they grow.

- **Lotus** *(Nelumbo spp.):* This large-leafed plant resembles the water lily, but possesses a much larger flower. It is relatively easy to grow and requires little care and maintenance. They do not overwinter, so they need to be moved inside or replaced in spring.

Shallow Plants

These are sometimes called "bog plants." Shallow plants grow in shallow water with most of the plant exposed above the surface. They tend to produce vegetation that is lush and are nice additions

fantail

Photo by Mark Smith/Photo Researchers, Inc.

ryunkin

Photo by Dr. Paul A. Zahl/Photo Researchers, Inc.

Photo by Mark Smith/Photo Researchers, Inc.

oranda

veiltail

goldfish

Photo by Mark Smith/Photo Researchers, Inc.

Photo by Joseph T. Collins/Photo Researchers, Inc.

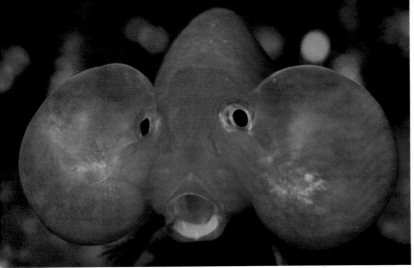

Photo by Tom Meyers/Photo Researchers, Inc.

bubble-eyed goldfish

Photo by Mark Smith/Photo Researchers, Inc.

marigold Chinese lionhead

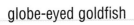

globe-eyed goldfish

Photo by Mark Smith/Photo Researchers, Inc.

red cap oranda

Photo by Mark Smith/Photo Researchers, Inc.

butterfly koi

Photo by Mark Smith/Photo Researchers, Inc.

blue metalic guppy

electric blue

kennyi

yellow rainbow

tropheus dubosi

Photo by Mark Smith/Photo Researchers, Inc.

black molly

betta

Photo by Mark Smith/Photo Researchers, Inc.

Photo by Mark Smith/Photo Researchers, Inc.

gold barb

Photo by Mark Smith/Photo Researchers, Inc.

cherry barb

Photo by Mark Smith/Photo Researchers, Inc.

neon tetra

discus

clown pleco

clown loach

angelfish

tiger oscar

red devil cichlid

Photo by Tom McHugh/Photo Researchers, Inc.

arowana

seahorse

Photo by Mark Smith/Photo Researchers, Inc.

Jack Dempsey

Photo by Mark Smith/Photo Researchers, Inc.

tricolor shark

Photo by E. R. Degginger/Photo Researchers, Inc.

Photo by Mark Smith/Photo Researchers, Inc.

orange-spotted goby

Photo by Mark Smith/Photo Researchers, Inc.

Photo by Pelcolatto/Photo Researchers, Inc.

gold-rimmed tang

Photo by Mark Smith/Photo Researchers, Inc.

threadfin butterfly fish

common anemone fish

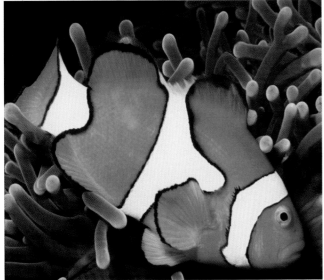

Photo by Nancy Sefton/Photo Researchers, Inc.

strawberry gramma

Photo by Mark Smith/Photo Researchers, Inc.

wreck fish

Photo by Mark Smith/Photo Researchers, Inc.

albino African frog

Photo by E. R. Degginger/Photo Researchers, Inc.

Photo by Mark Smith/Photo Researchers, Inc.

pajama cardinal fish

foxface

sharp-nosed puffer

Photo by Mark Smith/Photo Researchers, Inc.

Photo by Fred McConnaughey/Photo Researchers, Inc.

to the fish pond when scattered along the margins. They prefer to keep their roots wet but do not care for total immersion. Common shallow plants for the koi pond include:

- **Arrowhead plant** *(Sagittaria latifolia):* One of the many arrowhead species. It has spikes of white flowers accented by dark green arrow-shaped leaves.
- **Pickerel weed** *(Pontederia cordata):* This plant has heart-shaped leaves that penetrate the surface. It blossoms with blue flowers on short spikes.
- **Water iris** *(Iris spp.):* Here's a beautiful way to add color to your pond. The aquatic iris is a flowering plant that blooms in the spring. It comes in many colors. They are relatively tolerant of colder climates.

Submerged Plants

Submerged plants grow on the bottom of the pond and stay fully immersed below the water's surface. These plants play a role in combating algal growth by consuming excess nutrients, such as nitrate. Unfortunately, they are easily uprooted and eaten by koi and goldfish unless the measures outlined above are taken to protect the plants. Common varieties of these plants include:

- **Cabomba** *(Cabomba spp.):* This plant has fans of purple-backed green flowers with white flowers that bloom in the summer months. This hardy plant is tolerant of temperate climates.
- **Anacharis** *(Elodea canadensis):* This bright green, lush fern-like plant is the most common of the submerged plants. While this is a hardy plant, unfortunately, the fish love to feed on its lush vegetation.

So Many Plants, So Little Space

Yes, the plants are quite pretty, but don't forget about the fish! Make sure you're not overplanting your fish pond. For one thing, overplanting prevents you from seeing the fish. A good approach is

The Potato Chips of the Pond

Unfortunately, koi and goldfish will sometimes eat floating plants as soon as they are introduced into the pond. This problem can be remedied by using floating flora islands. These are made of fine mesh netting around a foam frame that you can anchor or allow to float free. The plants will provide shelter and shade to the koi, and any roots that grow through the netting can be consumed by the koi without harm to the plants.

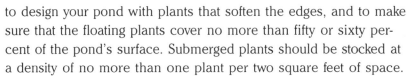

to design your pond with plants that soften the edges, and to make sure that the floating plants cover no more than fifty or sixty percent of the pond's surface. Submerged plants should be stocked at a density of no more than one plant per two square feet of space.

As there are for fish tanks, there are many other kinds of decorative objects you can add to your fish pond. Much depends on your personal tastes. Bridges, ceramics, and external vegetation will augment the natural beauty of your pond. Be creative and add features that aesthetically please you.

Water Quality and Filtration

The most important requirement of healthy fish is clean water. There are many aspects of water that the pond keeper must be concerned with. Since freshwater fish have adapted to a wide variety of habitats around the world, each species has its own water preferences. Koi and goldfish are considered to be very hardy species that are tolerant of differing water conditions. However, great care must be taken to avoid dramatic or rapid changes in your pond's water chemistry. Two very important parameters that characterize the quality of your pond water and need to be monitored are pH and hardness. This was covered in Section 1.

When conditioning a pond, it is important to monitor the levels of ammonia, nitrite, and nitrate to determine when the conditioning period is over. You should continue to test your pond water periodically to be sure that nitrogenous wastes are not accumulating to dangerous levels. Your dealer sells test kits that determine the levels of the compounds in your pond.

Filtration

There are three basic methods of filtration: mechanical, chemical, and biological. Again, these were covered in Section 1.

Biological filters use a substrate such as sand, gravel, or bioballs to support bacterial colonies essential for water purification. The key to successful filtration is surface area. The greater the surface area, the higher the population of nitrifying bacteria, and the better the filtration. The better the filtration, the greater the

Weight Is Good

If you're a plant in a pond, you need to be anchored to survive and flourish. Make sure you take the opportunity to weigh down the buckets that your plants are in. Not too much weight, you don't want to cut off the roots. But make sure they won't move when some big fish starts pushing up against them, as goldfish and koi are wont to do.

carrying capacity of the system and, hence, the more fish you can successfully keep in your pond. An operational biofilter does not need to be cleaned more often than once or twice a year. If you clean it, you actually kill the bacteria that are essential to the effectiveness of the filter. Biofilters do not work properly in temperatures lower than 55°F, so they are generally shut down during the winter months. Otherwise, they are left running continuously 24 hours per day.

Common interior filters are simple in design and are usually used in smaller ponds. Interior filters provide good mechanical filtration and some biological filtration, but their efficiency is very limited. They generally consist of a small box containing a pump to move the water through filter media, such as gravel or sand. The pump used by these smaller systems is submersible, which means that it is placed inside the pond, beneath the water's surface. Make sure that you choose a properly sized pump for your pond if you plan on using this type of filtration system. The pump should have a flow rate that is able to "turn over" the pond volume every three hours.

More advanced filter designs are used to maintain larger ponds. The most popular filter used by koi enthusiasts is the outside biological filter. If properly designed, the outside filter provides excellent mechanical, chemical, and biological filtration. The design of the outside filter is very similar to that used for most swimming pools. Water is drawn from the pond, pumped through filter media, and returned to the pond. Intake ports can include surface skimmers, bottom drains, and side-mounted drains. Water is purified by the filter and returned to the pond via outlet pipes, fountains, and waterfalls, which provide aeration as well. Outside filters are efficient, easy to build, and easy to maintain.

There are three kinds of biofilters: down-flow, up-flow, and lateral flow biofilters.

Down-Flow Systems

The down-flow system is also known as the gravity flow system. Water is drawn from above through heavier waste that accumulates on top of the filter media. This causes clogging of the media over

---

Today, The Role of Mother Nature Will Be Played By

Just like in any aquarium, or your living room for that matter, it's important to remember to vacuum your pond. Just like you would skim and vacuum your pool (if you do, or if you did, have one), you need to do the same to your pond. In nature, water currents do much of the work. However, in this pond it's you.

Fighting Back Against Algae

If you seem to have excessive algal growth, there are several measures that you can employ to reduce the presence of algae in the pond.

- Use a UV sterilizer.
- Keep the pond well planted; nitrates will be consumed by healthy aquatic plants instead of being available for algae.
- Make sure that all rocks, plants, decorations, and gravel going into the pond are free of algae.
- Remove excess nitrates which will fuel algal growth by carrying out partial water changes in a timely fashion.

time, leaving only a few channels where water can flow through the filter. Surface area is therefore diminished.

Up-Flow Systems

Some call this the reverse-flow system. This system works the same as the down-flow, but the water is directed up through the filter media. Other than that, the system works on the same principles.

Lateral-Flow Systems

In the lateral-flow system, the water flows laterally, and heavier wastes drop to the bottom of the filter where it can be drained off periodically. Channeling will not occur in the lateral flow system, and the filter will work more efficiently.

Filter Media

Media is the most important part of any filter. It is important because the media is the surface that houses the nitrifying bacteria. The most commonly used medium is gravel that is graded by size. That is, fine gravel is placed on top of a coarse layer of gravel in the filter. The smaller-sized gravel provides more surface area near the surface of the filter bed where most of the nitrifying activity takes place. This layering provides excellent filtration. The total filter bed should be about two to three feet deep from the finer gravel on top to the larger rocks on the bottom.

It is strongly recommended that you use the guidelines above and purchase a manufactured filter system with the advice of your dealer. Don't be tempted to build your own biofilter, though. It's the domain of experts. If you want to be a do-it-yourselfer with this pond, get a shovel and dig. Don't play with the safety of the fish.

Skimmers

Skimmers pull water from the surface of the pond and deliver it to a filtration system. As they do this, they remove film, floating algae, and other materials that often collect on the pond's surface. A collecting basket connected to the pond skimmer allows for floating debris to be readily removed before it reaches and overburdens the filter.

Ultraviolet Sterilizers

Ultraviolet sterilizers are routinely used by large aquariums to kill algae, parasites, and bacteria. They will cure a green water problem, but they may be expensive. They are definitely optional for the new pond keeper. The UV sterilizer can be useful if the correct kind is employed. If you choose to use a UV sterilizer, consult with your dealer to select the proper one for your pond. Remember that the efficiency of the sterilizer will diminish over time and even though the light is lit, it may not be emitting enough to be effective. UV sterilizers should be placed after your biofilter and should be cleaned regularly.

Aeration

Aeration is always important. Fish need to have a lot of oxygen available for respiration. This is especially true for ponds that are maintained at their fullest carrying capacity of fish. Although most filters provide water circulation and aeration to the pond, it is a very good idea to direct your water flow to aerating features, such as waterfalls and fountains in your pond. Supplemental pumps can be added to larger ponds to circulate water and provide aeration. It is important to circulate all the water in the pond and to not allow stagnant areas to develop. Ask your pet store owner or dealer to help you select the one that's right for you.

Algae

What exactly is algae and do all algae cause problems for your pond? As we said earlier, algae are actually plants that belong to the class known as Thallophyta with the fungi. Most species of algae occur in the waters and, like fish, have adapted to all kinds of water conditions. In your pond, they can be found on the surface, suspended in the water, or on the surfaces of rocks, gravel, and pond decorations. The four types of algae are: green algae, diatoms, whip algae, and blue-green algae.

In low levels, algae can be somewhat beneficial to the pond, providing the same benefits as plants. They supply oxygen during the day as a by-product of photosynthesis, and they consume nitrogenous compounds like nitrate which normally build up in the pond. Koi and goldfish both consume algae, so they provide an additional food source for your pets. Unfortunately, when conditions are right, the algal population in your pond can explode, creating problems. Excessive algal growth will overrun a pond unless water quality is properly maintained. Rapid multiplication of algae depletes trace elements that are required by other plants. In warm conditions, algae will rapidly deplete the oxygen in your pond at night.

High nitrate levels and sunlight will promote algal growth. Avoiding these conditions and using a UV sterilizer will minimize algae as a pond nuisance. Don't become obsessed with algae. Expect to live with algae in your pond.

Building Your Pond

You've spent a long time taking into account a great many things regarding your pond. Now, you are ready to begin building. If you're a do-it-yourselfer, this could be a lot of fun. However, make sure to seek the assistance of a certified electrician and plumber for the wiring and piping of the pond. It's better to spend a little more money up front and have a first class job to rely on.

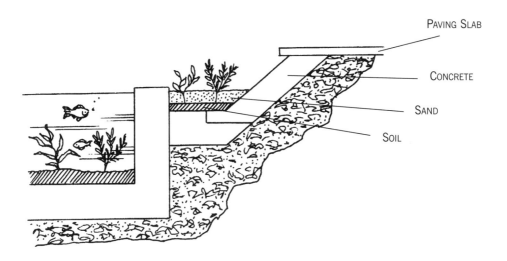

PAVING SLAB
CONCRETE
SAND
SOIL

Cross-section of a Pond

Usually, your filter system will be piped and installed along with the pond. In this section on pond construction, it is assumed that you have chosen an efficient and properly sized filtration system for your pond and are prepared to install it.

Excavation

This is otherwise known as digging. First, you want to lay out your pond. To do this, carefully lay out the perimeter of the pond with a rope or garden hose. Using brightly colored spray paint, make a line outside the hose or rope layout. Now you have a guide to help you the rest of the way. Using a spade or shovel begin digging, following the line. Depending on your pond design, you want to remember to add your plant shelves. If you intend to conceal your liner under a coping shelf, carve this shelf first. In general, dig a coping shelf about 12 inches deep by 12 inches wide. You may need to alter this, depending on the size of your coping material. Terrace the pond as you dig deeper, adding shelves for plants. In general, shelves are about 12 to 20 inches deep and 12 to 20 inches wide. Work your way toward the center excavating the interior of the pond. If you plan on installing a waterfall, move some of the soil to that area and build the grade.

When the pond is excavated, be sure to check for rocks that may damage your liner. If you notice large tree roots, this could pose a future problem. Tree root systems may ultimately damage a pond. If you encounter roots, you should consider moving your pond.

After excavation has been completed and the plumbing (filter, overflow pipe, and drain) have been hooked into the pond, you should prepare the bottom of the pond by laying down the layer of sand. This will protect the liner from punctures. After filling holes, a 1- to 2-inch layer on the shelves and bottom should be sufficient. Smooth and firm down the sand layer.

Once the underlay is in place, the liner can be added. Unfold or unroll the liner and refold it in a fashion that makes it easy to install from the center of the pond. You always want to lay the pond out from the center. Lay out the liner flat against the walls of the pond making sure that it is flush with the bottom and sides. You may need to use rocks or bricks to hold the liner down. It is best to have somebody assist you in placing the liner.

If You're Diggin' on Diggin'

If you are digging the pond yourself, remember the following tip: Always dig a little deeper than the desired depth because you are going to add a layer of sand on the bottom.

Waterfalls

Now is the time to add your waterfall. Working with the soil mound that has resulted from your digging, shape the waterfall so that a small pool at the top leads to cascading steps down to the pond. Be sure that the waterfall is deep enough so that water does not spill over the edges. Once shaped, the waterfall can be lined and seamed to the pond liner. Seaming kits come with detailed instructions and techniques in seaming will vary from kit to kit. Stones can now be added to the falls at each tier to direct water and to conceal the liner. Be sure to properly plumb the waterfall during the construction phase so that piping will be concealed as well.

Filling the Pond

Now you can finally fill the pond! A good idea is to use a garden hose and slowly fill the pond up to the level of the coping shelf. Now, and not before, is the time to add the coping shelf by adding rocks, bricks, slate, or other materials. These stones and materials hide the liner and give the pond a more natural, finished appearance. The coping stones should overhang the coping shelf by an inch or two. Add a layer of capstones around the periphery of the pond to conceal the edges of the liner.

When you trim the lining, make sure not to cut too much off. Settling and weather may put more stress on your lining. It's always better to have a little too much rather than too little. Trim excess liner, but be sure to leave at least eight inches of overhang. If necessary, you can trim the excess after the pond and ground have settled.

Now, hook up all the plumbing. At this point you may have a filtration system, pumps, skimmer, UV sterilizer, bottom drain, and overflow lines. Next, make sure the electrical systems are in place and tested—not just for use but for safety as well.

Now your pond is ready to be turned on! Congratulations!

Startup

At this point, you're probably eager to add your fish. However, just because the filter is pumping away and the waterfall works and everything is running, it doesn't mean it's time to add your fish.

Your pond may look ready, but it isn't. Take the time to make sure that all systems are running smoothly. Check for obvious leaks or overflow. Scrutinize the pond for a couple of days to be sure that all is well.

Before you can add large numbers of fish, it is important for the pond to be conditioned. Like new aquariums, ponds need to go through a conditioning or maturation period during which the filtration system becomes established. This period is generally four to six weeks long. During this time, it is fine to add aquatic plants. You can even add a few koi or goldfish to the pond. You will be able to increase your capacity once good water quality is established. Frequent water testing will determine when your pond water is conditioned and your filter system is well established.

Introducing Your Fish

Before introducing fish directly to your new pond, many experts feel that it is important to quarantine the fish for a period of two to three weeks. Quarantine prevents the inadvertent transmission of infectious diseases. Although your new fish may appear healthy, they could be carrying a number of diseases. This is especially true for the first fish that you add to your new pond. If the first fish introduced to the new pond are diseased, treatment of the pond could be very detrimental to the conditioning process.

New fish can be quarantined in a special quarantine tank that is set up for this purpose. Depending on the size of the koi or goldfish, these tanks can vary from 20 gallons to tanks substantially larger. The tank must be well equipped with a biological filter and a heater that maintains a constant temperature. Water quality should be monitored in the quarantine tank to insure that the fish are being held in optimum conditions.

You'll need to follow the same directions as in the earlier section on introducing your fish to the aquarium. Examine your fish during the quarantine period for signs of disease. Feed them lightly during this time and don't be alarmed if the fish do not feed immediately. They are recovering from the stress of shipment, and it may be several days before they begin eating properly.

Plumbing Tip

Make sure to consider both an overflow pipe and a drain when you have a plumber come over to help you attach the filter. Larger ponds should have an overflow pipe and a bottom drain to prevent problem associated with overflow. This plumbing in addition to external filter plumbing should be done at the same time.

After the quarantine period, your fish can be transferred to the pond. Before doing so, make sure that the pH, water hardness, and temperature of the pond and the tank are correct. Feed your fish sparingly in the fist few days until they settle down in their new home.

When stocking your pond for the first time, add your fish gradually, starting with just a few, until the pond is well established. Continue to monitor water quality, making sure that your filter is working properly.

Pond Care and Maintenance

Once your pond is well established and your fish are vibrant and active, it is time to think about continuous care and maintenance of your small pond ecosystem to insure the continued health of your pets. A well-established pond does not need a lot of maintenance, but you must keep it clean and free of waste and debris.

It is very important to test and monitor the quality of your pond water and, therefore, the efficiency of your filter. At least once a week, test your pH, hardness, ammonia, nitrite, and nitrate levels. If there are any sudden changes in the pond chemistry, something is wrong and measures need to be taken before your fish suffer.

Check your biofilter regularly and gently rinse heavy debris and waste materials from it. Filter pads can be easily hosed off and returned to the filter within a few minutes. The pump should be checked for clogging. These procedures take just a few minutes but will guarantee the health of your system.

Water will continuously evaporate from the pond, so you should add water with your garden hose on a periodic basis. Waterfalls, fountains, and high temperatures will cause higher rates of evaporation. You cannot control this, so be sure to watch the pond's water level.

Cleaning the Pond

Just like an aquarium, the most important aspect of pond maintenance is keeping it clean of debris and waste. When left in the pond, waste will foul the water. Make sure to remove leaves that enter the pond. And of course, there's always vacuuming to do. Use a pond vacuum to remove any fine silt or dirt that collects on the bottom of the pond. A pond vacuum can be purchased at your pond dealer. They are usually driven by a garden hose and can be very effective at sucking up debris. If you have a bottom drain, this can be opened periodically to remove dirt.

Seasonal Care

Your pond and fish will be exposed to changing seasonal conditions, depending on where you live. For those living in southern climates where the weather is relatively consistent, routine maintenance will not change appreciably throughout the year. However, for those living in areas of dramatic seasonal climatic change, routine maintenance tasks will change with the seasons.

The following section will specifically address pond care and maintenance in areas that experience seasonal changes in temperature only.

Winter

Certainly for those who live in more severe climates, winter poses numerous challenges. The first thing to know is that koi and goldfish (the ones herein recommended) are extremely tolerant of cold temperatures and will survive through the winter even in areas where ice forms, provided that the pond is deep enough to ensure it will not freeze through. As water temperatures decline in the fall and winter, the activity levels of these fish will diminish as well. You will not need to feed your fish during this time. It's practically the only time these guys ever pass up a meal.

As the fish become less active, they generate less waste, and the filtration system will be taxed less. Nonetheless, even in the dead of winter, fish will generate some nitrogenous wastes. Therefore, you must continue to remove these wastes, or at least allow them to escape from the surface. What does this mean? It means you can't let the pond freeze over.

If ice forms on your pond, you need to keep an opening in the ice. This will allow for oxygen exchange. It will also allow the

For Everything There Is a Season

Each season requires something different of the pond keeper. In the spring and summer there are algae and predators, in the fall there are leaves and other detritus, and of course in the winter there are snow and ice. The pond keeper is always working.

removal of toxic nitrogenous compounds. Beyond this, you can do a lot of other things to prevent your pond from completely icing over. If your biofilter can be kept from freezing, keep it running. If you have a waterfall, shut it down during the coldest months. The waterfall will cause too much circulation, mixing the deeper warmer water with colder surface water, and making the pond too cold. A small amount of water movement provided by your biofilter will keep the pond's surface from freezing over. Your biofilter may not be properly plumbed to keep it running, so you might need to shut it down.

If your filter has to be shut down, you can add a very small pump to the pond to bubble the water and keep it from freezing. Place the pump on one of the shallow shelves so that it does not mix the water layers. Some dealers recommend that a small pool heater or a water tank de-icer be placed in the pond, but this can be expensive and a bit excessive. Regardless of what you use to keep the pond from freezing, it is important to cover the pond with a pond cover or plastic sheeting. This will not only help insulate the pond, but will keep organic debris like leaves from degrading the water quality of the pond. This is especially important if you must shut down your biofilter. Be sure to leave some part of the water exposed. Also, make sure that the plastic sheeting is tightly held down, and won't eventually fall into the pond.

If your filtration system cannot withstand the extreme cold and must be turned off, be sure to clean it thoroughly before storing it for the winter. Other measures that should be taken during the winter include the removal and storage of your UV sterilizer if you have one. Also, turn off, clean, and store your fountain, and turn off your waterfall. Lower the level in your pond by a few inches to allow for the natural addition of winter snow and rain. Be sure to remove any tropical plants for inside storage and clean the pond thoroughly, removing all waste and debris, using the methods described above.

In most climates, these measures will insure that your fish survive the winter. However, in areas of extreme cold (Idaho, Maine, upstate New York, Michigan, Minnesota, and the Dakotas), fish should be moved inside for the winter. This will require setting up a temporary aquarium in your home.

GOLDFISH FOR YOUR POND

There are numerous goldfish that can be put in a pond. Here is a listing of the more hardy of the pond breeds. Any metallic or calico colorations will be fine.

- Common goldfish
- Comet goldfish
- Black moor
- Fantail goldfish
- Pearlscale
- Shubunkins
- Wakins

Depending on where you live, the bubble-eye and the black bubble-eye are also considered to be hardy enough for pond life. The weather must be on the warmer side, and there should be no sharp edges anywhere in the pond.

As with any goldfish, you should keep only like fish together. Read the variety section to make sure of the varieties you plan to foster together. And take size into account, as well. Ponds support larger fish. But a 12 inch goldfish will not tolerate a 2" inch goldfish for very long—especially if he's not fed enough.

Spring

Nature uses rain to do its spring cleaning. And your pond will definitely need it, too. Spring is a great time to conduct an annual, thorough cleaning of your own. You should examine the condition of your pond, the filter, and other factors. You can thoroughly clean your pond without causing great stress to your fish by removing them from your pond and putting them in a holding tank, such as a child's small plastic swimming pool. You may even use your quarantine tank if it is large enough. Do not use a small or mid-sized container such as a garbage can because these generally do not provide enough room for large fish like koi. Use your pond water to fill the tank and aerate it if you have a small pump. Be sure to cover it so that your fish do not jump out. Keep the holding tank out of direct sunlight so that the temperature remains stable. Now lower your pond level so that it's easier to catch your fish. Using a large, soft, shallow net, gently remove your fish one at a time and place them in the holding tank.

Yes, you must get in the pond to accomplish this. If you're going to clean, you've got to be willing to get dirty. While they're in the net, carefully, but quickly, examine each fish for signs of disease. When spring comes, fish are at their weakest and are susceptible to disease. It is an excellent opportunity to check them.

Now it is time to clean your pond. Empty the pond. Scrub the pond walls and bottom with clean, fresh water, but do not use any kind of soap or cleaning solution. Pump out all this water before filling the pond again and thoroughly rinse your biofilter. Make sure there are no tears in the liner or cracks in the concrete. Once you've finished cleaning and inspecting, you can fill your pond again.

Basically, it's like starting your pond all over again. Once the pond is filled, start up your filtration system. At this time you can also start your UV sterilizer, waterfall, and fountain, and add your plants. Test the water chemistry and make sure that it is ready for the re-introduction of your fish. If your biofilter was not shut down for the winter, it will not require too much time to get it fully functional. If you did remove it for the winter, you should seed it with a bacterial start-up product to bring it up to speed as quickly as possible.

Re-introduce your fish to the pond slowly and methodically as if you were putting them in the pond for the first time. You may now start feeding your fish again after a dormant winter period. Be sure to start this by feeding your fish a little at a time.

Summer

It's summer time, and the living is easy. The seasonal temperatures are highest at this time of year, so you'll be enjoying your pond on a regular basis. High water temperatures and bright sunlight are the engine of algal growth, though, so you'll have to take steps to control algae. Make sure that all systems are running smoothly and properly. The filter bed of the biofilter should be routinely raked once a month to minimize clogging. To do this, simply draw a rake over the surface of the filter bed down about an inch to break up the clumps of algae. This should be done throughout the year when the filter is running. Be sure that your UV sterilizer is running properly if you have installed one. Regularly clean out the surface skimmer and vacuum debris from the pond before it accumulates. Clean and inspect the pumps weekly, as well. If excessive algal growth occurs, remove it with a brush, but don't overreact to the presence of some algae in your pond.

Especially during this time of year, you should conduct a partial water change on a monthly basis. This will help keep the water from deteriorating in the warm summer months. During the three hottest summer months, at least 25 percent of the pond water should be changed monthly.

Fall

As temperatures drop and the weather begins to cool during the autumn months, your fish will slowly become less active. You should continue to monitor and test your water regularly and remove debris from the pond. Because fall is a time when many trees lose their leaves, your pond will be continuously burdened with organic matter. Be sure to skim the leaves from the surface before they drop to the bottom and begin to deteriorate. This is important, because this kind of debris can foul your water in an instant.

You'll need to make fewer water changes as the winter approaches. Keep an eye on your water chemistry and water temperature. Make sure to reduce the amount of food that you are feeding your fish as the temperatures drop in late fall. It's important at this time of year to remove your plants early. Better safe than sorry. Again, dying plants can ruin your water quality very quickly, and it takes a long time to recover.

Predator and Pest Control

You're not the only one interested in the fish swimming in your pond. Animals, such as birds, raccoons, cats, and muskrats, will be attracted to the prospect of finding a free meal in your fish pond. Unfortunately, there is little you can do to keep these creatures from getting to your pond. By definition, your ornamental pond should be an aesthetically pleasing habitat for you and your fish. Hence, the erection of any kind of fencing to deter these pests will diminish the tranquillity and beauty of your pond. Raccoons and muskrats can be humanely trapped and relocated away from your pond, but be sure to check with your local wildlife agency to determine how. Cats are curious natural hunters that will be attracted to the pond. While they will try to catch the fish, they rarely succeed. On the other hand, predatory birds such as herons, kingfishers, and osprey, are very effective fish hunters. There are few solutions to this problem other than simply scaring the bird away when it approaches. A heron net or monofilament meshing covering your pond may deter a regular visitor, but this will certainly detract from the beauty of your pond. The net can be used when you are away from your home and nobody is present to frighten away the birds.

If your pond is properly designed, these predators will have a hard time catching your fish. Deep water areas provide protection, and shelves that are crowded with plants make it difficult for predators to access the fish. Steeply angled pond sides are also effective in keeping pests out of your pond.

CHAPTER FIVE

Freshwater Tropical Fish

Common Freshwater Fish Groups

What's the difference between tropical fish and cold freshwater fish? Water temperature. Most of the fish found in this section come from warmer climates, but still live in fresh water. The tropical fishes are those you are most likely to have in your new aquarium. The diversity of these fish is daunting. Although most are now bred in captivity for the aquarium trade, these fish are found throughout the world.

Fish, as with other living things, are classified into species. Any particular species has a common name, which can differ depending on the region or the language. However, all species of living creatures have a scientific name that is used to identify that species anywhere in the world. In general, most authors prefer to combine freshwater aquarium fish families into two major groups based on their reproductive biology: live-bearers and egg-layers.

This classification is based purely on the method employed by these fishes to reproduce. In the following section, we're going to outline the major families of each group. These are grouped by families that have similar characteristics. By no means is this a complete list of tropical freshwater fish families; only those that you are most likely to find in local pet stores or in tropical fish catalogs.

Live-Bearers

These are the common aquarium fishes known as guppies, mollies, platys, and swordtails, as well as the various breeds and strains of each. The live-bearers include four major families, Anablepidae, Goodeidae, Hemirhamphidae, Poeciliidae, that are kept in captivity. These are especially hardy fish that readily breed in captivity. The males of these families are easily recognizable by their possession of a gonopodium. This modified pelvic fin is used by the male during mating with the female.

There's One Born Every Minute

Some of the most popular catfish are sucker catfish. These are fish that have incredible mouths that they use to attach themselves onto rocks, other decorations, plants, filters, etc. They love to eat algae. They do this to extract foods and minerals. They are the ultimate bottom feeders. They are especially fond of glass, where they can get a clean hold, and you can see their mouths at work.

Plecostomus is the catchall name for these fish. They tend to move around at night, rather than the day. They all tend to be brown though some have wonderful highlights, some come brightly spotted, and others have colorful fins. They are a great addition to any tank.

Egg-Layers

Barbs and Rasboras

Barbs and rasboras belong to the family Cyprinidae and Cobitidae, which contain over 1300 species of fish. It also includes the loaches, which are very popular aquarium fishes. Other fish include the tiger barb from Indonesia, the zebra danio from India, and the clown loach from India. The red-tailed shark, which is not a shark but actually a rasbora, is also a member of this family. It originates in Thailand.

Catfishes

There are 15 families and 2000 species of catfishes that contribute to the aquarium trade. The so-called armored catfishes include the popular plecostomus fishes and other algae eaters found in home aquariums. This group also includes the 140 species of Corydoras catfishes with their large heads and short bodies. These South American catfishes are notorious for their propensity to feed just below the surface of the gravel, thereby cleaning the tank bottom. Other families include the banjo catfishes, the naked catfishes, the glass catfishes, and the pim catfishes. Most of these catfishes are peaceful and easily adapt to a community tank.

Characins

Characins are most commonly known as tetras. This group contains 13 families of fish. There are over 1300 species of tetra. They originate mostly from South America, but some come from Africa. Common characteristics of this group include the possession of a toothed jaw and a second dorsal fin. In many species, males can be distinguished from females by the possession of hooklike spines on the anal fin or projecting from the base of the tail. These fish are generally school-forming in their natural habitat. Two of the most popular characins with very different dispositions are the neon tetra and the red-bellied piranha. A small school of the former is an attractive addition to the aquarium, but the latter belongs in a single species tank. Most members of this group are peaceful and make excellent additions to the community aquarium.

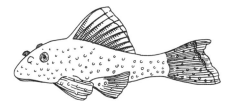

GOLD NUGGET PLECO

RED-TAIL CATFISH

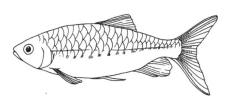

RED-EYE TETRA

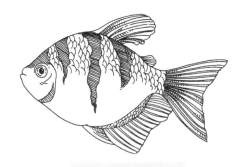

BLACK TETRA

JAGUAR CHICLID

Cichlids

This is certainly one of the most prolific and wide ranging groups. The cichlid family has fish originating from Central and South America, parts of the Caribbean, southern India, and across Africa. This species is made up of more than 900 fish. Cichlids inhabit a wide range of habitats throughout these areas, including saltwater and high temperature water (104°F). Most cichlids are small to medium-sized, with a single dorsal fin that is usually composed of hard and soft rays. Some species, like the freshwater angelfishes, are compressed laterally and have long ornate fins. Temperament in this group ranges from the pugnacious and intolerant to very peaceful. Care should be taken when selecting cichlids for the community aquarium. Common cichlids include the Jack Dempsey, oscar, angelfish, and discus. Cichlids can be extremely territorial and some fish mate for life.

Killifishes

Killifishes are an odd group, usually confined to very experienced aquarists. These fish belong to primarily two families, the Aplocheilidae and the Cyprinodontidae. They are very diverse fishes with more than 450 species spanning almost all the continents with the exceptions of Australia and Antarctica. Killifishes have permeated salt, brackish, and freshwater habitats throughout their range. Distinctive rounded scales and a lateral line system only on the area around the head are features that are characteristic of this group. Some of the more common members of this group include the lyretails, rivulus, and lampeyes.

Labyrinth Fishes

The most popular of the labyrinth fishes belongs to the family Belontiidae, which includes the gouramis, paradise fish, and bettas. The paradise fish is extremely hardy, but becomes very territorial in an aquarium as an adult. The betta is better known as the Siamese fighting fish, so-named because the males fight and tear their finnage to shreds. Although sometimes displayed in very small fish bowls, these fish should not be kept in less than a liter of water;

they are very sensitive to temperature changes. The gouramis are very popular additions to the community tank, they are peaceful fish with ornate fins, and that prefer heavy vegetation. The only member of the family Helostomatiidae maintained in captivity is the popular kissing fish. Found in Thailand, these fish are actually displaying aggression when "kissing" another member of the species.

These are some of the most popular and recognizable of fishes. This group of four families is so-named for the special organ inside their head called the labyrinth. This organ allows the fish to breathe in air at the surface. Air inhaled through the mouth is passed through the labyrinth, and from there the oxygen is extracted and passed into the system. This incredible system enables these fish to thrive and survive in oxygen-depleted waters. Many of these fish come from Thailand, Indonesia, Cambodia, and Malaysia.

Rainbow Fishes

Mostly originating from New Guinea and eastern Australia, this group is made up of three families. Members of the rainbow fish are peaceful, active, schooling fish with oval, laterally compressed bodies. A common member of this group is the splendid rainbow.

Knife Fishes

These fish are so-named for their laterally compressed blade-shaped tapered body form. Most knife fishes are nocturnal and peaceful, but they should be kept with fish of similar size. The unique group of knife fishes is comprised of four families. The speckled knife fish (Apteronotidae), the banded knife fish (Gymnotidae), and the American knife fishes (Rhamphichthyidae) are found in Central and South America. The fourth family, Notopteridae, comes from the freshwaters of Africa and Asia. Some of the Notopterid knife fish, however, are aggressive and are best kept alone.

Mormyrids

The mormyrids are also called elephant-nose fishes. This species of the family Mormyridae have a mouth that is extended

Snails

Snails are both good and bad. They are excellent at helping to keep your tank clean. They move along slowly. They are always attached to something. They are excellent at battling algae. However, they multiply rapidly and can take over a tank, so one or two is all you need. Also, they have been known to carry disease from one tank to another. So make sure you get them from a healthy tank.

like a elephant's trunk. Found in Africa, these fish use this modified mandible as a sensory organ. They also possess an organ near their tail that generates weak electric signals. When an elephant-nose becomes nervous, its electric pulse rate increases. The continuous pulsing of the electric organ can disturb other aquarium fish as well as other elephant-nose fish.

Miscellaneous

There are at least 40 families of fishes kept in aquariums that have not been covered above. They are so diverse in form and behavior that discussion of each would require too much space.

The Best Aquarium Fish for Beginners

Why is an aquarium sometimes referred to as a community tank? The community tank differs from a species tank in that it contains different species of compatible fish. While these are all fish that get along, they are not found in nature together. The species tank on the other hand contains only a single species of fish. The beginner should establish a community tank to start with because these fish are versatile enough to thrive in anything but the very hardest or softest waters. The species tank concept is best for those who want to maintain fish that require special tank conditions or are extremely aggressive.

There are a wide variety of fish that are well suited for the community aquarium. The important thing is to balance the types of fish in your tank. You will recall that species of fish have adapted to varying lifestyles and different habitats. Therefore, there are fish that live in the top-water, the mid-water, and on the bottom. In the community tank, you want to recreate this kind of environment by having fish spread throughout the tank.

In addition, many species of fish school by nature. This can be a very attractive addition to the community tank. These schooling fish should never be kept solitary but rather in a minimum size group of at least five or six individuals.

Some fish tend to be aggressive. These should be avoided by the beginner because a single antagonistic fish in a community tank can wreak havoc on the other species.

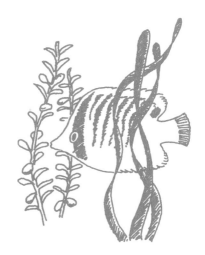

Another aspect of choosing fish that the novice sometimes overlooks is the maximum size of a particular species. A fish will grow continuously throughout its life. Some species grow faster than others. You don't want to put a fish in your tank that will attain a length of 12 inches in less than a year. This will not only disrupt your aquarium capacity, but the larger fish will undoubtedly dominate the tank. Some species are very compatible with other species when they are juveniles, but become solitary and aggressive as adults. These fish do not belong in the peaceful community tank.

Think Before You Buy

When your tank is fully established, the water chemistry is balanced, and you are ready to stock your aquarium, you should have a plan in mind. You don't just go shopping, as many people have done, and have no idea what you are talking about. While it's important to have an informed salesperson, it's also important to have an informed buyer. Otherwise, buyer beware. You don't want to end up choosing fish that are incompatible. Instead, pre-choose the kind of fish you want to start with. Read carefully. Look through fish encyclopedias that have a wider range of fish, if you are not struck by any of these. In other words, give it some thought and come up with a list of fish you'd like to begin with. Remember to choose a variety of species that will live throughout the water column from the top to the bottom.

Be selective when you get to the pet store. Buy fish only from healthy-looking aquariums with clear water, clean panes, and no dead fish in the tank. Make sure that the fish you want are healthy looking. If the fish has any cuts, scrapes, or fin problems, don't buy it. Watch for possible symptoms of disease, such as white granular spots, cottony white patches, frayed fins, or dull skin. Watch the behavior of the fish. Healthy fish swim in a lively manner and are not shy.

It is important to introduce your fish to the aquarium in batches, buying fish in lots every 10 to 14 days. This is especially important for the newly established aquarium. This allows fish to acclimate to each other and prevents aggressive behavior towards a single fish when it is introduced.

Fish, Big and Small

Freshwater fish range from fish as small as the neon tetra to the sturgeon huso huso, which grows up to 14 feet long and weigh as much as a ton!

The smallest fish is a goby that is found in the Philippine Islands.

The largest of all fish is the whale shark, which is a saltwater fish and may grow as long as 70 feet! (Remember, a whale is a mammal, so they don't count.)

The following is a list of species that are particularly easy to take care of. They are well suited for the beginner's community tank where pH ranges from 6.5 to 7.5 and temperature is maintained between 75°F and 79°F. I have arranged these fish according to the part of your tank that they are most likely to inhabit: top-water, mid-water, and bottom. Both the common and scientific names are listed. Some examples of each are also listed.

Top-Water Fishes

Just because it's called a top-water fish doesn't mean it's not going to swim around the tank. The top-water fishes are not restricted to the upper levels of the tank, but are more likely to be seen there. In particular, feeding and spawning occurs at or near the surface of your aquarium.

Guppy *Poecilia reticulata*
Origin: Central America to Brazil
Size: Males 1.5 inches, females 2.5 inches
Food: Omnivorous
Temperature: 64–81°F

This guppy is one of the most popular single species in the world. It is a definite favorite among beginners because it is a very hardy fish. They tend to spawn easily and may give birth to live young every month. The males are very colorful with ornate finnage and a gonopodium; females are dull in coloration. Selective breeding has resulted in the production of over 100 varieties. These fish are vigorous swimmers, preferring small groups of four to six members. Provide plenty of cover and floating plants and you may be able to successfully raise the fry (offspring).

Green Swordtail *Xiphophorus helleri*
Origin: Central America
Size: Males 4 inches, females 4.5 inches
Food: Omnivorous
Temperature: 68–79°F

The green swordtail is another popular community fish because it breeds readily in captivity. The males possess a long sword-like extension on the lower part of their tail, which has given the species its common name. This trait is not so obvious when they are young, but develops as the fish matures. The males can be temperamental and will harass the females, chasing them relentlessly. It is best to have many females and one male. Males tend to fight as they compete for breeding rights. These fish breed every 28 days at 74°F. Like the guppy, dense vegetation will provide cover for developing fry. Another benefit of this species is its tendency to consume algae.

Black Molly *Poecilia sphenops*
Origin: Mexico to Colombia
Size: 2.5 inches
Food: Omnivorous
Temperature: 64–82°F

The black molly is also known as the Mexican molly. The many varieties prefer temperatures on the upper end of the range indicated above. Other varieties include the green, marbled, albino, and lyretail mollies. This species is another live-bearer that is gentle, and it's basically a vegetable eater. Like the swordtail, the molly will consume aquarium algae, keeping it in check. This species is lively and prefers small groups of four to six members. Although not as hardy as other live-bearers, the molly will prosper if aquarium conditions are kept constant.

Beginner Fish

Best community fishes for beginners:

- Guppies
- Mollies
- Swordtails
- Platys
- Bettas
- Barbs
- Neons
- Angelfishes
- Gouramis
- Catfish

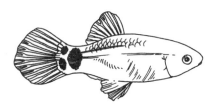

MICKEY MOUSE PLATY

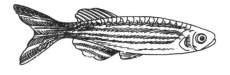

ZEBRA DANIO

Platy *Xiphophorus maculatus*
Origin: Mexico and Guatemala to Honduras
Size: Males 4 inches, females 4.5 inches
Food: Omnivorous
Temperature: 72–79°F

Some aquarists believe that the platy is the ideal community fish. The platy belongs to the same genus as the swordtail and is therefore a very close relative. As with most live-bearers, many color varieties have been commercially bred for the home aquarium. Plenty of cover in dense vegetation will lead to successful breeding and the survival of the fry in a community tank. The platy will consume algae and prefers to live in small groups of five to seven fish.

Zebra Danio *Brachydanio rerio*
Origin: India
Size: 2.5 inches
Food: Omnivorous
Temperature: 64–75°F

These are fish that like to school. Torpedo-shaped danios are very active fish. Their schools should be kept in groups of at least seven or eight fish. This egg-laying cyprinid has been commercially bred to both albino and long-finned strains. Males are generally slimmer than females and usually remain loyal to one female once they have spawned. This species likes to spend time at the surface where it is open and bright.

White Cloud Mountain Minnow *Tanichthys albonubes*
Origin: Southern China
Size: 1.5 inches
Food: Omnivorous
Temperature: 64–72°F

This minnow is another schooling fish. As a very undemanding, active cyprinid fish, it should be kept in a group of eight or more. Males are slimmer and have more intense coloration than females. These are peaceful fish. They prefer cooler water and should only be kept in temperatures less than 72°F! That's pretty cool for tropical fish.

Common Hatchetfish *Gasteropelecus sternicla*
Origin: Brazil, Guyana, Surinam
Size: 2.5 inches
Food: Carnivorous
Temperature: 73–79°F

These hatchetfish are surface dwellers. They are a close relative of the marbled hatchetfish. They need to be kept in schools of at least six fish. The unusually deep body of these species make them an interesting addition to any community aquarium. All hatchets are excellent jumpers so be sure to keep the hood in place on the tank. A few floating plants will provide adequate cover for these gentle fish.

Siamese Fighting Fish *Betta splendens*
Origin: Cambodia, Thailand
Size: 3 inches
Food: Carnivorous
Temperature: 75–84°F

Siamese fighting fish are more commonly known as bettas. This beautiful labyrinth fish is a popular addition to the community aquarium. Selective breeding over the years has enhanced the brilliant ornate finnage of the males. However, only one male may be kept per aquarium, otherwise vicious fighting will occur; duels between males can result in the death of one. This is why bettas are kept in separate bowls on shelves unseparated by dividers in pet stores. They are kept close to one another so that they will display their finnage, as if they were ready to fight. That's because they are. Males are generally peaceful with other species unless they have similar fin veils. The smaller, shorter-finned females are more drab but may be kept together in a community tank. This egg-laying species builds a bubble nest at the surface of the aquarium where the eggs are guarded by the males.

Mid-Water Fishes

Many of the mid-water fishes mentioned in this next section tend to be fish who school in groups of eight or more. Many of these mid-water swimmers belong to the groups of fishes referred to as the cyprinids and the characins. With this being the case, you should consider only one or two species of schooling mid-water fish.

Rosy Barb *Barbus conchonius*
Origin: Northern India
Size: 3 inches
Food: Omnivorous
Temperature: 64–72°F

The rosy barb is a very peaceful species that adapts well to a community aquarium. But it prefers cooler water than other community fish. In cooler waters it is generally more colorful. Barbs get their name from the small barbels that act as sensory organs near and on their mouths. They are fast and agile, and contribute great vitality to the mid-waters of the tank. Barbs, however, can cause harm to smaller fish and to fish with ornate finnage.

The tiger barb *Barbus tetrazona* is a related species. Do not introduce these fish singly or by pairs. They tend to be wild and disruptive, and even downright aggressive. But, if you keep them in schools of eight or more, they tend to establish a hierarchy within the school, and will ignore the rest of the tank. It is recommended that schools contain both the more colorful males and the heavier females. Unlike the rosy barb, these Indonesian fish prefer warmer waters in the range of 68–79°F. The ruby barb, *Barbus nigrofasciatus,* is also a peaceful addition to the tank in much the same way. Originally from Sri Lanka, the ruby barb also prefers warmer water and the company of other barbs.

Red Rasbora *Rasbora heteromorpha*
Origin: Southeast Asia
Size: 2 inches
Food: Omnivorous
Temperature: 72–77°F

This rasbora is another popular fish that is better off in a school of eight or more. The red rasbora has a deeper body than its close relative, the red-striped rasbora, *Rasbora pauciperforata,* which is streamlined in shape. Red-striped rasbora grow about an inch larger and have similar temperature preferences. They, too, are better off in groups of eight or more. Egg-laying species of rasboras are not as easy to breed as the barbs, but they are extremely peaceful.

Neon Tetra *Paracheirodon innesi*
Origin: Peru
Size: 1.5 inches
Food: Omnivorous
Temperature: 68–79°F

The neon tetra is certainly one of the most popular fishes included in community aquariums. Two of the main reasons for their popularity are their exciting colorings and their hardiness. They are capable of tolerating a wide range of temperatures, which makes them very desirable. Like other mid-water fish, the neon tetra should be kept in a school of six or more individuals. The iridescent coloration of this fish will glow if the tank is properly lighted.

Two related terta species include the cardinal tetra, *Paracheirodon axelrodi,* and the glowlight tetra, *Hemigrammus erythrozonus.* They will travel in schools peacefully throughout your aquarium.

Another ideal community fish is the black neon tetra, *Hyphessobrycon herbertaxelrodi.* It has a stouter body than the neon tetra.

Angelfish *Pterophyllum scalare*
Origin: Central Amazon to Peru, Ecuador
Size: 6 inches
Food: Omnivorous
Temperature: 75–82°F

The angelfish is certainly one of the most exotic and recognizable fish in all the community aquarium world. However, angelfish are not for the beginner. You should have a well-established aquarium and be experienced if you want to take the step towards keeping these fish. They cannot withstand extreme fluctuations in water quality and temperature. These placid fish require tall decorations (like plants), which they will stay quietly among. They are best kept in small groups of four to six with other even-tempered fish such as neon tetras and black mollies. The angelfish is actually a cichlid. Surprisingly, they are probably the only ones of this species that has a somewhat peaceful disposition. When they grow to full maturity, approximately six inches or more, they will eat smaller fish. There are many varieties of angelfish.

Blue Gourami *Trichogaster trichopterus*
Origin: Southeast Asia to Indo-Australian Islands
Size: 4 inches
Food: Omnivorous
Temperature: 72–82°F

The blue gourami and its relatives are peaceful labyrinth fish. They do not need to be kept in schools, but are quite well known to be happy in pairs. They have elaborate finnage and beautiful colors. They should not be included with fin nippers, like tiger barbs. Although listed here as mid-water fish, the gouramis will swim among the bottom decorations as well as make frequent excursions to the surface.

Included among gouramis are the dwarf gourami, *Colisa lalia*, the snakeskin gourami, *Trichogaster pectoralis,* and the pearl gourami, *Trichogaster leeri*. These fish are egg-layers. They build bubble nests during spawning like other labyrinth fish. The paradise fish, *Macropodus opercularis,* closely resembles the gouramis. The paradise fish is also a very hardy fish and can tolerate temperatures down to 61°F. Warning, this species may cause trouble. It may annoy, nip, or threaten other community species if they are very slow. Don't put two males in the tank, as they will fight bitterly.

Glass Catfish *Kryptopterus bicirrhis*
Origin: Eastern India and Southeast Asia
Size: 4 inches
Food: Carnivorous
Temperature: 72–79°F

GLASS CATFISH

The glass catfish is one of the few catfish species that does not hang out on the bottom. This fish likes to school in groups of four or more. The glass catfish has a transparent body, so the internal organs can be seen. Although sometimes difficult to acclimate in the aquarium, this hardy fish is a worthwhile addition to the community tank. It's better-suited for a slightly more experienced aquarist.

Bottom Fish

Bottom fish are the fish that hang out on the gravel or near the bases of plants. This category is dominated by the catfish, but there are a few other species as well. The bottom fish are usually also tank cleaners, eating bottom detritus and algae. They are living vacuums. Therefore, no community tank would be complete without a few.

Corydoras Catfish *Corydoras* species
Origin: South America
Size: 1.5 to 2.5 inches
Food: Omnivorous
Temperature: 72–79°F

Many of the Corydoras catfish are a genus of fish that are very similar, yet they come in many varieties. They have whisker-like barbels, which gives them their name. They are generally very hardy fish that feed on the substrate. These fish have a flat bottom so that they can stay close to the bottom of the tank. They have an adipose fin and armored bony plates rather than scales. They tend to be nocturnal, so they like to do their work at night, foraging and cleaning the tank's bottom surface. During the day they may seem somewhat inactive, some even like to hide. They like to live with others of their species, so keep three to five together. While they may not race up to the top during feeding, add a little extra food for them, as the substrate is not enough to feed these fish. You should augment their diets with other foods.

Other popular species include the bronze corydoras, *Corydoras aeneus,* the arched corydoras, *Corydoras arcuatus,* axelrod's corydoras, *Corydoras axelrodi,* the leopard corydoras, *Corydoras julii,* and the dusky corydoras, *Corydoras septentrionalis.*

Flying Fox *Epalzeorhynchus kallopterus*
Origin: Borneo, Indonesia, Thailand, India
Size: 6 inches
Food: Omnivorous
Temperature: 75–79°F

The flying fox species is a loner so it does not require the company of others of its kind. These fish are territorial, but only with other flying foxes. If you have a big enough tank, you can keep more than one, but the idea is that they each have enough territory to claim. The flying fox is not strictly a bottom species because it will also rest on the leaves of broad-leaved plants or graze algae on large flat stones. Several can be kept in an aquarium if ample space is provided for each to establish a territory.

Clown Loach *Botia macracanthus*
Origin: Borneo, India
Size: 6 inches
Food: Omnivorous
Temperature: 77–86°F

This uniquely colorful species of loach is an excellent addition to any community tank. It has whiskers like a catfish and the same bottom cleaning propensity. It is recommended that you keep several young as a school together, but only one mature adult in your aquarium.

Red-Tailed Shark *Epalzeorhynchus* bicolor
Origin: Thailand
Size: 4.5 inches
Food: Omnivorous
Temperature: 72–79°F

You really shouldn't keep the red-tailed shark. They are very aggressive. If you are determined to keep this fish, it should only be one, as they are very territorial with each other. Two might stage a major brawl. It is easily found in many pet stores and retail outlets, and it is very popular because of its look. Put them together only with fast, small fish or with easy going larger fish.

Clown Plecostomus *Peckoltia arenaria*
Origin: Peru
Size: 4.5 inches
Food: Herbivorous
Temperature: 72–80°F

Clown fish are a favorite among hobbyists. It would be impossible to cover the bottom fish without including at least one plecostomus. These fish are infamous for their "window cleaning" abilities. This species is one of the smaller sucker-mouthed catfishes that is ideally suited for the community tank. Others will attain lengths in excess of 10 inches and are not well suited for the beginner. This species has been known to be aggressive to its own kind, so it is

No Rookies: Fish for Experienced Hobbyists

The fish listed below either require very exceptional environmental conditions or are non-compatible with community fish or others.

Discus
Oscars
Red devils
Jack Dempseys
Tinfoil barbs
Red snakehead
Mudskippers
Clown knife fish
Arowana

Some fish need to be kept only with their own kind. A large arowana is usually kept only by itself. While oscars and discus can't be kept together, they can tolerate other fish, but they should be hardy and tough. Make sure to talk to your local pet professional when you desire to mix any of the above species.

best to keep only one in your aquarium. Plenty of cover and caves should be provided for this fish.

Predators

So far we've covered quite a few fish. However, there are certainly more. The fish covered in this section are not well suited for the beginner's aquarium for a number of reasons. Some may be highly sensitive to fluctuating water quality conditions, a frequent problem in a new aquarium. Others may require special water conditions, such as softer water or brackish water. The beginner should not try to provide this type of habitat without acquiring some experience.

Finally, there are a number of species that are not socially compatible with the peaceful community tank. This group includes large carnivorous fish that eat smaller fish, territorial fish that do not tolerate trespassing, and mature fish that display aggression and combative behavior during spawning or pre-spawning periods. In short, you have to know what you're doing if you want to handle one of these bad boys.

Many of these species are offered by the pet store and may even be promoted by the dealer because they are smaller juveniles that he considers "harmless." Don't be fooled by this argument. These fish grow fast and develop aggressive attitudes early in life. The small flake-eating baby will become a neon-eating carnivore in a matter of months.

Do not buy fish that require special water conditions. Beginners are usually not equipped to handle these requirements. These fish may live for days or weeks in your tank, but chronic stress will set in, and its immune response will fail. Ultimately, the fish will die due to disease.

As a novice, you must avoid the following fish. Here is a brief description of those species that should not be included in your community aquarium. As you develop your talents as an aquarist, you will expand your capabilities, and be able to keep some of the more sensitive species of fish. You may even want to establish an aquarium of "compatible" aggressive species or a species tank. As you will notice, many of these fish are cichlids.

Green Discus *Symphysodon aequifasciatus*
Origin: Amazon
Size: 6 inches
Food: Carnivorous
Temperature: 79–86°F

The green discus are outright beautiful fish. This very peaceful fish would be an attractive addition to the community tank. In the end, it really is best kept in a species aquarium. Why? Because it requires soft acidic water and becomes territorial when breeding. As aggressive as the discus can be, it falls into an unusual spot. It is too aggressive for most community tanks, and is not aggressive enough to be kept with the following fish.

Oscar *Astronotus ocellatus*
Origin: South America
Size: 13 inches
Food: Carnivorous
Temperature: 72–77°F

Oscars are often sold when they are very young and unassuming. However, you have just bought Frankenstein. They grow quickly. And they grow very large, given enough space. They can also be aggressive and they are quite strong. We once saw an oscar pull a large net right out of a hobbyist's hand. They require small fish or meaty food to satisfy their hefty appetites. Common goldfish, sometimes called feeder goldfish (because they are bought by the dozen), are a common food for domesticated oscars. Otherwise, they can tolerate a wide range of water quality parameters.

Red Devil *Amphilophus labiatus*
Origin: Central America
Size: 10 inches
Food: Omnivorous
Temperature: 75–79°F

The red devil, a cichlid, is an aggressive territorial fish that will eat anything and everything. This species can only be mixed with species that can take care of themselves, like the large oscar, Jack Dempseys, and jewel cichlids. They cannot be kept with discus.

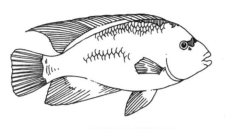

RED DEVIL

Jewel Cichlid *Hemichromis bimaculatus*
Origin: Central Liberia to Southern Guinea
Size: 6 inches
Food: Omnivorous
Temperature: 70–73°F

The jewel cichlid is noted for its extremely aggressive behavior when breeding. This belligerent fish will establish a territory and aggressively protect it.

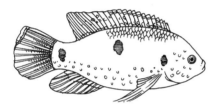

JEWEL CHICLID

Jack Dempsey *Nandopsis octofasciatus*
Origin: Central America
Size: 8 inches
Food: Omnivorous
Temperature: 72–77°F

The Jack Dempsey is another of the cichlid species that is intolerant of other species. The Jack Dempsey belongs in a species aquarium; otherwise, it will incessantly harass other species.

Rummy-Nose Tetra *Hemigrammus bleheri*
Origin: Colombia, Brazil
Size: 2 inches
Food: Omnivorous
Temperature: 72–79°F

This species of tetra is highly sensitive to water quality conditions. Any buildup of nitrates will cause chronic stress and ultimately lead to disease and illness.

Tinfoil Barb *Barbus schwanefeldi*
Origin: Southeast Asia
Size: 14 inches
Food: Omnivorous
Temperature: 72–77°F

The tinfoil barb is often mistakenly recommended by retailers as community fish. They are not. These fish are very active and grow far too large for the average aquarium. They require a lot of space, are best kept in schools, and have a tendency to dig up the substrate.

Sucking Loach *Gyrinocheilus aymonieri*
Origin: India, Thailand
Size: 11 inches
Food: Herbivorous
Temperature: 77–82°F

Most loaches are algae eaters. That's why we like 'em. However, this species can be aggressive toward its tank mates. And it becomes territorial as it gets larger! Its large size also precludes inclusion in the community tank.

Red Snakehead *Channa micropeltes*
Origin: India, Burma, Thailand, Vietnam, Malaysia
Size: 39 inches
Food: Carnivorous
Temperature: 77–82°F

This is another monster. These are for serious aquarists only. This large carnivore requires warm temperatures and small live fish to feed on. Although juveniles are considered "cute," they grow rapidly and consume the community.

Mudskipper *Periophthalmus barbarus*
Origin: Africa, Southeast Asia, Australia
Size: 6 inches
Food: Carnivorous
Temperature: 77–86°F

The mudskipper is becoming increasingly more popular in the aquarium trade. The problem with this fish is that it requires brackish water, which it needs to leave periodically. These requirements make this a challenge, even for experienced aquarists. Its territorial nature can also be a problem.

Clown Knife Fish *Notopterus chitala*
Origin: Southeast Asia
Size: 39 inches
Food: Omnivorous
Temperature: 75–82°F

The knife fishes usually become too large for the average community aquarium. This species and its relatives can be extremely aggressive and are best kept alone or with other large fishes.

Arowana *Osteoglossum bicirrhosum*
Origin: Amazon
Size: 47 inches
Food: Carnivorous
Temperature: 75–82°F

The arowana is an elegant and menacing fish that enchants the novice as well as the expert aquarist. It is a predator of the highest rank. Its large size and predatory nature exclude it from the community aquarium. Many arowana are kept alone in large tanks.

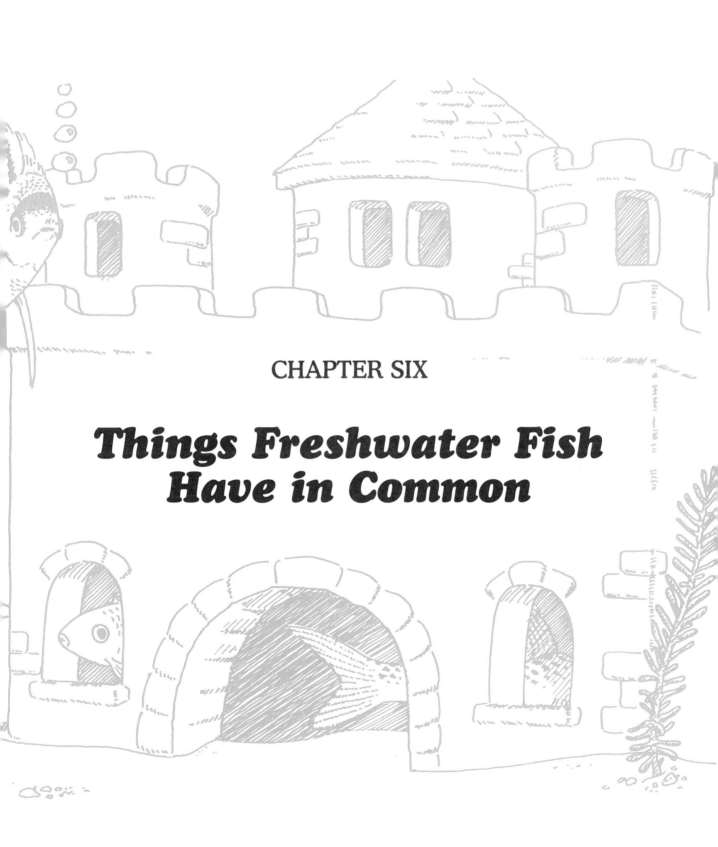

CHAPTER SIX

Things Freshwater Fish Have in Common

Tropical Fish Diseases

Fish are like kids in the first few years of grammar school. Eventually, they get everything. And the longer you have fish, the more diseases you will have cured or will have seen your fish fall victim to. Treating ailments in your fish is often difficult and upsetting. Sometimes it's very costly. One of the things that separate an experienced aquarist from a novice is the expert's ability to observe and identify some of the following maladies early on, so that he or she can help the fish in question and maybe save the rest of the tank.

Freshwater tropical fishes are subject to all kind of maladies. Parasites, bacteria, and viruses are present in all aquariums. Many are introduced with new fish or live plants, and many are highly contagious. However, whether or not diseases actually break out depends on the resistance of your fish. Poor living conditions will weaken your fish, cause chronic stress, and ultimately lower the fish's resistance to infection. That's when your fish is most vulnerable to disease.

That's why the importance of maintaining a healthy aquarium cannot be stressed enough. In spite of doing everything possible to have a disease-free environment in your tank, even the experts fall victim to these problems.

The Prognosis

First, you were mother nature. Then you were mother hen. Now you're Marcus Welby, MD. The first step to treating any kind of ailment in your aquarium is to recognize and identify the problem. You will be able to determine that a fish is not healthy by its appearance and its behavior. Since you have been spending time examining your fish while you feed them, you will be able to identify problems as soon as they manifest themselves. Tell-tale behavioral symptoms include no desire to eat, hyperventilation of the gills, gasping for air near the surface, erratic swimming behavior, lack of movement, rubbing of body or fins, twitching of fins, and excessive or agitated rubbing against plants or rocks.

Swimming Trouble?

If your fish is having trouble swimming normally, it's usually a sign that something is wrong. Usually it is a sign of swim bladder problems.

External symptoms include a variety of physical abnormalities of the head, body, fins, gills, scales, and anus. As we review the various diseases associated with aquarium fish, you will learn the symptoms of each.

The Hospital Tank: The Emergency Room

Earlier in this book we explained that some aquarists isolate new fish in a quarantine tank. In this way, the fish can be evaluated for signs of disease before introduction into the main aquarium. We didn't recommend a quarantine tank for the beginner community tank, because of the complexities associated with having to maintain two aquariums.

However, many experts do recommend that you set up a hospital tank to isolate fish that are suffering from disease. This tank will reduce the likelihood of the disease spreading to others in the aquarium. It will provide refuge to a fish that may ordinarily be harassed by healthier fish. The hospital tank will make it easier to treat the fish without subjecting other fish to the treatment. And it will make it easier to observe and diagnose the ailing fish.

As your expertise in this hobby increases, you will start to accumulate more expensive fish that you simply do not want to risk with disease. At this point, a hospital tank will be mandatory. It will also act as a quarantine tank, provided that it has not recently housed a diseased fish.

The hospital tank doesn't need to be large. A 10-gallon or a 5-gallon tank will do. It does need adequate filtration and aeration, but plants and gravel should be left out. It doesn't need to be pretty, and those are just more things that will hold onto to whatever parasite you're fighting, creating more work when cleaning up. Try to provide some kind of cover for the fish, though, in the form of rocks or flower pots as a source of security.

Commercial Remedies

For a cold, many of us take NyQuil or Contac, or whatever brand you prefer. In the fish world, there are name brands, too. You didn't think the drug industry was going to let the entire pet industry get away, did you?

Not Hungry?

Observation is the key to detecting illness early! One of the first clues that a fish is suffering illness is loss of appetite. If a fish repeatedly ignores food two or three feedings in a row, something may be wrong!

Rubbing Against Rocks?

Repeated rubbing against rocks and other aquarium decorations is one of the first signs that something is wrong. Basically, your fish is trying to wipe something off itself. It usually is a sign that a skin or scale disease is about to rear its ugly head.

It is very important that beginners use commercially available treatments instead of homemade remedies. Some experts recommend chemicals, such as malachite green or potassium permanganate. These must be handled in very exact dosages. If a fish is overdosed with one of them, it will kill the fish faster than the disease would have. Discuss all the possible remedies of a disease with your local pet dealer and let that person advise you on the best commercial remedies the store carries.

If you are still not satisfied, don't be afraid to call your veterinarian and ask a few questions. If your veterinarian does not handle fish, he can usually recommend somebody who does. Finally, when you apply the remedy, make sure that you follow the directions exactly.

Emergency Cleaning

This is as bad as it gets. This is the most severe treatment any tank can receive. If any of the infestations mentioned below strike more than three or four fish, you need to take drastic measures and perform an emergency cleaning. Place all the fish in the hospital tank and begin treatment. Then, turn your attention to the aquarium.

In essence, you are starting over again because your tank was overrun by disease. You must now take apart everything in your tank. Empty the water. Take out all the plants and rocks and anything else. You must start all over again from scratch. First, you must clean the tank thoroughly. Then the gravel. Before you put anything back into the tank, it must be thoroughly cleaned and totally restarted. Throw out filter media and save as little as possible. Rinse the walls, the gravel, and the filter with bleach. Of course, make sure that you rinse everything extra thoroughly. Do the same to the plastic plants. Throw out the rocks and buy new ones. If you have any live plants, dispose of them, too. Replace the filter media and airstones. Wash the heater with bleach as well, making sure to rinse it thoroughly. Also, wipe down the insides of the tank with bleach. Remember to rinse thoroughly!

THE OLD-FASHIONED SALT BATH

This is also called the progressive salt treatment. Every experienced hobbyist who's had fish for a length of time has done this at least once in their tropical fish career. This is the most time-tested cure-all of the fish world. Many times the hospital tank is used for just such a treatment. This very simple procedure has been known to cure a number of fish diseases, including ich, fungus, velvet, and tail rot. Many experts swear by it.

It's very simple. You add one teaspoon of table salt (not iodized) for each gallon of water to the hospital tank that houses your fish. Add the same amount of salt that night and twice the next day, once in the morning and once at night. If there are not improvements by the third or fourth day, add one more teaspoon of salt each day. On the ninth and tenth days, make progressive water changes and check for results.

Diseases, Infestations, Parasites, and Other Hangers-On

There are literally hundreds of possible maladies that can afflict fish. Some are specific to certain species, and some can easily be transferred between species. Not all are common in the average home aquarium. The causes of common aquarium ailments may be bacteria, viruses, fungi, or parasites. The following provides a general overview of those diseases you are most likely to encounter in your aquarium. For a more complete listing of tropical fish diseases and their treatments, consult the references in chapter 6.

General Ailments

Constipation or Indigestion (not contagious)

A fish that is constipated or suffering from indigestion is often very inactive and usually rests on the bottom of the tank. In addition, its abdomen generally swells or bulges. This can be caused by an incorrect diet, food that doesn't agree with the fish, or overfeeding. You will need to change the food you are feeding the fish. Some experts add one teaspoon of epsom salts for each five gallons of water in the hospital tank. Starve the fish for three to five days until it returns to being active. When it resumes normal behavior, feed it live or freeze-dried food for one whole week. After one week, return the fish to its normal tank. This is a problem that tends to recur, so make it a point to watch this fish.

Swim Bladder Problems (not contagious)

This is an easy one to diagnose. The fish can't swim properly. It suffers from a loss of balance, swimming on its sides or upside-down, or sometimes somersaulting through the water. Swim bladder disease can result from constipation; from bruising of the swim bladder during handling, fighting, or breeding; or from bacterial infection associated with poor water quality. These problems have been known to correct themselves as the bruised area heals, but you can't always count on this. If you suspect a bacterial infection, improve water quality and treat the fish with a broad-spectrum antibiotic. If this problem is associated with constipation, your fish is more likely to experience a recurrence. Feed your fish something

OR—Stat!

Some veterinarians are known to operate on fish to save them from various problems. Mostly veterinarians can help with a range of things, from removing obstructions to removing tumors and other cancerous growths. Koi owners and goldfish owners are known to operate on fish, too.

else, as diet can be one of the biggest reasons this disease develops at all.

Dropsy or Kidney Bloat (may be contagious)

This is also known as "pinecone" disease because the belly bloats noticeably and the scales stick out like a pinecone. In general, this disease causes the body to swell due to a buildup of fluid in the tissues. This disease is thought to be caused by water quality problems or some kind of organ failure. Fish generally don't live more than a week after full-blown dropsy makes itself known. Like constipation and swim bladder disease, fish that survive dropsy tend to have recurring attacks. While dropsy is not thought to be contagious, it is best to remove the fish at once. The tank should receive an emergency cleaning.

Many experts still feel that dropsy is not treatable and that the fish should be immediately removed and painlessly destroyed. Others feel that medicated food is one way to treat dropsy. Still others suggest mixing Furanace with water, 250 milligrams to the gallon. This bath should last only one hour and should not be repeated more than three times in three days. It is thought that Furanace can be absorbed by the fish through the skin. If you choose not to use this remedy, you can always try the old-fashioned salt bath (see sidebar). If your fish does not respond to treatment in two or three days, it should probably be destroyed.

Tumors (usually not contagious)

Obvious lumps, bumps, or protrusions, tumors sometimes look like a large blister or wart. They have been known to grow to the size of a large screw head. They can be surgically removed, but only by a veterinarian.

Pop-Eye (Exophthalmus; not contagious)

This disease causes the eyes to bulge from their sockets and is, therefore, easy to recognize for most tropical fish. The condition is generally caused by poor water quality and the subsequent chronic stress. Recovery may take several days if efforts are made to improve the water quality. Some feel that food should be withheld for two or three days until tank conditions are corrected.

Marcus Welby Meets Flipper

Many veterinarians see people whose patients are fish. To find out who takes fish on as patients near you, call your local veterinarian. He or she will usually refer you to another vet who specializes in aquatic life without too much difficulty.

Bacterial, Viral, and Fungal Infections

Furunculosis (Ulcer Disease; contagious)

This bacterial infection will go for some time unnoticed, but then it will spread rapidly. These bacteria infect the flesh under the scales somewhat like skin flukes, which we'll cover later. However, this infection is first manifested by the appearance of bumps underneath the scales. A short time later, the bumps rupture and create large bleeding ulcers. That is why this ailment is sometimes referred to as "ulcer disease." There is no certain cure for this.

While some fish have actually survived, large scars resulting from the infection often prove a problem for them. Fish with these kinds of ulcers should probably be destroyed. The remaining fish should be treated with tetracycline immediately. Tetracycline treatment can last up to ten days. Some experts argue that all foods should be immediately changed and that any remaining existing foods be disposed of. You may want to elevate your aquarium temperature to 80°F during that time if you do not have any fish that are intolerant of high temperatures. Furunculosis is a cold-water disease and the high temperature is thought to kill it.

Ulcers (Hole-in-the-Body Disease; highly contagious)

This is an infection that tends to be internal and that manifests itself in large red ulcers, boils, and dark reddening at the bases of the fins. It cannot be mistaken for anchor worms, which are covered later, because anchor-worm ulcers swell up, whereas these tend to eat away into the body.

A salt bath may be too harsh, but the infected fish should be isolated immediately and fed medicated food. At times, antibiotics are required, and you will need a veterinarian for this. Consult your local pet store before proceeding.

Fungus (highly contagious)

The most common species of fungus infecting tropical fishes is Saprolegnia. It is a fuzzy growth, different from velvet (see below) because it is whiter and easier to notice. The primary cause of this infection is damage to the mucus layer on the skin. This allows fungal spores to germinate and grow into the skin. Injury, environmental conditions, and parasites can damage the protective mucus layer.

Some experts treat this fungus with methylene blue, which they paint on the infected areas. This fish is then placed in a 10-day saltwater treatment. Again, commercial remedies are also available and the entire aquarium should be treated with a fungicide.

Body Slime Fungus (highly contagious)

This deadly affliction can kill your fish in two days if not caught in time. The protective mucus coating grows white and starts peeling off as if the fish were shedding its skin. The fins are gradually covered as well. Eventually, the body becomes red with irritation.

Do not hesitate to call your pet store immediately. Commercial remedies are available, but must be administered quickly. A salt bath with warm temperatures may be a temporary solution, as it should retard growth of the fungus. However, a cure must be found and a salt bath won't do it. Some have found that the severe salt treatments used as ich cures are effective.

Mouth Fungus (Columnaris Disease; contagious)

Mouth fungus is caused by the bacteria Flexibacter and manifests itself as a white cottony growth on the mouth. It can also be associated with the gills, back, and fins. If left untreated for any length of time, this infection will destroy the entire infected region and lead to death.

Commercial cures are available, but you can begin by isolating the fish and administering the saltwater treatment. Some aquarists will start with a salt bath, then use a general fungal or bacterial control. Consult with your pet store once you have diagnosed the problem.

Fish Pox (probably not contagious)

Fish pox affects goldfish, koi, and carp more than it does other aquarium fish, but it should be covered in this chapter. This is a viral infection that causes milky white or pinkish gray waxy film to develop over the fish's skin and fins. The usual pattern is that it appears, gets worse, and then disappears.

It is not definitively known what triggers fish pox and what eventually happens. However, it does not appear to be contagious. Nonetheless, take the necessary precautions and isolate the infected fish until the film goes away. This usually takes seven to ten days.

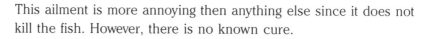

This ailment is more annoying then anything else since it does not kill the fish. However, there is no known cure.

Fin or Tail Rot (contagious)

This is sometimes caused by fighting among your fish—the fins get damaged and then bacteria infect the injured area. It can also be triggered by poor water quality. It is easily detectable as the fins have missing parts and eventually become shredded. As the disease worsens, the entire fin will be eaten away. There are many broad-spectrum medications that will help you deal with this situation. Consult your local pet store dealer.

Some experts argue that the best way to treat the infection is by dipping your fish into a bath made up of eight crystals of potassium permanganate to three quarts of water for five minutes. Then you cut off the infected areas of the tail or fin and paint them with methylene blue or mercurochrome. Steps like this may be for experts only.

Be sure to treat the aquarium water, too, because fin rot is usually contagious. You can choose from any number of commercial solutions available in pet stores today. Follow the instructions. Also, take the steps necessary to remedy the cause of the infection. Separate fish that cause injury to the fins and make sure water quality is at its best.

China Disease (highly contagious)

This is not a very common disease, and you must be absolutely certain of your diagnosis. This is the most contagious disease listed here and it is the most deadly. There is no known cure for China disease.

The symptoms are very easy to spot. The tail fin and other fins begin to fray, very much as in fin rot. However, with China disease it begins at the base of the fin and works its way outward. Also, the infected areas begin to blacken. Even the ventral region begins to turn black.

Unfortunately, the infected fish must be painlessly destroyed and the other fish put in the hospital tank. A 10-day progressive salt treatment isn't a bad idea.

In the meantime, you need to perform an emergency cleaning in the tank. This must be done immediately to prevent further damage by this disease.

Parasite Infestations

Fish Lice (highly contagious)

Fish lice are parasitic crustaceans of the species Argulus that are very easy to recognize on the surface of your fish. They are round disk-like crustaceans with prominent eyes, sucking disks, and a stiletto mouthpart that clamps onto its host, refusing to let go. They can move about the host with ease and tend to take on the color of the fish that they parasitize. Often the infected fish will rub up against objects in the tank in an effort to scrape these pests off. Some fish have been known to jump out of the water in an attempt to cleanse themselves of these parasites. These creatures feed by sucking the blood and tissue fluids out of the fish through the skin and scales. Sometimes they occur on the fins, but this is not as satisfying for them. Fish lice can also transmit other microscopic diseases, and wounds may develop secondary bacterial infections.

Fortunately, there are a number of high-quality commercially produced products on the market to control parasites. Your local pet dealer can help you select one. The fish should be quarantined and the tank disinfected with the same parasite control. Make sure to follow the directions carefully, as overdoing the treatment is just as damaging.

On larger fish, experts have been known to remove fish lice with forceps or drip hot paraffin wax from a candle onto the parasite. Others recommend giving the afflicted fish a bath for fifteen minutes in a mixture of potassium permanganate and water, which should be extremely light pink. Consult your local pet store first. Lice are treatable, but both the fish and the aquarium must be treated.

Most often recommended for aquarium treatment for fish lice, anchor worms, and leeches are Dipterex, Masoten, Dylox, or Nequvon. All bite marks or wounds on the fish must be treated. Dab a little antiseptic m0ercurochrome, malachite green, or methylene blue on the site. Do not use Formalin to kill the parasite; you may also kill your fish because the margin for error is so slim.

Final Rites— Saying Goodbye

What do I do with dead fish? Well, there have been various things that many pet owners have done.

Some folks flush away their sadness (along with their loved ones). Do this with small fish only.

Some people bury them in the backyard. If you do this, there's a 90% chance that some roving canine will express his interest in your loved one.

Anchor Worm (highly contagious)

These elongated crustaceans of the genus Lernaea also attach to the skin of the fish. Several species of this parasite have been described, but all females have a head with an anchor shape that embeds in the flesh of the host. The fish will rub against anything it can in an attempt to scrape off the parasite. Like fish lice, these creatures cause irritation and localized bleeding at the point of attachment; from this protrudes a white worm that can sometimes grow quite long. Secondary bacterial infection can occur at these points.

Treatment of the anchor worm will include taking the fish out of the water and removing the worm from the aggravated area with a forceps or tweezers. Be sure to carefully follow the instructions accompanying any parasite-control product that you buy.

To remove the worm, place a wet cloth in your hand. Hold the fish in the hand holding the cloth. Make sure to position the fish so that the worm is facing you. With a pair of household tweezers, gently press as close to the ulcer as possible, but only extract the worm. Be sure not to rip any flesh off the fish and be careful not to break the parasite. This is very dangerous to the fish and you must be extremely cautious when approaching this. It is best to get someone experienced to do this for you.

As in the case with fish lice, be sure to treat the infected area with an antiseptic after removing the parasite. Antibiotic treatment may also accelerate the healing of lesions. Consult your dealer for a general full-spectrum antibiotic.

Leeches (highly contagious)

Leeches are another group of parasites that may be found on the skin and scales of your fish. These are not the leeches we see as free living creatures in lakes and ponds. These are parasitic, wormlike creatures that attach at both ends to your fish, feeding on flesh and blood. They need to be removed as quickly as possible, but *not* with forceps or tweezers. These parasites are very strong, and you are likely to do more damage to your fish than to the leeches by trying to pull them off. Call your pet store for advice for commercially produced cures.

Another solution to leeches involves preparing a salt bath with eight level teaspoons of salt for each gallon of water. Once the salt is sufficiently dissolved, add the fish for no more than ten minutes. The leeches that do not fall off can now be removed with tweezers very easily.

Again, the aquarium needs to be treated immediately with commercially produced chemicals for parasite control. Check all your fish for parasites when one is discovered and always isolate the infected fish.

Flukes: Skin and Gill (highly contagious)

Like all infestations, weakened fish fall victim first. The gill fluke (Dactylogyrus) is easily detectable. It causes the gills to swell up pink and red, and the fish spends a lot of time near the surface trying to suck in air. Sometimes, a pus-like fluid will be exuded from the gills at this time. These flukes are microscopic parasites that lodge themselves in the gills. Other symptoms include severe color loss, scratching, and labored respiration. The skin fluke (Gyrodactylus) causes localized swelling, excessive mucus, and ulcerations.

As with all other parasitic manifestations, the host fish is constantly trying to rub itself against objects to scrape off the infestation. Again, pet stores have pest-control remedies for this problem, which is more easily treatable than the ones I have already listed. Be sure to treat the tank as well to make sure that this parasite does not spread.

Some experts recommend a formaldehyde bath. Do this only if commercial solutions are unavailable or are not effective. Place the fish in a gallon of water. Add 15 drops of formaldehyde every minute for 10 minutes. Then remove the fish and place it in a hospital tank. Repeat this process daily for three days. Formaldehyde will kill your fish, so do not haphazardly administer this chemical. Follow the instructions and time it precisely.

Ich (White Spot; highly contagious)

Raised white spots about the size of salt or granules that appear on the body are the parasite Ichthyophthirius. This is one of

A Guide to Symptoms
at a Glance

If a red agitated area on the fish's body is the base from which a white worm protrudes, and the diseased fish rubs against anything it can, attempting to scratch off the parasite, then your fish has ANCHOR WORM.

If the protective skin mucus grows white and starts peeling off, as if the fish was shedding or molting, and the fins are eventually covered as well, then your fish has BODY SLIME FUNGUS.

If, at the beginning at the base of the fins and working its way outward, tail fins and other fins begin to fray, infected areas begin to blacken, and the ventral region begins to turn black, your fish has CHINA DISEASE.

If your fish is very inactive, usually rests on bottom of the tank, and abdominal swelling and bulging occurs, then your fish has CONSTIPATION, INDIGESTION.

If the scales stick out like pinecones and the abdomen bloats notice-ably, your fish has DROPSY (KIDNEY BLOAT).

If, at first, the fin have missing parts, then they become shredded, and rays become inflamed and the entire fin may be eaten away, then your fish has FIN OR TAIL ROT.

If round, disk-shaped transparent crustaceans clamp onto the host fish and refuse to let go, and the infected fish rubs against objects in the tank in an effort to remove the parasites, your fish has FISH LICE.

If whitish or pinkish waxy film develops over fish's skin and fins, then your fish has FISH POX.

If your fish has a fuzzy growth, different from velvet because it is more whitish in coloration, then your fish has FUNGUS.

If your fish has raised bumps under the scales that eventually rupture and cause bleeding ulcers, then your fish has FURUNCULOSIS.

If your fish's gills swell pink and red, and the fish spends time at the surface gasping for air, and pus-like fluid is exuded from the gills, then your fish has GILL FLUKES.

If your fish has white stringy feces and enlarged pus-filled sensory pores in the head, plus erosion of the skin and muscles, which eventually extends to the bones and skull, then your fish has HOLE-IN-THE-HEAD.

If your fish exhibits raised white spots about the size of a salt granule on the body and fins, then your fish has ICH.

If your fish has long worm-like parasites attached at both ends to the fish, which do not come off easily, then your fish has LEECHES.

If white cottony growth on the mouth sometimes spreads to the gills and other parts, then your fish has MOUTH FUNGUS.

If the fish's eyes protrude from an inflamed eye socket, then your fish has POP-EYE.

If your fish exhibits ulcerations on the skin, localized swelled areas, and excessive mucus, and if the fish is constantly trying to rid itself of these parasites by rubbing against aquarium objects, your fish has SKIN FLUKE.

Does your fish swim on its sides, upside-down, or turn somersaults in the water? And can it be found either on the top or the bottom of the tank? Then your fish has SWIM BLADDER DISEASE.

Does your fish have obvious bumps, lumps, or protrusions that sometimes look like a large blister of wart? Then your fish has TUMORS.

Does your fish have large red lesions, boils, dark reddening, and bleeding? Then your fish has ULCERS.

Does your fish have fuzzy areas that grow with a yellow or golden color? Then your fish has VELVET.

the most common parasites among aquarium fish. It should not be taken lightly, as it will kill your fish if given enough time.

This ailment is so common that there are many commercial ich remedies on the market. Many of them are good, so don't buy the cheapest one, buy the best. Follow standard procedures and remove the fish showing the symptoms and treat it in a hospital tank. However, the entire aquarium must be treated as well. Follow the directions carefully.

If an ich treatment is not available to you, raise the aquarium temperature to 85°F and add one teaspoon of salt for every gallon of water in the tank. Give the infected fish in the hospital tank the 10-day saltwater treatment. It is important to kill this organism before it has an opportunity to infest the entire population.

Velvet (highly contagious)

The parasite Oodinium causes a golden velvety coat on the body and fins, which is referred to as velvet. In orange-colored fish, like goldfish, velvet is sometimes very difficult to detect at first. Commercially produced remedies are best for this parasitic afflic-tion. Some experts use malachite green or the old-fashioned 10-day salt bath. Use the commercial product, but if one is not available, try the salt bath. You should administer some kind of antifungal chemical in the water of the aquarium to disinfect the tank as well.

Hole-in-the-Head Disease (contagious)

This disease is caused by the parasite Hexamita, which is an internal parasite that is harmful when the fish is weakened by stress, age, or poor water quality. It is generally characterized by white stringy feces and enlarged pus-filled sensory pores in the head. Other symptoms include erosion of the skin and muscles that eventually extends to the bones and skull. The lateral line is also a preferred site for these lesions.

Transferring the fish to larger tanks and imple-menting frequent water changes is sometimes enough to cure the fish. Improved nutri-tion supplemented with vitamin C has been known to improve the condition as well. The prescription drug metronidazole prepared in a bath of 50 mg for every gallon of water is effective in treating this disease. It is recommended that you repeat this treatment after three days.

Breeding

As you gain experience in the husbandry of fishkeeping, and as your aquarium becomes more involved, it is inevitable that you will want to get into breeding your fish.

Fish breeding can be simple or complicated, depending on how extensively you wish to breed. It can be as simple as letting your guppies breed in your community tank, or as complicated as breeding in a separate breeding tank. Nonetheless, serious fish breeders ultimately take the latter route if they intend to produce viable young.

Enthusiasts can list a great number of reasons why they chose to breed their fish. Maybe it is just the pleasure associated with knowing your fish are behaving naturally. Home breeding also allows you to produce different varieties of fish. It can also offset the costs of purchasing new fish. Whatever the reason, fish breeding is a vast and complex topic that has been covered by a wide variety of books. Here, I will cover the basics of fish reproduction, spawning behavior, and breeding techniques.

Natural Reproduction

As fish have evolved through millions of years, different species have found different methods of reproduction. The methods, of course, depend upon the type of habitats that the fish were adapted to. For example, fish in the open ocean tend to broadcast large numbers of eggs and sperm into the water column where they develop in the plankton community. They are never seen again by their parents. On the opposite end of the spectrum is the fish from a lake or river where numerous hiding places allow for nest building and parental care.

While the habitats might vary from place to place, one things remains the same—it takes two to tango! The gonads which pro-

Fish Farming!

Unlike 20 or 30 years ago, many tropical fish these days are actually bred here in the United States, at places known either as fish farms or more properly as hatcheries. Most of them are in the South. They vary from place to place. Some use natural waterways and others use pools. They are large operations and are expensive to run. They supply a large portion of the tropical fish sold in the United States today.

duce eggs and sperm (testes and ovaries) are internal in fish, lying inside the abdominal cavity. For this reason, it is not always easy to tell the sexes apart. Live-bearing fish are the exception.

Live-Bearers—The Live Performance

The scientific term for live-bearing species is "viviparous." Not many fish in the fish hobbyist's world are live-bearers. Live-bearers give birth to living young. In general, with live-bearing fishes, males and females mate, and the sperm is transferred to the females via specialized pelvic fins called gonopodia or claspers, depending on the species. The ovarian eggs are fertilized internally and develop within the female for a period of days, weeks, or months, depending on the species. Live-bearing females then give birth to a relatively low number of fry. Those fry are at an advanced stage of development and do not require a lot of parental care. Since the female is able to store the sperm in her body for several months at a time, a live-bearing female can go on to produce multiple broods on her own. There are fourteen families of live-bearing fish, and many are sharks and rays. In the tropical fish world there are four families of live-bearers.

Egg-Layers—Eggs-alent Beginnings

The vast majority of fish are egg-layers. Egg-laying species are referred to as "oviparous." Generally speaking, the fish in this group reproduce by means of fertilizing the eggs outside of the female's body. The eggs are deposited or released into the water where they are fertilized by the male. To sustain development over a period of time, the eggs of these species contain large amounts of yolk. Depending on the species, the embryos develop within the egg for a period of time, ranging from days to months. This is a very dangerous time for the eggs. During this time and immediately after hatching, these fish are extremely susceptible to predation. Fry are not only sought out by carnivores, but by omnivores, as well. These are a yummy, live, nutritious treat. Therefore, oviparous species generally release very large numbers of eggs to insure the survivorship of some of their young. The theory that mother nature subscribes to here is that there is power in numbers. There is also a tendency among these fish to protect and care for their eggs and fry to increase survivorship.

Getting to Know You

In the human world, it takes a long time to get to this point. There's the first date—usually a safe lunch. Then lots of excuses in case you don't like each other. Or you move on to the second date. Maybe dinner and a movie. Some dark little restaurant. Candlelit, with violins. Good food and wine. And l'amour. It's all terribly inefficient, but we do it anyway.

Natural reproduction in fish is quite different and is usually stimulated by a variety of natural conditions. Different areas and seasons encourage fish to mate at different times of the year. In temperate areas where seasonal changes occur, fish have a tendency to reproduce in the spring and summer when the temperature is highest, days are longest, and food is plentiful. In tropical areas, fish will reproduce all year long because these factors do not change greatly. For most freshwater tropical fishes, however, this may not be the case. Fish in freshwater lakes and streams may not be subject to large variations in temperature, but they can experience changes in rainy and dry seasons, changes in day length, and changes in water chemistry (pH, hardness). These factors can combine to trigger breeding several times a year. If you intend to become a serious fish breeder, you will need to mimic the natural conditions which stimulate fish breeding. In other words, you have to trick them.

In nature, predation is a part of life. And it is certainly part of the reproductive cycle. There is a point where young fish are expected to "leave the nest," regardless of whether they are born or hatched. In the former, this generally occurs right after birth. For oviparous species, the young may be protected to a certain size and then they move away. If a young fish enters an area which is inhabited by an adult fish, the adult may assume it is not her own and she will probably eat it. This is a survival strategy which has evolved to insure survival of her own kind. Similarly, weak or sickly young may stay close to their mother, where they are also likely to

Live-Bearers Aren't Mammals

Some fish species bear live young; others lay eggs. However, those that bear live young are not considered mammals, because they still use gills to breathe. Many of the fish listed here also do not nurse their young, another feature of mammals.

Nature, however, does provide examples of "fish" that are actually mammals: whales and dolphins. These breathe air, do not have gills, bear live young, and nurse them as well.

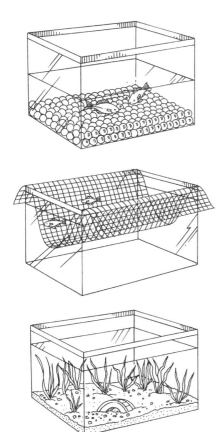

Breeding Setups

be consumed. This behavior leads to greater energy supply for the next brood and again insures survival of the species. Another thing that will cause a parent to eat its young could be a drastic change in environmental conditions.

Reproduction in the Aquarium

When you are considering breeding your fish in your own home, there are many factors that must be taken into account. The idea is that you are trying to mimic the tell-tale signs of the fish's natural environment. You must consider the type of reproduction and the natural conditions that will trigger spawning. You also need to consider the parental care and behavior patterns, too. You must take into account whether the fish is a live-bearer or egg-layer and what type of egg-layer. You must consider the natural requirements of your fish that will not only initiate breeding, but will maximize survival of the young. Finally, you must know when the adult is most likely to consume their young and separate them from each other. Even considering the best of aquatic parents, there comes some time in a young fish's life that the parents will expect them to leave the nest. Either they move out, or they become dinner.

The Breeding Tank or Love Shack

Many species of fish that are kept by hobbyists, particularly the live-bearers, will breed right in the aquarium. There's no telling how successful they'll be. However, the serious breeder usually sets up a separate tank. These are called breeder or spawning tanks. The idea of these tanks is twofold. You can select the prospective parents and breed a better specimen of fish, like they do with dogs. And you can insure the survival of the young fry. These tanks will allow you to establish special tank conditions that will trigger spawning, and it will isolate the parents and the fry so that they can be closely monitored. Some species of fish, like cichlids, become extremely aggressive and territorial when they are breeding. Moving these fish to a breeding tank will spare your other fish the grief associated with this behavior. The breeding tank should be set up according to the type of fish you intend to breed.

These tanks do not have to be well decorated. They will have to be filtered, heated, and aerated. Tank size, gravel, plants, decorations, heating, and filtration requirements will vary according to species. In most cases plants are useful. In general, the types of plants and gravel will depend on whether the fish is a live-bearer or an egg-layer. In most cases, filtration should be kept simple. Large power filters will suck delicate fry to a certain death. A box filter or small power filter with fine screens over the intakes will suffice in the breeding tank. Especially in a breeding tank, make sure there's good aeration.

Parents and the Family Tree

Be sure to pick good stock to breed. Too many times a beginner breeds a pair without thinking. They usually don't breed two better specimens of the species and end up with dull-looking fry. For all the work that this will cause, you really should take care to breed the two best-looking specimens you can buy.

When you breed, you want to produce viable, healthy offspring, so you must start with excellent parent fish! You should choose as carefully as possible. Select fish that are healthy and energetic with flawless form, coloration, and finnage. In most cases, it is best if the parents are not related since indiscriminate inbreeding will result in inferior offspring. There are exceptions to this when you are trying to perfect a certain variety or strain of fish, such as goldfish or guppies.

Culling

This part is going to sound heartless, but again, nature has always done it to insure the survival of a species. You should cull inferior offspring. If you are going to raise your fry for sale or for further breeding, don't waste time and energy raising inferior fish. You should always cull those fish that are deformed or unable to function well. In nature, these fish are always culled out. Remove deformed or undersized offspring and feed them to other fish.

Love Is in the Air

Few tropical fish mate for life, if any. In some cases, they will mate with multiple partners insuring that the eggs will be fertilized.

Green discus, on the other hand, pair up and seem to mate for life. They are excellent parents and raise their young together.

Live-Bearers

Almost all of the fish that are live-bearers in the freshwater species are relatively peaceful community tank members. Mollies, guppies, swordtails, and platys are live-bearing species that you are likely to have in your first aquarium. As we have already explained, the sexes in these are readily distinguishable by the presence of a gonopodium on the male. In addition, the males tend to be brightly colored, while the females of these species tend to have a more drab coloration. Gravid (pregnant) females are also easy to spot because of their bulging abdomen. As we pointed out earlier, many female live-bearers can store sperm and will, therefore, give birth to multiple broods from a single mating. Young can be produced every few weeks and brood sizes can be quite large. A live-bearing mother can have a brood of up to one hundred fry!

Small Fry in a Community of Fishes

As with certain egg-layers, these fish will have little problem mating and giving birth to fry in your community aquarium. Breeding in a community tank presents its own problems. Again, predation rears its ugly head. Most or all of the young will be consumed by other fish if a large amount of cover is not provided for the fry. The best way to prevent is to separate the gravid female into a spawning tank. Or you can insert a commercially produced tank divider.

While tank dividers solve some problems, they can amplify others or create totally new ones. A tank divider is simply a piece of fine-holed plastic that fits into the aquarium, thereby dividing it into two separate sections. The gravid female can be placed in one section, and the other fish can remain in the main section. The divider allows the passage of water, but not the fry, between sections. The problem lies in the fact that you must have a large enough aquarium to be able to commit a section to breeding live-bearers. Also, tank conditions cannot be modified to meet the requirements of the young and at the same time not disrupt the rest of the community. Nonetheless, in a pinch, the tank divider will suffice until the breeding tank can be established.

Breeding Tips

Live-bearers are usually the easiest to breed the first time around. Guppies are especially easy and they are very hardy.

Live from a Breeding Tank Near You

Do most beings want a lot of folks around when they give birth? No, although some humans do. Nature isn't as fond of the group experience when it comes to birth. Fish especially would like to be far from other fish, as they are trying to pass on their traits to their progeny, not feed their progeny to their competitors.

So that she may give birth to her young without endangerment, the gravid female is placed in a breeding tank by herself. Gruesome though it may sound to us, even with live-bearers, you need to protect these young from their mother. The mothers are not exempt from an easy meal either. To protect the small fry, you should have a heavily vegetated tank. The young fry will use these plants as protection. Floating plants are the most ideal for this purpose.

Some experts use the spawning trap. They are easily found, and can be bought at your local pet store. The spawning trap is a fine-meshed "cage" that fits into the tank. How does it work? The gravid female is first placed into the trap. Once there, she will give birth to her young. While the hungry, struggling mother is restrained via the mesh, the tiny fry can pass through the screen-like gauze to safety. After the female has given birth to her young, allow her to rest for a couple days separately before returning her to the main aquarium. You can't put the small fry into the community tank any time soon. Without question, the minute fish stands a very high risk of being eaten. You must have enough patience to wait out time. Patience will reward you with fry that grow to adulthood, and will be able to take care of themselves. You must wait until the babies are of comparable size before putting them into the community tank. You should wait approximately 6 months before introducing these fish into the adult community aquarium.

Laying an Egg
(Doing It the Old-Fashioned Way)

This brings us to the age-old question: Which came first, the fish or the egg? One of the most famous examples of egg-laying fish is the salmon (although you cannot keep one in an aquarium). Their eggs are used for one variety of that expensive and most sought-after

Definition Please: Milt

Milt is a milky fluid secreted by male fish to fertilize fish roe, or eggs.

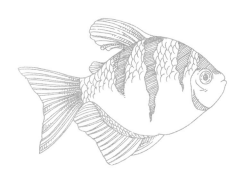

of all delicacies: caviar. Sturgeon's eggs are also used for caviar. While man views caviar as a great and expensive treat, salmon and sturgeon see it as a gruesome end to their descendants.

It's important to note that the vast group of fish can be further divided based on how they deposit or release their eggs. In large part, how each of these three groups lays their eggs, will largely determine how you set up your breeding tank. We have divided the egg-layers into three groups: (1) egg-scatterers, (2) egg-depositers and buriers, and (3) nest-builders and mouth-brooders.

Scrambled Eggs

Fish that expel their eggs and milt throughout the tank are called egg-scatterers. Fish that use this method usually spawn in schools or pairs. The fertilized eggs will float in the current or fall to the bottom among the gravel and stones, after they have been mixed with milt in the column of water. Many of these eggs remain unguarded. Obviously, this is a method of reproduction that has served many species well. In the wild, these eggs are carried far and wide. And while they risk being eaten in a wide range of places, because the eggs span far and wide, there is greater chance for some small amount of fry to survive. This is one of the most difficult groups to breed. Some barbs and some tetra are scatterers. By the way, one of the main predators could be mom or dad.

Egg-scatterers need to be put in the mood. They require a little coaxing. Many authorities agree that one of the best ways to breed egg-scatterers is to condition the sexes separately. After both have been prepared, you should place them together in the spawning tank. Check the special water quality requirements of the species you intend to spawn. Make sure your spawning tank matches these requirements. For example, some fish, like cardinal tetras, require some change in water chemistry to initiate spawning. In this case, the change would be slightly acidic pH and softer water.

One of the things you want to do is prepare to prevent the egg-scatterers from eating their fry. There are two ways to do this. Some hobbyists cover the bottom of the tank with glass marbles so that eggs may fall between them. This system works well, because it prevents the parents from eating them, since they are not known to move gravel in the same way a strong goldfish might. Feathery plants will also provide suitable cover for these eggs.

You might refer to this method as the dragnet method. You need to drape a piece of fine mesh netting in the water. Then you place the spawning fish in the tank. When the eggs are scattered, they fall through the mesh. In that way, they are held away from the mouths of the hungry parents.

No matter which method you use, the parents should be removed from the breeding tank as soon as the breeding is over.

The Savings Plan

Some fish lay their eggs on flat surfaces or in vegetation. These fish are called egg-depositers. Rocks and fine-leafed plants are ideal surfaces for these species. First, the female deposits her eggs. Then the eggs are fertilized by the male. In most cases, egg-depositers will guard their eggs and fry. This group includes some of the cichlids, like the angelfish, killifish, rainbow fish, as well as catfish like the corydoras.

Depending on the species, the breeding tank for egg-depositers will vary. Killifish and rainbow fish prefer fine-leafed plants or spawning mops. Flat rocks, broad-leafed plants, and flower pots should dominate the breeding tank when breeding cichlids and catfish. Some hobbyists remove the eggs attached to the surface of a stone or spawning mop so that they can be hatched in another tank. Despite the fact that these, in large part, tend to be more caring parents, eventually you'll need to remove the spawning pair. Make sure to do some research to see what kind of fish you are attempting to breed and acquaint yourself with their habits.

Buried Treasure

Some fish will lay their eggs and bury them in the soft substrate. These are called egg-buriers. Killifish are the most well known of all the egg-buriers. The best way to accommodate these fish is to provide suitable soft substrate like peat so that they can bury their eggs. Some aquarists recommend that the eggs and substrate be removed, dried, and stored for several weeks before hatching.

Cannibals! In My House?

It might sound like something out of a weird science fiction movie, but sometimes both the mother and father have to be separated from their young. Some species tend to eat their young. So it's important to know whether the breed you're chosen must be separated or not.

Nesting

While nesting is always popular, these are the folks who started the craze. Nest builders include many species of fish that dig holes or small pits in the gravel. Then they deposit their eggs there. And voilà, you have a nest, or what some hobbyists call a den. Many cichlid species build these kinds of nests or dens, and they will defend these areas quite aggressively.

There are those who go the Don Ho "Tiny Bubbles" route when it comes to nesting. For example, gouramis build another kind of nest referred to as a bubble nest. The male will construct a bubble nest by expelling air from his mouth. In the case of the Siamese fighting fish, the female will first release her eggs. The male will then deposit them into the bubble nest he has prepared. The eggs will hatch within 48 hours, and then the male will tend and defend the nest. He will guard the den for up to 10 days. If you're thinking that maybe father does know best, think again. As with other species, he should be removed after 10 days before he eats the fry.

The one nice thing about nest builders is that they require little equipment. They don't need netting or spawning mops. The most difficult part of mating these kinds of fish is that they are very picky. Basically, you'll be running a dating service. And since cichlids are very particular about who they want to mate with, you will run into many instances where Harry dislikes Sally very much. These are choosy fish. You should try to keep several juveniles together to allow natural pairing. The pair should then be transferred to a breeding tank by themselves for courtship and spawning. Everyone likes a honeymoon—even fish!

Bubble nest builders require no special breeding setup in the spawning tank. In some species, such as the Siamese fighting fish, the male is very aggressive. In the case of these fish, it's best if the sexes are kept separate, at least until spawning time. A tank divider is very effective in keeping the sexes apart until they are ready for spawning. Females should be removed after spawning while the male tends to the eggs and fry. And you thought "Mommy Dearest" was tough.

Big Mouths

Some fish will actually hold the eggs and fry in their mouths for days or weeks, depending on species. These are called mouth-brooders. This is a very high level of parental care that results in the successful rearing of well-developed fry. The most popular species of mouth-brooders are the African lake cichlids. In some cases, both sexes participate in the parental care. In others, only the females will brood the eggs in her mouth. In general, a female deposits eggs on a flat surface then picks them up into her oral cavity where they are held until they hatch. Fertilization will occur either on the flat surface or while in the female's mouth. After hatching, the fry may continue to seek shelter in her mouth.

Like the nest builders, the breeding tank of the mouth-brooder does not require any special setup. Mostly, they just need a flat surface for the initial egg deposition. There are, however, special water quality considerations that must be maintained when trying to breed some species. Some excellent examples are African lake cichlids.

Feeding the Fry

Different species will need to begin feeding at different times. It's best to do some research before you begin your breeding so that you can be prepared. The fry of live-bearers and mouth-brooders are generally larger and more developed fish. They are usually ready to eat right after separation from their parents. The fry of egg-laying species are different. Many of those will sustain themselves off their yolk sacs for several days after hatching. At this stage, they do not swim but stay on the bottom or remain attached to the spawning substrate. They become free-swimming fry after all their yolk is fully absorbed.

You'll notice when these little ones are hungry. From their groggy start, they will suddenly start actively looking for food. They will begin to dart across the tank, back and forth. It is very important that you try to feed the fry at this point. This should be done three times a day: once in the morning, once at midday, and once at night.

Definition Please: Fry

Fry is the word used by aquarists to describe the baby fish or hatchlings during the first 4 weeks of its life. They are very small, and sometimes take a lot of careful inspection before you actually see them. Fry are to fish what a litter and puppies are to dogs. Fry can identify either a single new fish or a group of small fish.

Oh, the Places You'll Go

When you are using a mating tank, make sure not to use an under-gravel filter or a box filter. Use a power filter with a screen on the intake tube. Many a small fry has been sucked down under the gravel or lost in a box or power filter. Take pre-cautions so as not to lose any.

Infusoria, the Breakfast of Champions

What you feed your fry mainly depends on their size. The larger fry of live-bearers can handle larger foods, while the tiny fry of some egg-layers will require microscopic aquatic organisms called infusoria. Infusoria is a bacterial culture that is highly recommended for most larval fish. It is easily digestible and very nutritious. If we have Cheerios or oatmeal, then the fish equivalent is infusoria. Another added benefit of infusoria is that you can make it at home. You should begin doing this when the eggs are first released from the female.

To make infusoria, fill a jar approximately three-quarters full with boiled water that has been cooled. Add a banana peel or three or four lettuce leaves (it's best when the lettuce is bruised). With the lid off, place the jar in a relatively sunny spot.

Warning! This stuff is going to stink! And you thought your three-day-old gym socks were bad. It's like someone took the garbage and left it out instead of throwing it away. So don't put the jar in a heavily used room!

For the first few days the water will be cloudy, and the jar will smell awful! After a couple more days, the water will clear up and, while it won't smell good, it will have a sweetness you can easily detect. Now you're cooking! This is infusoria! You can use a turkey baster or a spoon to feed the infusoria into the tank or you can just pour it in. Remember, only feed these fish as much as they can eat in five minutes, twice a day. Infusoria needs to be made every two to three days to keep feeding your fry without running out.

Toddler Foods: Please, a Shrimp Cocktail for the Child

Eventually, all the little babies need more adult-like foods. They don't use spoons or forks, but they need something to chew on. Nope, you cannot give them teething biscuits. The next step on the feeding ladder in terms of size are freshly hatched brine shrimp (*Artemia salina*). Use the steps that I outlined in Chapter 2 to raise brine shrimp at home. Be sure to start the culture two to three days before the fry are due to become free-swimming. This will be difficult to gauge with live-bearing fish. It's best to have a batch of brine shrimp going when the female's abdomen begins to swell. Each batch of shrimp should last about two to three days. Another thing hobbyists recommend is to be sure to rinse the brine shrimp in fresh water to remove excess salt before feeding them to your fry.

As your small fry grow to larger sizes, you will be able to vary their diets with a wide range of foods. Commercially produced flake foods crumbled to small particles can also be fed to your young fish. Increase the size of the foods that you feed your fry as they get larger. Try to feed live foods when possible because many experts agree that a high protein diet is essential to this stage of development. Tubifex, bloodworms, microworms, and daphnia are all recommended foods for fry. Caution must be taken with some of these foods because you don't want to introduce a disease to these young creatures. At this age, like with human children, these fry are not strong enough to fight off disease or fungus associated with certain live foods. You can never be too careful with kids. Eventually, they will grow to adulthood, and should follow the diets recommended in the feeding section of this book.

Fish Trivia

Fish didn't begin to develop jaws until approximately 80 million years ago!

Culling

As your fish mature you must keep in mind to cull inferior fish. Specialty breeds of fish, such as goldfish or guppies, are culled routinely to produce the desired variety. Culling is essential only if you have limited space or if you are trying to raise perfect fish for sale or display. If these are not your intentions, keep as many as you desire for your own personal interests.

Depending on the species, you will eventually be able to introduce the young fish into your community aquarium. Make sure that you don't put fry too small into a tank, or else, after all your hard work, they'll get eaten anyway. New fish introduced into an established tank should never be smaller than any of the others already in your tank.

CHAPTER SEVEN

Saltwater Tropical Fish

Two Old Salts

Years ago, back during the Punic Wars, when we were both kids, keeping a saltwater tank was by far the most expensive and difficult thing in the world to do. Anyone who actually kept one going without losing all of his or her fish within the first year was considered an aquarium god.

Today, this is not the case. Bitter as we may be over the ease of keeping a saltwater tank these days, we can safely say that you don't need to be Jacques Cousteau to have one in your home.

That said, you should have at least a year or two of freshwater experience before you go slogging into the saltwater world.

Introduction

There are many similarities between starting a marine tank and a freshwater tank. In order to set up a marine aquarium, you will have to read the first section thoroughly. However, you should read this section first! Marine fish require many of the same things that their freshwater cousins do—plenty of room, good filtration, consistent temperature, aeration, consistent maintenance, and a good feeding program. However, there are some substantial differences, i.e., plants (other than coral and algae, there are no plants in a marine tank), a small amount of equipment, water consistency, gravel, and diseases are just some of the things that are different.

Read this section thoroughly to understand the subtle differences you need to know before starting. There will be some repetition, though we've tried to keep it to a minimum.

Chemistry 101: Saltwater vs. Freshwater

You may think you know the difference between freshwater and saltwater, but the odds are you don't. And the odds are greater that you don't know why it matters.

There is one essential difference between freshwater and marine fishes: marine fishes are able to thrive in their saltwater habitat. Generally speaking, freshwater fishes seem a hardier species then their saltwater counterparts. Many experts pointed out that freshwater fish have better adapted to the rapid and sizable changes in temperature in their environment, and this has helped them to better withstand changes in their environment, as opposed to their saline cousins. Because many marine fishes come from warm, coral reefs, where they are not usually subjected to vast changes, but are more acclimated to their rather stable environments, hobbyists have a tougher assignment ahead of them. The problem is that marine fish do not adjust well to differences in water quality or temperature fluctuations. Of course, the home aquarium is more prone to temperature changes. Thus, marine fish need someone who's going to spend a lot of time worrying about them.

What is fresh water? Fresh water is the water we drink when we are thirsty. What is salt water? Salt water is water that has substantially higher concentrations of sodium chloride. Sodium chloride is salt! While sodium chloride is the most prevalent dissolved component in salt water, it is by no means the only component. There are many, some variations of salt and other chemical compounds, too. The amount of these dissolved "salts" in water is referred to as its salinity. All living things must balance their internal chemistry within very precise limits in order to survive. The salinity of cells must be maintained in the face of external salinity gradients. In the process called "osmosis," pure water flows through cell membranes from areas of low salinity to areas of high salinity. Fish are surrounded by the media in which they live and are therefore subjected to salinity gradients and the forces of osmosis. Fish in fresh water are constantly subjected to an influx of water because their cells are more saline than their environment. On the other hand, marine fish are always threatened by the loss of water from their cells because their environment is more saline.

Biology 101: Freshwater Fish vs. Marine Fish

So you used to sleep through biology? Now, you'll begin to understand why it was so important. Now, a pet's life will hang in the balance, so you'd better pay attention. No doodling, passing notes, or watching the clock.

Anatomically, the two groups of fishes are very similar in appearance. However, they have also evolved two very different ways of living in these chemically different environments. Freshwater fish need to maintain their internal salinity. What do they do to keep that balance within their bodies? Freshwater fish drink very little water and produce large quantities of dilute urine. Marine fish are almost completely opposite. Most marine fishes drink large quantities of water. And they eliminate salts in small amounts of highly concentrated urine and feces, as well as at the gills. Sharks and their close relatives, rays, are exceptions to this pattern in marine fish. These species concentrate urea in their tissues and blood to offset the loss of water. The ability to maintain internal salinity compared with that of the surrounding external water is called osmoregulation.

Fish Trivia

The earliest known fishes were the jawless Arandapis. Their bony plates have been found in Middle Ordovician strata which dates back 500 million years ago!

Why is all of this important to you? It is important to understand the basic principles of osmoregulation because it has significant implications for fish held in captivity. For example, now you understand why freshwater fish cannot be kept in salt water—because their bodies cannot adapt to the change. Another thing that's important to understand is that since marine fish must expend a lot of energy to prevent the loss of water and excrete salt, they require a lot of food and good health. Last and most importantly, marine fish drink large amounts of water. If that is the case, then the water quality must be very good. Abrupt changes in salinity will disturb the internal chemistry of marine fishes. That's why marine fishkeeping can be more difficult than the maintenance of a freshwater aquarium. It's a little more difficult, but not impossible. It's gotten easier in recent years than it was 10 or more years ago. And, of course, the greater the challenge, the more rewarding the sense of accomplishment when we refer to establishing a stable marine aquarium.

Anatomy

There are many similarities between freshwater fish and saltwater fish, despite the differences that allow marine fish to live in seawater. It's important to take a closer look at the unique adaptations of fish that have allowed them to live so successfully in the aquatic environment. Because there are no less than 12,000 kinds of marine fish, it is difficult to describe the "typical" marine fish. However, for the most part, all fishes have some common attributes. These similarities include the body shape, fins, scales, and swim bladder.

The Aquarium

Everyone talks about the old days. Well, according to tropical fish, the old days weren't so good. In the not-so-distant past, most tropical fish that were kept by hobbyists were originally captured from their native homes. This created a problem. In doing this, the pet industry contributed to the degradation of tropical habitats. It also depleted the populations of many species.

Thankfully, for both the fish and humanity, we are much better off today. Through breakthroughs in breeding in captivity and other modern husbandry techniques, we have taken tremendous pressure off natural stocks. Today, many of the common freshwater aquarium species are bred in captivity. Selective breeding has also given us hardier fish. Today's freshwater tropical fish are more adaptive to the varying water conditions of the aquarium and temperature fluctuations.

The Call of the Wild

Some of nature's most beautiful marine fish are not so lucky. Even today, while marine fish represent only a fraction of the pet fish sold, almost all of the saltwater species are harvested from the wild. Modern husbandry techniques have not yet been able to emulate or recreate the necessary environment to help commercial hatcheries supply a steady stream of hardy marine life for the vast pet industry. That's why it's so incredibly important to value the precious lives you are charged with when you take on a saltwater aquarium. The most popular saltwater fish come primarily from coral reef ecosystems.

Truth be known, we are not yet in danger of harming the coral reef systems around the world. Many coral reefs around the world, if properly managed, can be harvested without doing any real damage. Most coral reef systems are extremely productive. This is because of their size and the fact that many of their inhabitants are extremely competitive. It would be nice not to purchase fish that may have been harvested in areas that do not adhere to sound conservation of natural reefs, but unfortunately it is not possible to know.

If you are an experienced freshwater aquarist, you will learn that marine fish are less tolerant of sub-par water quality. You must be meticulous in the quality of your care. It's a good idea to keep records of all your experiences.

A Sample Community Saltwater Tank

The amount of fish per gallon is less than it is in freshwater. You cannot crowd a marine tank. You will not succeed, especially if you are not experienced. As an example, a 40-gallon aquarium should contain no more than 10 inches of fish for the first six months. These may be comprised of one 3-inch queen angel, two 1-inch clown fish, one 2-inch regal tang, one 1-inch bicolor blenny, and three 1-inch Beau Gregorys. After 6 months, additional fish may gradually be added to increase the total number of inches to 20.

Seawater Composition

How many oceans are there? Five! What are they? The Atlantic, the Pacific, the Indian, the Mediterranean, and the Arctic. Water covers more than 70 percent of the earth's surface. Most folks know that one. However, one of the most amazing things is that despite the vast differences in location, the chemical composition of seawater is extremely consistent throughout the world. It is also surprising that though seawater is 96 percent pure water (H_2O), it also contains many dissolved minerals. These dissolved minerals consist mainly of sodium and chlorine (85 percent), while magnesium, sulphates, calcium, and potassium comprise another 13 percent. Bicarbonate and 68 other components make up the remainder in trace quantities.

Now, of course, you're thinking of doing something that you really shouldn't. The obvious thing for any rookie is to try to obtain natural seawater for your new aquarium. However, there are several reasons you should not do this. Instead, you should use one of the synthetic salt mixes that are readily available at your pet store. Why, you ask? The answer is complicated.

While the composition of water basically doesn't change from place to place around the world, what lives in it does. The sea life from ocean to ocean and sea to sea varies tremendously. First, you probably do not live in the tropics. If this is true, and if you intend to maintain a tropical aquarium, your local seawater will be colder than sea water from a tropical region. The colder water will contain species of plankton that are adapted to these temperatures. This is why the water off New Jersey doesn't look anything like the water off Aruba. Elevating the temperature to tropical levels will cause these organisms to die or rapidly proliferate. What results is polluted or poor quality water—and of course, dead or diseased fish.

Second, even if you wanted to keep marine fish suited to your region, have you ever lifted 40 gallons of water? How about 10? It's heavy, heavier than most other elements. The logistics involved in traveling back and forth to the seashore for large quantities of water will seem, at best, futile and silly. Many of you don't even have the opportunity to go near an ocean.

Now, if none of these things seem sensible enough to stop you, maybe you could consider this last problem. It's called pollution. There are no guarantees that your water source is free of pollution. Seemingly clean seawater may contain high levels of toxic compounds and metals. There are no test kits available at your pet store—none that will detect pollution, anyway. Why take any chances?

Welcome to the wonderful world of science. The science of chemistry has yielded salt mixes that mimic the marine environment without the potential toxins. They are perfectly suitable for the home aquarium. And best of all, they are safe! These mixes can be dissolved in ordinary tap water (which presumably you have plenty of) when you set up the aquarium.

Salinity

Earlier we discussed the important relationship between marine and saltwater fish. Marine species are adapted to a specific level of dissolved salts in the water that they live in. So, it doesn't take a genius to figure out that the amount of dissolved salts or "salinity" of the water has to be maintained at this level. How in the world do you gauge that? To directly measure salinity, you need equipment that can sometimes be expensive for the average hobbyist. However, another way to gauge salinity is to measure the "specific gravity". What is specific gravity? Specific gravity refers to the ratio of densities of seawater to pure water at various temperatures. For example, a specific gravity of 1.031 is 1.031 times denser than seawater.

What do you use to measure specific gravity? You use a hydrometer to measure the gravity in your aquarium. This is a very important piece of equipment. The marine aquarist needs to use this every couple of days. There are two types of hydrometers: the floating tube type or the needle type. The needle type is easier to

A Special Stash

You should always mix up additional properly balanced salt water for water changes and emergencies. Batches of seawater should be stored in non-metallic containers in cool, dark places until needed. Five gallons is always a good amount. Make sure you mark these containers properly, as you don't want else mistaking these for drinkable water.

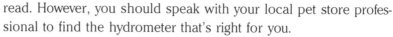

Home Brewer or Aquarist: You Decide

A hydrometer is a very popular instrument used in a number of other industries. Some hobbyists, though, who also use hydrometers are home brewers. Home brewers use the hydrometer to check the specific gravity of their beer before fermentation and after. By doing this, they are able to gauge the alcoholic content of the beer they're brewing. Here's a hint, though. Don't put your beer in the fish tank or your fish in the beer tank—neither is going to do very well.

read. However, you should speak with your local pet store professional to find the hydrometer that's right for you.

So, you're asking, what's the right reading for my aquarium? Generally speaking, you want to establish and maintain a range between 1.021 and 1.024. More importantly, it should be maintained at a very specific level within this range. It's an absolute must to know that even minor fluctuations in your aquarium's salinity can cause problems for your fascinating new pets.

Why Does the Salinity Change?

There are many different reasons or ways that the salinity of the water can be altered. Many are very subtle and take place over a few days or weeks. They are unseen and, left unmonitored, will go undetected by the human, until one day you come home and your fish are no longer of this world. One of the major culprits in the battle of maintaining salinity is evaporation.

Evaporation of salt from the tank is without a doubt the single largest factor in the quality of the water. Here's the scenario. First, the water evaporates in a marine aquarium. Remember, the water evaporates, not the salts. The salts remain in the solution, and the water becomes more concentrated. What's the result? The salinity and specific gravity have become increased. You must constantly monitor water levels in the aquarium to prevent these fluctuations.

Evaporation is easily remedied by adding fresh water to the tank, not additional salt water. If you add salt water, what happens? You don't return the tank to the proper salinity levels. You're adding more salt, as well as water. It's still 40 gallons. But now you have all the salt you once needed, re-hydrated, plus the extra you had in the salty water. Don't wait until levels have significantly dropped before you top off the tank; instead, do so regularly with small quantities from the tap.

Of course, there are other, less common ways in which salts can be lost. As waters evaporate, some salts are carried with the gases that are leaving the surface. These gases can leave deposits on parts of the tank. Crystallization on the hood and other fixtures may occur as well as losses from the protein skimmer.

What's the best way to fight this battle regarding salinity? The hydrometer. Keep an eye on the hydrometer! Evaporation will continue no matter what you do. You must be just as constant.

pH

We've covered this before, but we're going to do just a little recap before we explain its importance in a marine aquarium. The pH refers to the amount of acidity of the water. It ranges from 0 to 14 with a pH of 7 being neutral, a pH of 1 being very acidic, and a pH of 14 being very alkaline. This scale is logarithmic, meaning that each number is 10 times stronger than the preceding number. For example, a pH of 2 is 10 times more acidic than a pH of 3 and 100 times more acidic than a pH of 4.

Why is this important? Because, salt water is more alkaline than fresh water. If you had a freshwater aquarium, you probably maintained the pH within the range of 6.5 to 7.5. On the other hand, the pH of seawater is about 8.2, so it's imperative you maintain in the aquarium between 8.1 and 8.3.

pH is influenced by a variety of factors. The amount of carbon dioxide and fish wastes in the water are big factors. The water will acidify, and the pH will drop with the accumulation of either or both of these. Commercial test kits that are very simple to use are available at most pet stores. You should use one of these kits every week or two to detect any changes. An abrupt drop in pH may be indicative of an increase of carbon dioxide or nitrogenous fish wastes. A great countermeasure is to increase aeration or do a partial water change. This will be necessary to alleviate the problem before the lives of your marine fish will be compromised.

The Nitrogen Cycle

Again, we covered this in the freshwater section in depth. The nitrogen cycle applies almost exactly as it does in the freshwater scenario. Marine fish are living creatures. They obtain energy from food and burn that energy with the help of oxygen, which they breathe from the water. Of course, these processes generate waste products, as they do in all other living animals. These are returned

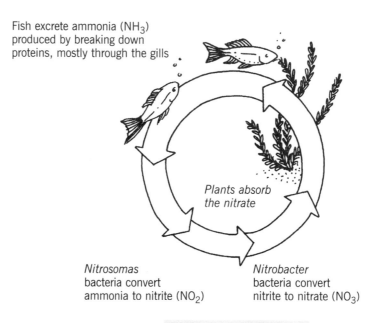

Fish excrete ammonia (NH_3)
produced by breaking down
proteins, mostly through the gills

*Plants absorb
the nitrate*

Nitrosomas
bacteria convert
ammonia to nitrite (NO_2)

Nitrobacter
bacteria convert
nitrite to nitrate (NO_3)

THE NITROGEN CYCLE

to the environment via the gills and the anus. The primary wastes
are carbon dioxide and nitrogenous compounds. Some of these
compounds include ammonia, and are extremely toxic to fish.
These wastes must be removed from the aquarium. Carbon dioxide
generally leaves the water through aeration at the surface. It also
occurs via photosynthesis by aquarium algae. Toxic nitrogenous
compounds, like ammonia and nitrite, are converted to less toxic
compounds via the nitrogen cycle.

This cycle is important because it helps to rid your tank of
wastes that are generated by its inhabitants. It's also important
because it helps feed algae, which, kept in check, is also a positive
in your tank. And besides, the nitrogen cycle must be maintained
because otherwise you'll spend lots of money on fish that will
suffer ill health, and suffer diseases that might cause death.

Foamy Fun—Protein Skimmers For Everyone

Today, the protein skimmer is commercially available to marine hobbyists at a reasonable cost. However, in the not-so-distant past, the protein skimmer really was the domain of the expert and aquarist. This is definitely one of the secret weapons used by the modern marine aquarist in maintaining a healthy marine environment.

The protein skimmer is not some kind of pool man that comes by a couple times a week. It is a piece of equipment that utilizes a process known as "foam fractionation" to remove dissolved waste products from the water. It's a simple enough contraption. It is a tube that hangs in the back of your tank. Air is pushed to the bottom of the tube, generating a cloud of very fine bubbles which flow to the surface. Protein and other wastes adhere to the bubbles and travel to the surface. As the bubbles spread out on the surface of the water, the wastes adhering to them collect in a removable cup. Your job is to empty the cup on a regular schedule. If you let it build up, it doesn't do its job as well, and the careful balancing act you're trying to maintain will fall apart. Most of the inexpensive models are driven by an air pump. This is perfectly normal, because it moves water through the unit, aerating it.

The protein skimmer is incredibly valuable. It can remove considerable amounts of waste. It is highly recommended for the beginner as well the advanced hobbyist.

Water Management Systems

What can't they do with modern technology these days? Today it is possible to buy complete water management systems for your new aquarium that are state of the art. Are they expensive? No, but they're not cheap. These new complete systems incorporate the biological filtration of trickle filters with chemical and mechanical filtration. They also include heaters, aerators, nitrate removers, and protein skimmers. These powerful maintenance machines represent the future of water quality management, especially for the marine hobbyist. They are efficient, keep the water circulating, heated and aerated, and maintain a constant filtration. Especially for marine

A Foamy Tip

To get the best performance out of your protein skimmer, make sure that it extends the height of the tank. That maximizes efficiency. It also adds to the water flow.

aquarists, it may be worth looking into one of these new systems. Ask about them before you buy any components.

Water Disinfection

What is this? Do your new fish have to be inoculated? No, but the water has to be treated in order to remove any unseen bacteria or other possible illness-causing elements. UV sterilizers and ozonators are two common methods for disinfecting water. Both are commercially available to the home aquarist. Some experts recommend one or both of these for the marine aquarium. Are they necessary? Not really. Should you risk your investment by not doing one or the other? Probably not. However, one or the other is more than enough.

Sterilization? What are we doing, going into an operating room? UV sterilizers are self-contained units that kill some microorganisms that may be harmful to your fishes. It exposes the water to ultraviolet light as it is passes from your power filter to the UV unit, before being returned to the tank. Does this really work? Well, the effectiveness of this method depends on many factors. It must be stated that its utility for the home aquarist has been questioned. UV disinfection is recommended only if you intend to maintain delicate species of fish and only to treat severe outbreaks of disease.

Ozonators produce ozone. Theoretically, ozone kills microorganisms in your aquarium. However, the chemistry of ozone in seawater is poorly understood. Plus, ozone can be harmful to humans. So, what should you do?

You probably don't need it, either.

The Heater

There is little here that is not stated elsewhere in this book, especially in the first section. However, it cannot be overstated how important it is to maintain temperatures with marine fish. Those fish most commonly seen in the marine aquarium are the tropical coral reef species. The term tropical refers to natural habitats where the waters are warm throughout the year. It should come as no surprise, therefore, that it is necessary to maintain your aquarium within a specific temperature range.

EQUIPMENT CHECKLIST FOR
SETTING UP A SALTWATER AQUARIUM

You will note that it is very much the same as for a freshwater setup.
Needed for the first day:

- ❏ Glass aquarium
- ❏ Fish tank stand or furniture with support board
- ❏ Electrical outlet or extension cord
- ❏ Five gallon bucket (never been used)
- ❏ Hood with light or hood and light

- ❏ Gravel
- ❏ Filter
- ❏ Filter medium
- ❏ pH kit
- ❏ Aeration devices
- ❏ Heater algae sponge
- ❏ Backdrop (optional)

Needed after establishment of working environment to maintain a healthy aquarium (2 days to 3 weeks later)

- ❏ Plants (real or artificial)
- ❏ Decorations (coral)
- ❏ Five gallon bucket and siphon hose

- ❏ Vacuum
- ❏ Two nets
- ❏ A much smaller second tank for emergency situations

Under-Gravel Filters and Gravel

Remember, you should always buy some extra gravel. You'll want it when you aquascape your tank. Under-gravel filters sometimes require more gravel when you're trying to do more interesting aquascapes. That way you have sufficient amounts to sculpture the bottom and provide relief.

It is strongly recommended that with any tank created for marine fish, you should use two heaters. You need these in case one heater goes on the fritz. You should also have two heaters to make sure there are no cold spots in the tank, and that the water temperature is as consistent as possible. This really is one of the best ways to spend your money to insure that your fish will live in an environment that will enable them to be spry and healthy.

At what temperature should you keep your tank? This depends greatly on what kind of fish you are going to keep. It is entirely species dependent, and you should consult your local pet dealer or one of many fish encyclopedias available at your local dealer or library. Make sure that you do not mix species that have very different temperature preferences.

Inside the Tank

The majority of marine aquarium inhabitants originate from tropical coral reef habitats. While we encouraged you to create as wild a setting as you desired for your freshwater aquarium, those hobbyists who venture into marine fish tanks are usually more serious. With this being the case, we're going to recommend that you strongly consider trying to decorate your tank like the reef-like ecosystems found in tropical regions around the world. These fish are taken from the wild. To get the most activity out of them, you want to make them feel as comfortable as possible.

Many advanced aquarists often make great efforts to duplicate specific reef systems. Many try to re-create those that might be found in Hawaii or the Caribbean. This can take a lot of effort and time, as well as a lot of experience. Since your basic marine community aquarium will feature a variety of fishes from multiple habitats, it is best to create an aquascape that is pleasing to the human eye as well as pleasing to the fish. This leaves a lot of leeway in choosing the components that you'll use in your aquarium. But remember, you need to meet the habitat needs of your marine fish.

Gravel

As in many fish tanks, the bottom substrate of your aquarium will consist of gravel. But, unlike the gravel in a freshwater aquarium, the gravel used in a saltwater tank must be of a specific type. Calcareous gravel have proven to be the best substrate for the marine aquarium. However, that doesn't mean that there's just one type of gravel. There are many types. These include coral gravel, dolomite, calcite, and crushed oyster shell. These gravel all contain carbonate which is thought to help "buffer" the seawater. Why is that important? Because it maintains pH levels.

If you are using an under-gravel filter, the grain size and gravel depth is very important. The depth of the gravel should be 3 inches. And the average grain size should be about 2 to 5mm (.08 to .2"). If you use an under-gravel filter, remember that your substrate will be the biological filter that drives the nitrogen cycle in your aquarium. Some experts recommend the use of two sizes of gravel together. You should layer the fine gravel on top of the coarse gravel. You can separate them with a plastic mesh or "gravel tidy." This may allow for filtration while minimizing the amount of substrate that can become clogged. The gravel tidy also protects the filter from burrowing tank inhabitants. This really is a very good idea, and is not viewable to the passerby once it is established.

Plants Are For Gardeners, Not Marine Hobbyists

For freshwater aquarists, plants are an integral part of the aquascape. However, there are few plants in coral reefs, from which many of these fish originate. With few exceptions, all of the ocean's plant life are classified in the primitive group known as algae. Remember, algae is a plant.

The term seaweed actually refers to the many-celled forms of algae, and are not common in the beginner's home aquarium. If you really must, plastic seaweeds are available and some marine hobbyists like their plant-like appearance. Experienced aquarists find the various species of Caulerpa algae to be attractive additions to the tank. There's no getting around it though—real marine aquarists decorate mainly with coral and algae.

Real or Artificial: Only Your Pet Dealer Knows For Sure

Here's a hint on how to make your aquarium look as realistic as possible. Let the algae grow on your coral! Once the coral is overgrown with algae, it is virtually indistinguishable from the real thing. Most importantly, fish can't tell the difference either. And who's to know?

Coral

More than plants, the most requested tropical marine decoration is coral. There are two different kinds of coral. There's real coral and artificial coral replicas. These structures give the aquarium a natural look, and they provide excellent shelter for tank inhabitants. They also provide ideal substrate for algal growth. Real coral and other calcareous objects, like shells, also provide the added benefit of buffering the water for pH maintenance.

What is coral? Coral is an almost rock-like substance composed of basically the skeletal remains of millions of living animals that lived as a colony. In a natural coral reef system, the outermost layer of the reef is the living coral colony! As the reef grows, layers are added. In other words, the new coral grows on the remains of the old coral.

Coral reef growth is extremely slow. In many cases, it takes decades to establish itself. Because of this, efforts must be made to protect coral reef systems. Live reefs should not be harvested for the aquarium trade. You can harvest dead coral from the shore that is perfectly suitable for the aquarium after it has been properly cleaned. It is recommended that you boil all coral and any other tank decorations collected from the seashore before you add it to your tank. It is very difficult to determine if the coral has been illegally killed. You will not be able to tell the difference. However, many aquarium stores carry corals which may have been harvested from living reefs.

A great alternative to dead coral is artificial coral replicas. These are becoming increasingly popular and readily available as coral reef protection is increasing worldwide. There is no shame is using artificial coral. These natural-looking synthetics are safe for the aquarium. They provide the same benefits as real coral, however, with the exception of water buffering. Many large commercial aquariums utilize artificial corals to mimic the natural reef system.

What if white's not my color? As you will probably see, most coral that you purchase will be bleached white. Don't worry about it. In a natural setting and a well balanced aquarium, this will not last for long. Algal colonization will add green and brown to the coral, diminishing its sterile look.

What if white *is* my color? Sorry! While some newcomers find the growth of algae over their once-white coral sort of dirty looking, remember, coral isn't white in the real world. In nature it's covered with all kinds of living things—few of which are white. The occasional removal of algae by boiling is recommended if growth becomes excessive or unsightly.

How many cool photos have you seen of beautiful marine aquariums? There are fish darting here and there. Life abounds! These systems are established by hobbyists who often have years of experience in aquarium keeping.

Other Decorations You Can Use

Of course, there are other decorative materials available to the marine hobbyist. Here are a few of them.

Tufa

Tufa is a popular alternative. Tufa is a naturally occurring calcareous rock. It is soft and easy to shape. One of the great things about tufa is that it has all the beneficial attributes of coral, including the buffering of water.

Slate

Slate is more often used by freshwater aquarists. However, it also works in the marine tank! That's no problem. Make sure to clean it thoroughly with an unused scrub brush and water only.

Shells

Everyone thinks of shells when they think of the sea. That's why shells are popular natural additions to the saltwater aquarium. Be sure to boil shells before using them in your tank. Never put an unwashed shell into your tank!

Sea Fans

Sea fans provide "plant-like" decoration to the aquarium, but must be soaked to expose the black skeleton before use. Some experts boil them first. Sea fans or sea plums are made up of both soft and hard coral. They are considered part of the coral family. You need to be delicate with them, as they will fall apart easily.

It's Alive! It's Alive!

If you're a rookie, you shouldn't add live coral to your tank. Just like with live plants for freshwater tanks, you don't need yet another living thing beside the fish to keep alive. Corals are invertebrate animals that have very special needs. They can be extremely difficult to maintain in good health and if they begin to die, can foul the water and endanger the other living things in your tank.

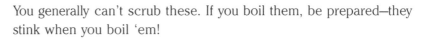

You generally can't scrub these. If you boil them, be prepared—they stink when you boil 'em!

Living Rock

The "living rock" is currently one of the most popular additions to the marine tank. They have become very popular in the aquarium trade. But what is a living rock? Is this from the same guy who came up with the pet rock? Is this some kind of gimmick?

Living rock is actually a piece of calcareous stone, which is harvested from the sea. It is encrusted with many forms of living animals and algae. Small sponges, shrimps, crabs, worms, various species of algae, and a number of microorganisms live on the surface of the rock.

Living rock is not recommended for the beginner. Yes, it is certainly a part of the natural reef ecosystem, like live coral, but it's also very difficult to maintain. Much like coral, keeping these animals alive can be very challenging for the novice. Death of any or all of them will significantly degrade the water quality of the aquarium, causing trouble for other tank inhabitants.

With so many possibilities before you, what should you do? Have fun. Pet stores sell a variety of tank decorations and some come in the forms of plastic or ceramic creations. Other pieces are simply well-selected rocks and stones. No matter what it is that you want to do, or what you want to create, especially for beginners, make sure you purchase them from a pet dealer. By purchasing these tank decorations from the dealer, you are avoiding the addition of toxic substances. You'll also avoid adding unwanted water-modifying agents to your tank. It's also strongly recommended that you avoid the temptation to collect your own rocks. Until you know how to identify each kind of rock, stone, piece of wood, and other marine life, and its influence on the water, you need to stick to the stuff that's not going to cause you any additional problems.

Setting Up the Aquarium

Setting up a marine tank is very much like setting up a freshwater tank. We're going to repeat some of the steps, so that you know the exact order to set up your tank. In this way, you won't need to go back to the first section during the setup.

First, you want to assemble all the components in the area where you plan to place the aquarium. Make sure you have everything. Make sure that you are not lacking any important components. The one thing you don't want is to be well into setup and find that you are missing something. Once you are confident that everything is in order, take the following steps to set up your aquarium.

1. This is primo and most important! Make sure everything is clean. It can't be too clean. Give the gravel, tank, filter, heater, aquarium decorations, and anything else you expect to put in the tank a thorough rinsing with clean warm water. *Never use commercial cleaners!* Some experts use a little salt, but this must be rinsed off with as much water as possible.

   Why should you rinse these items if you bought them from your local pet store? Residues, dirt, and other toxic agents can accumulate on your equipment between the time it is manufactured and the time it gets to your home.

   Also, you should boil some aquarium decorations, such as coral and shells. Make sure to boil them in freshwater only!

   Cleaning your gravel is also very important. Never put unrinsed gravel in your tank. Uncleaned gravel adds dust to the aquarium, making it cloudy. It also makes it unhealthy for your fish. It's easy to clean gravel. First, empty it into a large container, such as a 5-gallon bucket. Then fill the container with water. Thoroughly stir the water and gravel, making sure you've swirled it around as much as possible. Then dump out the water. You're not done, though. Do this several times, until the water that you pour off is clear. Four to five rinsings is necessary for brand new gravel, and sometimes more.

2. Make sure you place the tank on its stand. You want to make sure the aquarium is exactly where you want it to reside. You know how heavy a gallon of water is? You are

Planning Makes Perfect

Before buying any decorations for your aquarium, take the time to design the kind of setting you want to build for your fish. Remember to provide a space where fish can hide or seek shelter. It's also important to plan for sufficient swimming space. Remember to plan for the heaters, filters, and protein skimmers. Be sure to plan for water currents and aeration, too.

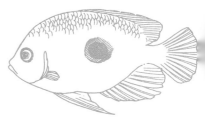

not moving a 10-, 20-, 30-, or 40-gallon tank of water. Once the thing is filled, it is where it's going to stay. This isn't a couch. Do not expect to move the tank once it is filled.

Now, you can begin assembling the interior of your tank. It is time to aquascape your tank. Start with the thoroughly rinsed gravel. Place your under-gravel filter first. Gently pour the gravel into the tank. Remember, coarse gravel first. Then the net. Then the finer gravel. Terrace the gravel so that it is slightly higher in the back than in the front of the tank. This adds a natural field depth to your aquarium.

3. Now for the artsy stuff. This is like laying out the living room of your house. You can play with this for hours. But if you've done your homework, you'll already know what you want and this will go quickly. However, take your time. This should be one of the fun parts of owning an aquarium.

   First, add any larger pieces of coral, rock, etc. Don't attempt to add smaller decorations, yet. If you add the smaller ones now, when you pour the water in, they'll be disturbed by the rushing water, and you'll have to rearrange everything. The large, immovable things get placed in the tank first. Remember to leave spaces for heaters, filters, and other equipment.

4. This is a great time to add the airstones to the aquarium. Make sure to take the opportunity to conceal air supply tubing behind larger decorations. It will be more difficult to do this once the tank is filled.

5. Now add the water to the tank without disrupting your aquascape. To do this, place a clean plate or bowl on top of the gravel and pour the water onto it. In many cases, tap water will be fine. Check with your local water company if you suspect that your tap water contains

chemical impurities, such as nitrates, sulphates, or phosphates, or is chemically treated with chloramine. In some cases, you may need to purchase water or purify the tap water with de-ionizers or nitrate-removing resin. In most cases, the tank-aging process, combined with filtration, will eliminate minor tap water problems.

Keep track of the amount of water you use to fill the tank. Then you can add the artificial salt mix to the aquarium. Read the directions carefully. Follow the manufacturer's instructions as closely as possible.

6. Now is the time to add the heater. Place the heater in the tank near sources of water circulation, such as filter outlets or airstones. This helps to maximize its output. Don't plug in the heater before you place the heater. Only plug the heater in once the tank has been fully set up. If you plug it in and let it warm up, when you place it in the tank, the glass may crack.

    Set up the heater only—not the external power filter. You don't want to add it yet. You should wait until the water has matured before using chemical and mechanical filtration. Also, do not set up the protein skimmer until the tank has matured and is ready for its inhabitants.

7. Now you can place the smaller decorations in the tank. You can add the thermometer as well. This is also a great time to fine-tune your aquascape.

8. Fit the aquarium hood, making sure that the external components and electrical equipment are properly placed. Make sure the hood is not yet plugged in or turned on. Add the light on top of the canopy and make sure that it is correctly hooked up.

9. All of you who like to play with sockets can have fun now. When you are confident that the electrical wiring is safely insulated from sources of water, plug the aquarium units in and turn on the system. Make sure the heater is properly adjusted. Don't be impatient. This may take a day or two. Check the operation of the under-gravel filter, air pumps, and light.

Avoid All Chemicals

Never use any kind of soap when cleaning your aquarium components. This can cause immediate water quality problems and may result in the death of your fish. Remember, fish don't require a Lysol clean environment. Don't make this common first-time mistake.

10. Now you want to check the gravity. Use your hydrometer to check the specific gravity. The floating hydrometer is the most popular. Use it this way. First, take some aquarium water and pour it into a suitable container. Usually, this is the plastic tube that the hydrometer came in. You want to fill it up high enough to make sure that there is enough water to float the hydrometer. Now, place the hydrometer in the tube.

Make sure that it is floating freely. Read the hydrometer at the waterline. This reading is the specific gravity of the water in your aquarium. Some experts feel that it is important to convert specific gravity to salinity. However, this is not the case. It is not required as long as the temperature in your tank is kept relatively constant. If the specific gravity is not ideal, don't add freshwater or additional salt. Let it sit for 24 hours. This allows for all the salt to dissolve and reach an equilibrium. After 24 hours, add more salt if the specific gravity is less than 1.024. Or, remove water and add tap water if the salinity is greater than 1.024.

11. Do nothing! Leave everything alone. Do *not* turn on the filter. Let the tank sit for a few days. You need to let the tank water mature.

Aquarium Maturation

"Okay," you're saying, "Now I have a tank full of water and I'm not even using the power filter that I paid a small fortune for. I've shelled out a lot of money, and all I have is a lot of water in a glass cube. It's got to get better than this." Don't worry, it does. But you also have to make sure that you have mature water first.

The problem is that you do not yet have the working, well-balanced artificial habitat for fish that hobbyists call an aquarium. How do you get that? What do you do? Nothing. You just need to let the water sit there a while. You need to let the tank mature. Remember, your fish, especially marine fish, require suitable water qualities. What are suitable water qualities? Suitable water qualities include these four areas of concern: appropriate levels of water pH, salinity, temperature, and biological filtration.

For example, your tap water may harbor treatment additives. These are not found in the native waters where your fish once lived. Usually these are harmful to your new marine fish. Another important factor your tank must have is an established nitrogen cycle. These water parameters need to be established and maintained long before you just start adding fish into the water! Water circulation, temperature regulation, and filtration will help your water to mature. How long must you wait? Five weeks. Yes, *five weeks*. This is how long it can take to establish bacterial colonies sufficient to drive the nitrogen cycle.

Water Maturation—the Fast Lane

Hey, I don't want to grow old before I'm allowed to add fish. Are there any tricks to jump-starting the water maturation process? It just so happens there are. In fact, there are a couple of proven methods for accelerating this process. The best methods of these will speed up the process so much that you will be able to introduce fish within a couple of weeks. Of course, this depends on how fast ammonia and nitrite levels peak and then drop off.

One of the faster methods involves the introduction of commercially prepared maturing fluids and bacterial cultures. As you might suspect, there are several kinds of these products on the market. Speak with your aquarium professional to learn more about which product is best for you. Be sure to follow the manufacturer's instructions. It is preparations like these that will introduce the necessary ingredients to give your bacterial filter a head start. Of all the effective jump-start methods, this one is the most strongly recommended.

Of course, there are other methods, too. Another trick used by experienced aquarists is extremely effective. It involves the inclusion of substrate from an already matured and established tank, which may have been up for some time, into your own gravel. If your aquarium is set up and brimming with water, you can either go to a friend who has a healthy, established system, or you can go to your local pet store. Take a small cup or mug, and ask for gravel

Saltwater Tip: Check the pH!

Just because this is a saltwater aquarium, doesn't mean you don't have to worry about the pH. pH is still extremely important, and you must check it regularly.

from one of their already established systems. You may ask for more than that—the more you get, the faster your jump-start. Ask ahead of time if they'll do this. Not all pet stores offer this. Make sure the gravel they give you is from a good tank, where there are healthy, active fish darting around the tank. If the fish are lethargic and look ill, don't do it. It'll ruin your aquarium. Better to have to wait a few extra weeks than to have to overcome an illness right when you start your aquarium. When you get home, take this established substrate and mix it with your gravel. Some experts call this "seeding." What you have done is introduced bacteria and detritus into your aquarium. This will give your aquarium the opportunity to establish a bacteria colony which will form the bedrock of your filtering system and an excellent start to your nitrogen cycle.

Some people may advise you to a third and different approach, which I advise against. It's also a form of seeding. Some professionals recommend the inclusion of an established live rock. Their theory is that it, too, will seed a new aquarium. Don't do it. Live rocks are adding something living into your tank. You have no idea if the rock is healthy or not, and it may foul your water or introduce diseases to your water before the first fish arrives. Experts who have more than one marine tank often exchange substrate, but don't often seed with live rock. If someone recommends this to you, they are playing with fire. Better to wait, than be sorry.

Testing the Waters

No, we do not do this by dipping our toes into the tank. We do not stick our arms in to see if it feels good. Instead, we follow good, old-fashioned chemistry. In the beginning, it is imperative to test your water daily. You need to determine when the water is properly conditioned. And when it is, you can finally add fish to the tank. Usually, once you have introduced established substrata into your tank and helped to establish bacteria to jump-start the nitrogen cycle, the sequence of events will proceed as follows:

1. Initially, you will have low values of ammonia. These will slowly begin to increase after a few days. The bacterial

colony grows as ammonia builds. Ammonia is then converted into nitrite. This process increases. Don't be alarmed as the pH level will begin to decrease as these other levels rise.

2. The bacterial population will proliferate. And ammonia will then begin to decline. Now, nitrite will continue to increase. Your pH should stabilize about here, and it should not drop lower than 8.2. Depending on how much you seeded, this period can take days or weeks.

3. The ammonia will be consumed by bacteria. As this happens, nitrite will begin to be converted to nitrate. Obviously, the level of nitrate will slowly rise. Nitrite will peak and suddenly collapse. The nitrate will continue to rise.

4. Now, check the pH. From experience we can tell you that the pH may remain low. It may also rise as nitrogenous wastes are removed. If the pH is lower than 8.0, correct it after the tank has matured by performing a 50 percent water change. This will also remove nitrate that has accumulated in the aquarium during the conditioning process.

At this point, your aquarium is finally ready for the first few hardy species to hit the water! And you thought it would never happen.

Of course, if you have an under-gravel filter, the substrata will not be completely established for several months. With this being the case, make sure to be very conservative when you add your first fish. Begin with a few peaceful inexpensive fish. Don't introduce something like the damsel, which is extremely territorial. These fish will establish their ground in the absence of other fish, and make it more difficult to add new fish later on. Damsels can be very aggressive, especially if they think their space is being invaded. As you add the first few fish, you should carefully monitor the ammonia and nitrite levels in your aquarium. You need to do this to make sure that the biological filtration is handling the new load. You can start your protein skimmer at this time. If you have an external filter with activated carbon, you can also start it at this time.

Choosing Fish for Beginners

Common Tropical Marine Fish Families

OK. I want three yellow ones, the cobalt blue one, and, well, I'm not sure. No, red clashes. Sorry, this isn't the way we pick out fish, especially marine fish. Since you are interested in marine fish, we can probably assume that you are at least somewhat knowledgeable about fishkeeping as a hobby. With that in mind, let's talk a bit about marine fishes seriously.

The great majority of saltwater fishes sold in pet stores often originate from warm tropical coral reefs. They are popular because their brilliant colors, unique body shapes, and animated behavior make these fish extremely eye-catching. One of the great things about the coral reef system is that it serves an extremely diverse community of plants (algae), invertebrates, and vertebrate animals that function as a whole. The coral reef itself is a neighborhood. It is the great melting pot of the sea. It serves as the basis upon which the community is built.

This is great! Why? Because it affords you a huge and varied selection of life-forms that you can introduce to your new neighborhood. You can introduce both vertebrates, such as fish, or invertebrates, such as crabs. Generally, there are three ways to fill your new marine tank: the fish-only tank, the invertebrate tank, and the mixed fish-invertebrate tank.

About 97 percent of all animals in the world are invertebrates. What are invertebrates? Invertebrate animals are all those living creatures that do not have an internal skeleton. They have no backbone. Sponges, worms, insects, and snails are all examples of invertebrate animals. Vertebrates are like us. They have internal skeletons and backbones. Some obvious vertebrates are mammals, reptiles, birds, amphibians, and, of course, fish.

What are marine invertebrates? You'd be surprised what qualifies. Marine invertebrates include crabs, snails, coral, anemones, and shrimp, to name a few. They are more easily affected by water quality than marine fish. They are also more difficult to feed and more difficult to maintain in an aquarium than marine fish. If you are going to have a mixed tank, it's important to know that you need to keep a pretty delicate balance. If you mix them with too many fish, the nitrogenous wastes of the fish will kill them. Okay, if we haven't talked you out of invertebrates yet, then we'll say it outright: we recommend that the beginner avoid trying to establish an invertebrate or mixed species aquarium until you have a lot more experience.

Of course, there is one exception—the introduction of a single anemone. Why? Because you would take the anemone to accompany clown fish in an established aquarium. They have a symbiotic relationship. And let's face it, anemones are cool.

If Fish Are in Schools, Does That Mean They Are in Class?

All animals, including humans, have been classified into species. Any particular species has a common name. These differ from region to region and country to country. But biologists have taken pains to establish names that do not change from place to place. To biologists, all species of living creatures have a scientific name that is used to identify that species anywhere in the world. The scientific name of a species is based in Latin and is in two parts: the genus and the species. For example, the scientific name of the threadfin butterfly fish is *Chaetodon auriga* and that of the spotfin butterfly fish is *Chaetodon ocellatus*. The first name refers to the genus to which both species belong. A genus is a scientific grouping of very similar species. If you look at these fish, you can see that they are extremely similar. The second name refers only to that species and no other.

You will find in the fish listed below the various families of fish that commonly inhabit coral reefs. These are not the specific fish, but the groups of families in which specific species can be found. These fish are highly suitable for your tropical fish-only saltwater aquarium. As we previously discussed, the wide variety of these fish is incredible. These various fish are found throughout the world, and many are found around the warm waters near the earth's lower latitudes.

Let's be blunt now, to avoid any misunderstandings. In no way is this a complete listing of tropical saltwater fish families. However mind-boggling, there are, in fact, hundreds of families and thousands of species. This is an overview of the various families and the differences between them. If you wish to know more about a particular kind of fish, extensive research has been done by many experts in the field. Many of the books that contain this knowledge are listed in the bibliography at the end of this book. We recommend you consult them if you wish to acquire deeper knowledge of any of the species listed here. Keep in mind that some of the fishes listed here are not recommended for beginners.

Sharks

How cool is this? You can own a shark! A great white? Sorry. However, there are at least 31 families and 350 species of sharks in the world. Many of these have never been kept in aquaria. Sharks usually achieve lengths too long for the home aquarium. They can also be very aggressive and are very sensitive to water quality. However, some pet stores carry small fish in the shark family. But for the above reasons alone, sharks are not recommended for the beginner.

Moray Eels

Some people don't know that eels are actually a part of the fish family, since they look so much like a water snake. These fish belong to the Muraenidae family. The morays lack pectoral fins. However, they possess small gill openings and long fang-like teeth! Morays are generally nocturnal fish. They spend most of the day time hiding in crevices between rocks or in holes. They feed on both fish and invertebrates at night. Hobbyists who keep these fish usually keep them well fed with a variety of live foods, including feeder fish. In nature, it is not uncommon to see these fish easily attain lengths in excess of five feet! But not in your aquarium. This won't happen in the average home aquarium. Moray eels will certainly eat almost anything. Obviously, they are carnivorous. If you have smaller fish in the tank with them, the small fish will soon disappear, usually during the night. Eels are not recommended for the peaceful community tank. And they are not recommended for beginners.

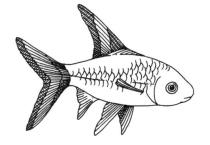

TRICOLOR SHARK

Squirrel Fishes

Squirrel fishes are red. They have long bodies with two dorsal fins: a longer fin of spines and a shorter soft-rayed fin close to the tail. They are from the Holocentridae family. In the wild, they are normally nocturnal creatures. They use their large eyes, which give them excellent vision in the dark, to feed at night. However, if kept in an aquarium, they can be trained to feed during daylight hours. Squirrel fish are highly active and need a lot of space to swim. Because they are so frenetic, they may be disruptive to a peaceful community aquarium. It's also important to note, that as they get larger, they may tend to eat the smaller fish.

Sea Horses and Pipefishes

Even cooler than sharks by a long shot are sea horses. Many people who get into fishkeeping don't know that sea horses are in fact real living things. Many have never seen a real one, not even on television. These are considered fishes, and they come from the family Syngnathidae. These exotic creatures are no strangers to the aquarium trade. The pipefishes are those that lack the prehensile tail, vertical swimming position, and angled head characteristic of the sea horse.

While sea horses and pipefishes are extremely cool, they are also extremely difficult to keep. For the novice, their eating and water quality requirements make them difficult to maintain in the aquarium for any length of time. One excellent example of why they are not good for the community tank is that they do not compete well with other species for food. These fish, while quite active, are slow and graceful, and very peaceful. Sea horses and pipefish will do best in a very quiet, serene aquarium.

One of the other cool things about sea horses is that they are characterized by unusual reproductive behavior. The female deposits her eggs outside her body. That, in itself, is not so unusual. What makes it fascinating is that the female deposits her eggs into an abdominal pouch on the male! The male then fertilizes and incubates the eggs in this pouch. Talk about a modern kind of guy! Suddenly, carpooling seems a whole lot easier.

Lionfishes and Scorpion Fishes

Lionfishes and scorpion fishes are some of the most famous of all aquarium fishes. There are no more exotic-looking fish than these. No saltwater aquarium section would be complete without mentioning these unusual fishes of the Scorpaenidae family. The Scorpaenidae family has over 300 species of fish. These are dangerous fish. Many have stocky spiny heads and spiny fins armed with venomous glands. They are generally deadly predators. They hover or lie in wait for their prey, suddenly lunging at and engulfing them. Their coloration helps to camouflage them, which aids them in their hunting. Their spines are also very dangerous to both other fish (which makes them not such a great meal for larger fish) and humans as well. It should be obvious at this point. Do we need to tell you that these fish must be handled with great care? Many experienced aquarists have kept these fish. They are quiet and extremely graceful. There is nothing sharp or quick about them, outside of their table manners. Like some of the above fish, however, they will consume some of their lesser tankmates. And, *no,* this fish is not for the beginner. You should be an experienced saltwater hobbyist before going near these types of fish.

Grunts

Grunts are named for the sound they make. These fish make noise? Yes, they grunt! Well, they don't actually grunt, but they emit a sound similar to a grunt. Their swim bladders amplify the sound generated by the grinding of their teeth. These fish belong to the family Haemulidae. They are hardy and active fishes. Grunts are omnivorous and will eat a wide variety of foods. However, as they are very active, they will require a lot of space. It is best to keep only small juveniles in small schools.

Sweetlips

Sweetlips are part of the Plectorhynchidae family. At one point, however, they were thought to be of the same species as grunts, especially because they are very active, like grunts. They originate in the Indo-Pacific region. As juveniles, they are often very brightly colored. As they get older they begin to lose some of that brightness, and their colors fade to more drab tones. When they mature, they also lose a little of their rambunctious nature and prefer a community tank without antagonistic neighbors.

Snappers

You want that with a lemon butter sauce or just broiled? This is, in fact, the fish of that snapper family! Several different snappers are exploited around the globe as food. Snappers are from the Lutjanidae family. There are more than 200 species in this family. Snappers are fast growing, highly active fish. As they mature, they become less and less suitable for the saltwater home aquarium. These fish are natural predators. Especially as they get older, they will need great amounts of space. They will easily and quickly dominate a home saltwater aquarium.

Groupers and Sea Basses

This is starting to sound a like a visit to a Red Lobster, isn't it? While many think of groupers and sea basses in the same way that they think about grunts and snappers, many of these families are actually of the Serranidae family. This species is generally comprised of fast-growing, large predatory fish. If you intend on keeping one of these kinds of fish for any length of time, you'd better install a pool. Why? Because these fish grow fast and big.

There are more than 350 species belonging to this family. Of that 350 there are several smaller species that are ideal for the community saltwater aquarium. Groupers are not the most exciting of fish. They are nocturnal. They will lay on the bottom most of the day or hide if they can.

Cardinal Fishes

Cardinal fishes are of the family Apogonidae. In the Apogonidae family there are more than 200 species of slow-moving, community fishes. Large eyes, two separate erect dorsal fins, and a large head are characteristic of these fish. Although nocturnal, cardinals can be trained to feed during the daytime. They have also been known to be more active than many other nocturnal species. These fish make ideal additions to your saltwater community tank. They are also fairly hardy, for saltwater fish, and are a good risk for the beginner.

Fairy Basslets

There are only three species of basslets of the family Grammidae. They originate from the Caribbean. These are shy fish. They will often search high and low to find a small area of shelter somewhere in the tank. If they do find some small area to hide, they will defend that area and become somewhat territorial. These beautiful, finicky fish are difficult to take care of and are best left to those who have a mixed-fish invertebrate tank.

Dottybacks

These fish of the family Pseudochromidae are very similar to the fairy basslets in size and appearance. Dottybacks are distributed in the Indo-Pacific while basslets are confined to the Caribbean. Some of the dottybacks can be highly territorial. If you are set on having a pair of these fish for your saltwater community tank, make sure to observe the fish you want closely for some time. You must take care to choose the right species for your peaceful marine aquarium.

Butterfly Fishes

Butterfly fishes are some of the most popular aquarium fish. They belong to the Chaetodontidae family. Many of the fish in this family have oval flattened bodies, terminal mouths, and stunning color patterns. The butterfly fish are extremely well adapted to life on the coral reef. They are well-known scavengers, feeding on the reef itself, often searching for and eating algae, sponges, and corals. Although among the most beautiful, these are not the hardiest of saltwater tropical fish. They are extremely sensitive to water quality changes. Some species can be territorial. These fish are more difficult to take care of. They are difficult to feed in captivity, and are really a handful for the beginner.

Angelfishes

Angelfishes are extremely popular fish with saltwater aquarists. They come from coral reefs from around the globe. Some may grow quite large—more than 24 inches! Other species within this family may not exceed more than a few inches. Angelfishes can be found in a wide variety of colors and patterns. These colors or patterns may sometimes change, as the fish matures from juvenile to adult.

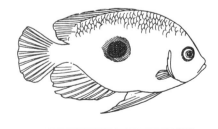

LEMON PEEL ANGELFISH

Angelfishes are sometimes confused with butterfly fishes. This is because they have deep flattened bodies and ornate colors. However, angelfishes are part of the Pomacanthidae family, which is quite separate from butterflies. One of the distinguishing characteristics that readily separates butterflies from angelfishes is the presence of a spine on the gill cover.

In terms of care, angelfish will consume a variety of foods, especially when they are young. Some species, as they mature, can be somewhat picky eaters, preferring sponges and corals. Some of the angelfishes that grow large are a little harder to manage. As they mature, they become much more territorial. Many experts feel that they are really only for expert aquarists with larger aquariums, and some are for public exhibits only. Don't despair, though, as many hobbyists will quickly recommend the pygmy angelfish as an excellent saltwater home aquarium inhabitant.

Clown Fishes and Damselfishes

These two very popular saltwater fishes are often paired together because they belong to the same family of fish: the Pomacentridae. Both the clown fishes and the damselfishes are extremely popular in the pet trade.

Certainly, more than many, the clown fish has its own peculiar story, which helps its popularity spread. Clown fishes are sometimes called anemone fishes. Why? Because in the wild, these small ornate fish are able to live unharmed among the stinging tentacles of anemones. Anemones are soft invertebrates related to corals. The anemones thrive by living on reefs and using their tentacles to incapacitate fish passing by. Most fish try to steer clear of them. However, the clowns and the anemones live in harmony. It's believed that both the fish and the anemone receive protection from each other against their predators. It is a fascinating symbiotic relationship, that many hobbyists have recreated in their home aquariums. However, it's important to note that anemones require lots of special attention. They are not recommended for the beginner's tank.

Many saltwater experts consider the damselfish to be the hardiest of the marine aquarium species. As a result, they are

often the first fish to be introduced into your marine tank. However, they have their own foibles, as well. They tend to be very territorial and aggressive. One of the problems involved with damselfish is that if they are indeed the first fish introduced to your tank, they will not take too kindly to the new fish on the block when you introduce your next fish a few days or weeks later. They are less difficult when introduced in schools, where it is assumed that they find safety in numbers. Regardless, many experts agree that some damsels are exciting additions to the new hobbyist's aquarium.

Wrasses

Wrasses belong to the family Labridae. This family is comprised of over 500 species from all over the globe. It is probably one of the most diverse families of fishes in the world. Contrary to many of the other saltwater ornamental fish families, many of these fish are not found in tropical waters. Differences in body shapes, behaviors, and sizes make this group quite different from one another. One thing many of the species have in common is that many wrasse species are capable of changing sex! They do this as needed for reproductive purposes. Some rest in mucus cocoons at night, while others are substrate burrowers that require sand. Others are the sanitation engineers of the oceans and reefs of the world, as they perform cleaning services similar to those provided by a few species of gobies.

These, again, tend not to be fish for the beginning saltwater aquarist. The more frenetic species of wrasses can disrupt a peaceful tank. They tend to be aggressive toward smaller fishes. And they are also very fast-growing fish for the average tank.

Blennies

Blennies are very active fish. They are long and slender. Most blennies rarely exceed 4 inches in captivity and many are peaceful additions to the new aquarium. They prefer hiding in places like caves and crevices. Blennies are very good for beginning saltwater enthusiasts. These fish belong to the family Blenniidae, which is comprised of more than 300 species.

Blennies are not finicky eaters. They generally eat a variety of foods from algae to flake foods, which is another reason they are recommended for beginners.

Gobies

Here's something really cool! Some gobies are able to live out of water for extended periods of time! They return to the water only to wet their gills!

Most gobies are brightly colored, peaceful, and relatively small in size. Gobies are sometimes confused with blennies by beginners. Like the blennies, gobies prefer hiding places and shelters. Some reef-dwelling gobies act as "cleaner fish," removing parasites from other reef fishes at specified cleaner stations on the reef. While gobies and blennies are somewhat similar in body shape, the gobies belong to the family Gobiidae. This family is the largest of the marine fishes. There are more than 1500 species and 200 genera in the Gobiidae family! Gobies have modified pelvic fins, which are united, forming a sucking disk.

These fish are not particularly discriminating eaters, and will happily dine on a wide variety of foods.

Surgeonfishes and Tangs

As you go from place to place, you will see that surgeonfishes and tangs are very common fish in the marine aquarium world. They are very hardy fish. These popular saltwater aquarium fish belong to the family Acanthuridae. They are characterized by high profile, flattened oval bodies. Their name is derived from the presence of two "scalpel-like" spines at the base of the caudal fin (tail). These are used in defense or during territorial disputes.

Surgeonfish and tangs are schooling fish. They are also algal grazers in the wild. They will happily continue in this vein in your tank. However, they can be trained to take other kinds of food in the home aquarium. In the wild, they may reach sizes in excess of 15 inches! But don't worry. Depending on the species, they rarely reach half that size in your tank.

Rabbit Fishes

Rabbit fish are part of the family Siganidae. This family of fish originates from the Indo-Pacific region, and contains about a dozen species. They are similar to sturgeonfishes because of their flattened oval bodies and small mouths. As a form of self-defense, rabbit fishes possess venom glands in their dorsal and anal spines. These deter predators. They should also deter you. You need to be extra careful when handling these fish.

Rabbit fish require lots of extra swimming space as they are active and because they are fast-growing. They love to munch on algae and other matter in the vast oceans of the Indo-Pacific, and will be more than happy to do so in your aquarium. However, they can be coaxed into taking vegetable foods in captivity.

Triggerfishes

Triggerfishes are named for their first dorsal fin, which locks into place. Triggerfish (called triggers by hobbyists) belong to the family Balistidae. The Balistidae has more than 130 species of fish in it. These fish move primarily using their dorsal and anal fins, saving the tail for emergency situations.

Triggerfish have sharp teeth. They feed on many things in the wild, including invertebrates. Their powerful teeth are very dangerous to other fish when they're aggressive. While some experienced hobbyists have been able to feed them well enough to render them less aggressive, these fish really are not recommended for the beginner.

Filefishes

Filefishes are close relatives of the triggerfish. Like the triggerfish, filefishes have a dorsal spine that locks into place. But the similarities end there. The filefish belongs to the family Monocanthidae. Unlike the triggerfish, the filefishes are less active and more peaceful. They are also smaller, which makes them a great addition to any saltwater aquarium.

Filefish do present one problem, though. They are very particular eaters. In the wild, these fish normally feed on coral and algae. While they have been kept in captivity successfully, you'll need to investigate what substitutes can be given to keep them from going hungry. Of course, letting algae grow in your tank is certainly one way to keep them happy.

Box Fishes and Trunkfishes

Box fish and trunkfish are of the family Ostraciidae. These fish possess box-shaped bodies covered with bony plates and no pelvic fins. Neither of these fish is really for the beginner. While they might sound very interesting in a marine special on television, they are, in fact, very ill-suited for the beginning saltwater aquarist. Why? Because these fish release poisons into the water when threatened. It is an act of self-defense against aggressive fish and predators. This makes them extremely poor choices for a home aquarium.

There's also another reason these bottomfeeders can present a problem to the home aquarist—they are generally intolerant of their own kind! Talk about a curmudgeon!

Porcupine Fishes

Porcupine fish seem like something out of a sci-fi movie. First, their scales have spines, which is very unusual. And second, these fish have the ability to inflate their bodies, making their spines that much more dangerous. The porcupine fish uses this tactic whenever it feels threatened by another aggressive fish.

They are relatively easy to care for in captivity. However, because they reach such large sizes, they can usually be kept by the home aquarist.

Puffers

Many novices confuse the puffer fish with the porcupine fish. Puffer fish will also inflate themselves as a defense mechanism, usually to avoid being eaten. Their flesh is poisonous when consumed.

However, the difference between the puffer and the porcupine is that the puffer fish's scales don't have spines. Puffers are also smaller than the porcupines, and they have fused beak-like jaws, unlike porcupine fishes. The puffer, in fact, belongs to a completely different family, called the Tetraodontidae. Some species in this family can be quite aggressive. These fish are easy and voracious feeders in the home aquarium.

Wanted: Polite Fish

What any aquarist really wants is fish that will get along. The problem with creating a community atmosphere is that one bad apple can spoil the whole bunch. Don't buy an aggressive fish because it's beautiful or because you get talked into it. One fish can cause many of the others to be unhappy. This weakens their systems and allows them to succumb to illness and disease.

Pick the polite fish, and you'll have healthy and active fish that will provide countless hours of fun and fascination.

Great Fish for the Beginning Saltwater Aquarist

First, many people get so bent out of shape when experts recommend things "for beginners." You can't think like that. Aquarists who wish to ascend to this level of fishkeeping should not bristle at this list of very colorful and interesting fish. As many of you aquarists have already experienced different levels of knowledge in this field, you need to leave your egos behind. Create a nice diversified tank by beginning with these fish. Learn to understand, as you have at other levels, the nuances of keeping marine fish and their many idosyncracies.

Now, for those of you who may not remember or who may not know, there are two types of aquariums that the home aquarist can plan: a community tank or a species tank. The community tank offers the home aquarist a wide range of species to choose from because it contains different species of compatible fish. The species tank, on the other hand, contains only a single species of fish. Usually these are difficult fish to keep and are for the more experienced hobbyist. It really is best that the beginner establish a community tank to start with. Community tanks are generally comprised of fish that are relatively hardy and get along with each other. They are easier to attain success with and, therefore, will be more fun for you. The species tank concept is best for those who want to maintain fish that require special tank conditions or fish that are extremely aggressive, or who want to mix fish with invertebrates. Generally, these are harder to keep and require more care, maintenance, and knowledge.

One of the nice things about establishing a community tank is the wide variety of fish that you can draw from. One of the most important things is to balance the types of fishes in your marine aquarium. Remember, many species of fish have adapted to different behaviors and varying lifestyles. You must keep in mind that in the wild some fish will use the entire living space of the water, while other fish stay exclusively in the middle to bottom levels. In the community tank, you want to recreate this kind of environment. By choosing your fish wisely, your fish will spread throughout the tank, minimizing competition and utilizing the entire aquarium.

Schools

You must also keep in mind that many species of fish school by nature. This is both an attractive and exciting addition to your community tank. It's always a bad idea to keep a single fish of a type that normally schools. These fish tend to be aggressive when left alone in a community environment. These schooling fish should be kept in a minimum size group of at least five or six individuals.

As we discussed in the general overview, you can see that some fish tend to be territorial or aggressive. These should be avoided by the beginner because a single antagonistic fish in a community tank can wreak havoc on the other species.

Another mistake that is often made by beginners is that the new marine aquarist will sometimes overlook the maximum size of a particular species. Fish will grow continuously throughout their lives. Some species grow faster than others. As cool as you think it sounds, you do not want to put a fish in your tank that will attain a length of 12 inches in less than a year. You really need to understand this. This will not only disrupt your aquarium capacity, but the larger fish will undoubtedly dominate the tank. In some cases that reads: eat their neighbors. Don't be fooled when you're buying younger fish! Some species are very compatible with other species when they are juveniles, but become solitary and aggressive as adults. These fish do not belong in the peaceful community tank. Remember to do your research before selecting your fish.

Before your tank is fully established (meaning that the water chemistry has balanced and the filtration system is working) and you are ready to stock your aquarium, you must have a game plan in mind. Don't blindly go to your pet dealer and look for fish for your tank. This can result in disaster. The end result will be fish incompatibility. Instead, you must pre-choose the kind of fish you want to start with. Read this section carefully. Talk with pet dealers and consult more in-depth books on different species. Read and learn everything you can before you make your decisions. If you do this, you will establish a good list of potential fish that you'll want to introduce into your new marine aquarium.

Remember, most saltwater tropical fishes are taken from reefs around the world and not bred in captivity. This makes tropical

Be Prepared!

One of the worst things you can do is just walk into a pet store and buy a few fish. No plan is the wrong plan!

If you think it through and choose well, you can create an excellent saltwater habitat teeming with lively, active fish. The time you put in beforehand, reading and learning out from pet industry professionals, will be rewarded in the long run. If you have a plan, more times than not, it will work, and you'll have a better and more fun experience. The result will be years of fascinating fun. The result if you don't plan? An empty tank gathering dust in the basement—another thing that didn't work out.

marine fishes more expensive than their freshwater counterparts. Therefore, you should be very selective when you get to the pet store. Buy fish only from healthy-looking aquariums with clear water, clean panes, and no dead fish in the tank. Make sure that the fish you want are healthy looking.

Insist on fish that are free of any cuts, scrapes, or fin problems. If they are afflicted with any of these, don't buy them. Watch for possible symptoms of disease, such as white granular spots, cottony white patches, frayed fins, or dull skin. Watch the behavior of the fish. You want fish that swim in a healthy and lively manner. You do not want fish that look shy, tentative, or scared. One of the tips that some experts insist on is seeing the fish feed before they buy it. They want to make sure that the fish has recovered from the stress of shipping, and has acclimated to life in the store's aquarium.

Most experts agree that it's important to introduce your fish to a newly established aquarium in batches. You should buy fish in lots every few weeks to a month. Why is this so important for the newly established aquarium? By doing this, you allow the fish to acclimate to each other. It also prevents aggressive behavior towards a single fish when it is introduced. One of the things you must guard against is to stock a marine aquarium too rapidly. And you must make sure to follow the tank capacity guidelines outlined earlier.

The fish that are outlined in this section are tropical marine species that are relatively hardy. This means that, for the beginner, they are easy to take care of. For a beginner's community tank, a pH should range from 8.1 to 8.3, and the temperature will be maintained between 75°F and 79°F. Included in the following list is information on which level of the water column in the tank that the fish is most likely to inhabit. Also listed are the sizes that these fish tend to attain in captivity, as opposed to those larger sizes of those found in the wild.

SALTWATER FISH FOR BEGINNERS

- Gold rim tang
- Lipstick tang
- Regal tang
- Black-finned trigger fish
- Midas blenny
- Bicolor blenny
- Lemon blenny
- Neon goby
- Orange-spotted goby
- Blue cheek goby
- Spanish hogfish
- African clown wrasse
- Cleaner wrasse
- Four-Spot wrasse

- Yellow sweetlips
- Dwarf angelfish
- Threadfin butterfly fish
- Wimplefish
- Common clown fish
- Clark's anemone fish
- Sergeant major
- Green chromis
- Wreck fish
- Foxface
- Sharp-nosed puffer
- Flamefish
- Pajama cardinal

Gold Rim Tang *Acanthurus glaucopareius*
Origin: Pacific and Indian Oceans
Size: 6 inches
Food: Herbivorous
Tank Level: All levels

The gold rim tang is so named because its black body is rimmed with a fluorescent yellow-gold. The shape of the gold rim is very typical of tangs. The gold rim has an oval body and steeply sloping forehead. This species is safe with small fishes, but is best kept as a single specimen in a large aquarium. This species, like other tangs, prefers a vegetarian diet, so tank algae and vegetables are a must.

Lipstick Tang *Naso lituratus*
Origin: Indo-Pacific
Size: 8 inches
Food: Herbivorous
Tank Level: All levels

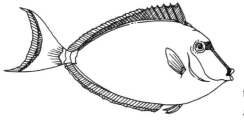

LIPSTICK TANG

This species is another peaceful tang that is an attractive addition to the larger aquarium. The common name refers to the red around the mouth of this fish. Remember that tangs have two scalpels on each side of the tail, so care must be taken when handling these fish. Although the lipstick tang and other tangs are listed as herbivorous, they can be acclimated to other protein foods and flake foods.

Regal Tang *Paracanthus hepatus*
Origin: Indo-Pacific
Size: 6 inches
Food: Herbivorous
Tank Level: All levels

REGAL TANG

The regal tang is certainly one of the most popular of saltwater community aquarists. The deep royal blue and bright yellow tail of this tang is beautiful and very distinctive. Many pet professionals sell these fish when they are very young. Beware! Regal tangs lose this coloring as the fish gets older. Experts disagree on the numbers of regal tangs you should keep. While some feel that the regal can be kept with members of the same species, it really is a better idea to limit your tank to one unless you have a very large tank. These vegetarians will also accept food, such as brine shrimp, most of the time.

Black-Finned Triggerfish *Melichthys ringens*
Origin: Indo-Pacific
Size: 10 inches
Food: Omnivorous
Tank Level: All levels

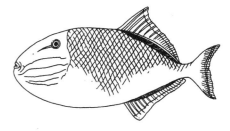

BLACK-FINNED TRIGGERFISH

Few triggerfish are recommended for community tanks. The black-finned triggerfish is one of the few species we would advise you to buy. Generally, the black-finned trigger is a gentle fish. It is generally thought to be safe with other small fishes. It is also considered to be relatively easy to keep in captivity. One of the drawbacks of this species is that it is difficult to obtain. And, of course, prices are a little higher for this fish. However, once in your aquarium, they are relatively easy to maintain and are generally easy to feed, as they eat almost anything.

Midas Blenny *Ecsenius midas*
Origin: Indian Ocean, Red Sea
Size: 3 inches
Food: Omnivorous
Tank Level: Lower level

The midas blenny is a yellow-hued fish that swims like an eel. Like most blennies, the midas blenny requires numerous nooks, crannies, and caves to frequently hide in. The nice news is that it won't always stay in its hiding place, once it's claimed one. Once assimilated, the midas blenny is quite lively. It will perch itself on rocks or other natural shelves in the aquascape to observe the rest of the aquarium. Since it's an omnivore, it has an excellent reputation as fish that is easy to feed and maintain. It is highly recommended for beginners.

Bicolor Blenny *Ecsenius bicolor*
Origin: Indo-Pacific
Size: 3 inches
Food: Omnivorous
Tank Level: Lower level

The front half of the bicolor blenny is brown and the rear half is orange. This is how this fish got its name. By nature, the bicolor is a tentative type of fish. It, too, lives in small caves or nooks. It is very interesting to watch it feed. It quickly zips out of its home to snatch the food and speedily returns to the safety of its den. It resumes its place in its den by "backing" in. The bicolor will gobble up a wide variety of foods. It is a fascinating species to observe.

Lemon Goby *Gobiodon citrinus*
Origin: Indo-Pacific
Size: 1.5 inches
Food: Carnivorous
Tank Level: Lower level

With its yellow coloration and blue streaks, the lemon goby is certainly one of the most beautiful marine fish you can purchase for your tank. But the lemon goby is not as active as it is beautiful. As most gobies go, lemon gobies tend to loiter among various aquarium decorations or plants, content on watching the rest of its fish world pass by.

As aquarium fish go, this is a very peaceful fish. It is recommended that you should not keep it with large fishes because of its size. As your new goby becomes more comfortable with its surroundings, this carnivore can be trained to eat many different foods. However, lemon goby experts will tell you that they have a well-known love of live brine shrimp.

Neon Goby *Gobiosoma oceanops*
Origin: Western Atlantic
Size: 1 inch
Food: Omnivorous
Tank Level: Lower level

There's all kinds of interesting information about this goby. The most interesting is that the neon goby is one of the rare fish that have been bred in captivity! But there's another reason this is a popular fish. It is the world's hardest working goby! The neon goby, while being beautifully colored, performs an invaluable service. The neon goby is famous for its cleaning services that it offers to fellow inhabitants. This is a popular marine fish that should be kept in a school of at least five or six. But take note—you cannot have these in the same tank with predatory fish.

The only drawback of a neon goby is that they live remarkably short lives. The average neon goby lives no more than approximately two years.

Orange-Spotted Goby *Valenciennea puellaris*
Origin: Indo-Pacific
Size: 4 inches
Food: Omnivorous
Tank Level: Lower level

The orange-spotted goby is another popular fish. First, they are fascinating to watch, with their sleek silver body, highlighted by orange neon spots. And second, they are very hardy, which makes them an obvious choice for beginners looking to make their first saltwater aquarium a success. You should have a relatively sandy bottom for these fish, as they love to dig and burrow into the substrate. Since the fish are omnivores, they are easily fed and will devour a wide range of foods offered.

Viva la Difference!

Remember to choose a variety of species that will live throughout the water column from the top to the bottom. Your fish won't be in a mad rush to compete for food and living space, and you'll be happier when there are fish throughout your aquarium, instead of all in one area.

BLUE-CHEEK GOBY

Blue-Cheek Goby *Valenciennea strigata*
Origin: Western Pacific, Indian Ocean
Size: 3 inches
Food: Omnivorous
Tank Level: Lower level

This is an incredibly useful fish and another of the hard-working gobies. Blue-cheek gobies love to root around in the substrate. They're like little living vacuums, constantly patrolling and devouring everything they can find in the aquarium's gravel beds. They are excellent for under-gravel filters, as they will pick off all the detritus that would otherwise clog your filter. Blue-cheek gobies are peaceful fish and can easily be paired with members of its own kind. Knowing how they eat, and knowing that they are omnivorous, lets you know that they are easy to maintain. Here's a fish the beginner would do well to have two of.

Spanish Hogfish *Bodianus rufus*
Origin: Western Atlantic
Size: 8 inches
Food: Omnivorous
Tank Level: All levels

The Spanish hogfish is part of the wrasse family. Depending on where they come from, their coloration may vary. But as they become older, red tends to become the predominant color. The problem with wrasses is that they can grow quite large. Not only will they dominate a tank, but they will become more aggressive as they grow. The larger they grow, the more likely that they will make a meal out of their smaller tankmates. Many experienced aquarists remove them when they become too large. Sometimes they establish a separate, second tank devoted only to a particular type of fish, such as the Spanish hogfish. A close cousin to the Spanish hogfish is the Cuban hogfish *(Bodianus pulchellus)*.

When young, Spanish hogfish are known as cleaner fish. However, the older they get, the less cleaning is part of their activities. As juveniles, they are quite peaceful and very hardy. As juveniles, they will eat a wide variety of marine foods.

African Clown Wrasse *Coris formosa*
Origin: Indo-Pacific, Red Sea
Size: 8 inches
Food: Carnivorous
Tank Level: Lower level

The African clown wrasse changes colors as it gets older. Its white stripes change to a blue-green. It is recommended that you keep just a single African clown wrasse in your aquarium. These fish tend to fight among themselves if there is more than one. The African clown wrasse is usually peaceful with other small fishes as a juvenile. But like some other wrasses, as they mature they become more combative. A close cousin of the African clown wrasse is the clown wrasse *(Coris gaimardi)*.

The African clown wrasse is a bottom-feeder. It prefers live food, especially marine invertebrates like brine shrimp and a variety of other meaty foods.

Cleaner Wrasse *Labroides dimidiatus*
Origin: Indo-Pacific
Size: 2 inches
Food: Carnivorous
Tank Level: All levels

This is the hardest-working wrasse in the saltwater community aquarium world. The cleaner wrasse is also one of the most popular marine aquarium fish in the world. This is a must for the novice saltwater aquarist. This fish provides a wonderful service for your aquarium. As you might have guessed from the name, the cleaner wrasse feeds on the parasites of other aquarium cohabitants. It is amazing to watch as it devours these parasites from the body, gills, and mouth of its understanding neighbors. The other nice thing about this fish is that it gets along with its own kind, so that you can keep more than one cleaner wrasse at a time!

One of the nice things about the cleaner wrasse is that is gets some of its nutrition from its job. You should, however, use a variety of other marine foods to complement this fish's normal diet.

Anemone and Friends

There is another animal that is impervious to the anemone's tentacles, and that is the Japanese anemone crab. They are colorful, beautiful, and cool to look at. They are also very difficult to keep and are recommended only for advanced saltwater aquarists.

Four-Spot Wrasse *Halichoeres trispilus*
Origin: Indian Ocean
Size: 4 inches
Food: Carnivorous
Tank Level: All levels

The four-spot wrasse is certainly one of the most beautiful marine fish that you can have in a saltwater community aquarium. This fish is known for its intense yellow body that is highlighted by four black spots that occur along its spine and tail. These are great fish for the beginning saltwater enthusiast. A close cousin to the four-spot is the banana wrasse *(Halichoeres chrysus).* Both are very peaceful fish. The four-spot wrasse is a carnivore and will readily devour any meaty marine food.

Yellow Sweetlips *Plectorhynchus albovittatus*
Origin: Indo-Pacific, Red Sea
Size: 4 inches
Food: Carnivorous
Tank Level: Middle and Lower Levels

The yellow sweetlips is ideal for the peaceful community tank. It should not be kept with lots of active or hyperactive fish, as it might tend to become much more shy. They are hardy fish. Yellow sweetlips are known for their vibrant yellow stripes. Like some other fish, these intense colors will fade with maturity. The colors change with age, and they become more drab with size. The beautiful yellow stripes muddy, and the fish becomes more brownish. Sweetlips mostly eat meaty marine foods.

Dwarf Angelfish *Centropyge* species
Origin: Atlantic, Pacific, Indian Oceans
Size: 3 inches
Food: Omnivorous
Tank Level: All Levels

As we discussed earlier, the angelfish are some of the more beautiful fish of the marine aquarium world. However, as they mature and grow they become a meaner species. They can become very aggressive and extremely territorial. And, of course, you need to have a large aquarium if you're going to keep them; otherwise, they'll probably get way too big for your tank and other fish. However, dwarf angelfishes fulfill the desire for angelfishes without all those problems.

Dwarf angelfishes don't have aggressive attitudes and are quite peaceful. They don't fight among themselves, which is extremely important. That means you can keep them in pairs with other dwarf angelfish.

Another good thing about dwarf angelfish is that they can cohabitate with many marine invertebrates. Therefore, if you want to expand the scope of your tank later, you can. One thing you need to do for dwarf angelfish is to supply as many aquarium decorations as possible without crowding the tank. You need to leave swimming space, which is always important, but dwarf angelfish like to seek refuge from time to time.

Dwarf angelfish are omnivores and enjoy a wide range of marine foods. Some of the dwarf angelfish you should investigate include the following:

- African pygmy angel (*Ceutropyge acanthops*)
- Cherubfish (*Ceutropyge argi*)
- Coral beauty (*Ceutropyge bispinosus*)
- Flame angel (*Ceutropyge loriculus*)
- Herald's angel (*Ceutropyge heraldi*)
- Lemonpeel angel (*Ceutropyge flavissimus*)
- Resplendent angel (*Ceutropyge resplendens*)

Threadfin Butterfly Fish *Chaetodon auriga*
Origin: Indo-Pacific, Red Sea
Size: 4 inches
Food: Omnivorous
Tank Level: Middle and Lower Levels

The threadfin butterfly is of the butterfly fishes family. The threadfin gets its name from the threadlike extension that grows from the dorsal fin of the mature fish.

Butterfly fish are generally not recommended for the beginner saltwater aquarist because they can be very difficult to maintain. However, they can be readily found in the pet trade, which helps to account for their popularity. And they are hardy, which makes them easy to care for.

Threadfin butterfly fishes will consume a wide variety of aquarium foods. They particularly enjoy dinning on live brine shrimp. Other butterfly fishes that can be recommended to beginners include:

- Vagabond butterfly fish (*Chaetodon vagabundus*)
- Klein's butterfly fish (*Chaetodon kleini*)
- Raccoon butterfly fish (*Chaetodon lunula*)

Wimple Fish *Heniochus acuminatus*
Origin: Indo-Pacific, Red Sea
Size: 6 inches
Food: Omnivorous
Tank Level: Middle and Lower Levels

WIMPLE FISH

The wimple fish is easily identifiable. The front rays of its dorsal fin can grow extremely long and protrude quite noticeably, like a car antenna. This extension continues to grow as the fish matures. When they are young, they tend to be cleaner fish, but this activity dies down as the fish becomes older. These are peaceful fish. Wimple fish are very compatible with one another and can be kept in groups of two to three. Make sure your tank is large enough and has enough space.

The wimple fish is hardy and easy to keep and to feed. They will eat any variety of foods.

Common Clown Fish *Amphiprion ocellaris*
Origin: Indo-Pacific
Size: 2 inches
Food: Omnivorous
Tank Level: Middle and Lower Levels

The common clown fish is certainly the most popular anemone fish in the aquarist world. They are bright orange, bright white, and black. They are very striking. These fish do best, however, when kept with an anemone. That's why they're referred to as anemone fish. When you add any type of anemone fish to your tank, you're not just adding two fish, you're also adding an invertebrate as well. In most cases, anemone fish should be bought in pairs to go along with an anemone. Common clown fish don't do well singly.

We know that no matter what we advise, some of you will not heed our warning and throw caution to the wind. But listen up! The excited novice must avoid these fish at least for a few months! You do not have the experience nor understanding of your tank's biological systems and reactions yet. To keep this delicate group of fish and anemone healthy and vibrant, the water quality and the environment *must* be established and stabilized. The water quality cannot fluctuate. And adding an invertebrate is adding a completely different life-form to the mix.

The common clown fish dines on a variety of well-diced frozen foods. It can also be trained to accept a small portion of flake.

Clark's Anemone Fish *Amphiprion clarkii*
Origin: Indo-Pacific
Size: 3 inches
Food: Omnivorous
Tank Level: Middle and Lower Levels

This is one anemone fish that can actually be kept without an anemone! And unlike the common clown fish, they need to be kept singly, as they will be aggressive with one another if more than one exists in a tank. This makes them better for beginners. The colors of Clark's anemone are difficult to catalog, since their coloration and markings change from region to region. The area where they were captured plays a large role in what kind of fish you'll see. A cousin to the Clark's is the tomato clown fish (*Amphiprion frenatus*). Clark's anemone fish will eat a wide range of foods, including flake, live foods, and green foods.

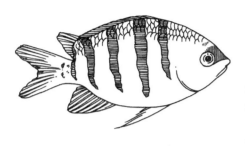

SERGEANT MAJOR

Sergeant Major *Abudefduf saxatilis*
Origin: Indo-Pacific, Atlantic
Size: 2 inches
Food: Omnivorous
Tank Level: All Levels

The sergeant major is a damselfish. Damselfish can be very territorial and aggressive. Obviously, this sometimes creates problems for the other cohabitants in the aquarium.

However, the sergeant major is less aggressive and less territorial than damsel brethren. Easily identified by his broad stripes, the sergeant major is a schooling fish and should be kept in groups of four or more. This fish is recommended as an ideal saltwater ornamental fish for the community tank, especially for the beginner. They are also quite hardy. The sergeant major is a gracious fish and likes to eat almost everything.

We can also recommend other damsels. In general, they are hardy fish that are usually pretty easy to keep. Again, they may be somewhat more pugnacious than the sergeant major, depending on the other cohabitants. They are all good for beginners. They include:

- Beau gregory (*Stegastes leucostictus*)
- Blue damselfish (*Abudefdul cyaneus*)
- Humbud damselfish (*Dascyllus carneus*)
- Yellow-tailed damselfish (*Chromis xanthurus*)

Green Chromis *Chromis caerulea*
Origin: Indo-Pacific, Red Sea
Size: 2 inches
Food: Omnivorous
Tank Level: Middle Levels

The green chromis is a schooling fish and should be kept in groups of six or more. The green chromis is a peaceful damselfish. When they are first introduced to a new tank, they may be a little skittish. As they acclimate, they will be less so.

If they eat little when new to the tank, don't worry. After they are accustomed, they will eat almost everything. They may be picky at first, but don't worry, they'll eat a wide range of meats and other food supplements.

Strawberry Gramma *Pseudochromis porphyreus*
Origin: Central and Western Pacific
Size: 2 inches
Food: Omnivorous
Tank Level: Lower Levels

The strawberry gramma is a dottyback. As with other dotty-backs, it can be aggressive towards other strawberry grammas or similar-looking fish. It is best if you keep this fish singly in your tank. The strawberry gramma is extremely well-known for its intensely rich, vibrant purple. They are very hardy. The strawberry gramma devours almost all marine frozen, live, and flake foods.

Wreck Fish *Anthias squamipinnis*
Origin: Indo-Pacific
Size: 4 inches
Food: Carnivorous
Tank Level: All Levels

Like the wimple fish, the wreck fish also has rays in the front of its dorsal fin which extend out like a car antenna. A school of these iridescent, multicolored fish is a very attractive and vibrant addition to any beginner saltwater aquarist's tank. The wreck fish belongs to the family of sea basses. It differs from its relatives in that it is a schooling fish. And an added bonus is that it doesn't become too big nor aggressive. In fact, it is a very peaceful fish.

Remember, the wreck fish is a carnivorous species. It needs live or meaty foods to remain healthy and active.

Foxface *Lo vulpinus*
Origin: Pacific
Size: 6 inches
Food: Omnivorous
Tank Level: Middle and Lower Levels

In some cases the foxface is also known as the badger fish. Regardless of the name, there is no mistaking this absolutely exquisite fish. Its striking black and white broadly striped face stands out starkly from its vibrant yellow body. The foxface is a rabbit fish. It is the most popular rabbit fish kept in captivity. It must be noted that foxfaces do not take kindly to their own kind and will show aggression toward another foxface. For this reason, they should be kept singly in your tank.

The foxface is an algae eater. This means you'll have to do less vacuuming because you have a helper. So let that rich, lush algal growth grow! Make sure to supplement the foxface's diet with a wide range of foods. And make sure you present plenty of vegetable matter.

Sharp-Nosed Puffer *Canthigaster solandri*
Origin: Indo-Pacific, Red Sea
Size: 2 inches
Food: Carnivorous
Tank Level: Middle and Lower Levels

The sharp-nosed puffer fish is certainly one of the most striking fish you will ever see, especially in the puffer fish group. Its dark body is highlighted by neon stripes and polka dots, and is also contrasted by its large, bright eyes.

This puffer fish is the smallest and most beautiful of common puffer fishes. Unlike other puffer fishes, it will remain small, and it will not outgrow your tank. It is a peaceful fish. However, it should be kept singly, as it will show aggression toward other sharp-nosed puffers. These fish will eat a wide range of well-diced seafood.

Flamefish *Apogon maculatus*
Origin: Western Atlantic
Size: 3 inches
Food: Omnivorous
Tank Level: Middle and Lower Levels

The flamefish is so named for the brilliant translucent, orangish-red color that seems to emulate that of a flame. The flamefish is a cardinal fish. They are very peaceful fish and are not hyperactive. They are excellent fish for new saltwater aquarists. It's important to remember that these are nocturnal fish. They will sleep or hide part or most of the day and be more active in the evening hours.

These omnivorous fish will devour almost anything. They are not difficult to feed at all. However, you may want to establish a late night feeding time for these fish, since they are nocturnal.

Pajama Cardinal Fish *Sphaeramia nematopterus*
Origin: Indo-Pacific
Size: 3 inches
Food: Omnivorous
Tank Level: Middle and Lower Levels

Cardinal fish are some of the most unique-looking fish you will ever see. They are easily identifiable due to the three distinct markings on their bodies. Their head is a solid silver metallic, their mid body is a black criss-cross pattern against the same silver, and the last third of the body from behind the dorsal to the tail is a series of black polka dots on silver. Its eyes also make it identifiable as they are large and colorful. Their eyes are large because they are nocturnal fish, and they use them for better vision in the dark.

Pajama cardinal fishes are peaceful fish. They do best when kept in groups of four or more in a peaceful tank. Keeping them with more active fish causes them to be more reticent about joining the frenzy, and they'll hang back.

Being omnivorous, they are happy to munch away on almost anything. Obviously, a combination of all three groups is an excellent diet and will allow for maximum health.

Clam up!

Clams are usually part of a reef tank. There have been clams in aquariums that have grown to almost a foot long, but may grow considerably larger out in the wild if given the opportunity. These bivalve animals will grow nicely, but need lots of natural light and supplements of calcium. They do not eat other fish, but in fact rely mainly on photosynthesis to survive.

The most popular claim is the Tridcana also known as the giant clam. They can be quite colorful and interesting. Make sure if you are going to choose a clam that the mouth closes completely, with no gaps. Gaps in its shell might allow the fish to pick at it. It also shows the clam may not be healthy.

Just Say No—Fish for Beginners to Avoid

Let's be honest for a moment. There are fish that you are not yet prepared to handle. And there are a number of reasons that you are not yet ready for them. Let's discuss them one at a time, shall we? First, you do not have enough experience in dealing with changing water quality conditions that are part and parcel of the new aquarium experience. You have yet to learn to counter pH changes or water temperature drops. Some fish are extremely sensitive to changes and may suffer ill effects, such as death! Second, others may require special water conditions, like brackish water. That may sound easier than it really is. You haven't learned to maintain healthy regular water yet; now, all of a sudden, you're going to recreate the brackish waters of the Amazon? The new established hobbyist should not try to supply this type of environment without gaining more experience. Third, you must remember that there are a number of fish that aren't socially compatible with the peaceful community tank. Simply put, some large carnivores eat smaller fish. There are also fish that are very territorial and do not allow trespassing. And, of course, there are fish that get big, old, and grumpy, so much so that they exhibit aggression and pugnacious behavior. And let's not forget that there are those fish that expel poison when alarmed. That's a major problem, especially in an enclosed tank.

You need to pay attention. Read the list of fish in the sidebar and know that they are not for the beginner. Many pet stores offer these same fish as juveniles, when they are at their brightest and most companionable. However, this won't last for long. Don't be fooled by this argument. Large predatory fish generally grow fast and develop aggressive behavior early in life.

Be strong. Don't be led. And don't be fooled into buying fish that require special water conditions. If you're lucky, these fish may live for a few days, or maybe even weeks, in your aquarium. Then what? Then, chronic stress will begin to take its toll. The fish's immune system will fail, and the fish will not be able to successfully fight off the diseases that will eventually destroy it. And there you are, looking like Alfred E. Neuman, going, "Aw, shucks." Don't let it happen to you!

I Want to Be a Star (Fish)!

These animals are for the moderately experienced saltwater aquarist. Maybe someone who's operated a successful community tank for a year or more without too much loss of life. Of course, starfish, and their many cousins, are not fish at all. They are part of the echinoderm group. These are sea animals with spiny skins. They will come running at feeding time once they understand it. They move slowly, but can move quickly if necessary.

You can buy a starfish or sea star that's missing part of a leg. Starfish regenerate quite easily. However, never buy a starfish that has any kind of sore or tumor, because that animal will not survive.

Some of the most popular starfish that will survive in a home aquarium are:

- Brittle stars Ophiocoma (species)
- Serpent stars Ophioderma (species)
- Blue starfish (Lincka laevigata)
- Red starfish (Fromia elegans)
- Chocolate chip starfish (Protoreaster)

Don't Mess with the Following Fish!

If you are a beginner, the fish mentioned in this section are not for you! The following is a list of species that you should avoid in your tropical community aquarium. You are likely to see these fish in your local pet store. They are arranged by their zoological family.

ANGELFISH
Three-spot angelfish *(Apolemichthys trimaculatus):* Delicate, territorial.

Purple moon angelfish *(Arusetta asfur):* Aggressive, territorial.

Bicolor cherub *(Centropyge bicolor):* Delicate.

Blue-faced angelfish *(Euxiphipops xanthometapon):* Delicate.

Queen angelfish *(Holocanthus bermudensis):* Aggressive, territorial, grows large.

King angelfish *(Holocanthus passer):* Very aggressive, grows large.

Rock beauty *(Holocanthus tricolor):* Very aggressive, finicky.

French angelfish *(Pomacanthus paru):* Grows large.

Koran angelfish *(Pomacanthus semi-circulatus):* Grows large, territorial.

Regal angelfish *(Pygoplites diacanthus):* Delicate.

BLENNIES
False cleanerfish *(Aspidontus taeniatus):* Predatory, biter.

Redlip blenny *(Ophioblennius atlanticus):* Territorial.

BOX FISH
Spotted box fish *(Ostracion meleagris):* Secretes poison, delicate.

BUTTERFLY FISH
Yellow long-nosed butterfly fish *(Forcipiger flavissimus):* Delicate, needs perfect water quality.

Pakistani butterfly fish *(Chaetodon collare):* Difficult to feed.

Saddleback butterfly fish *(Chaetodon ephipippium):* Finicky eater; aggressive.

Banded butterfly fish *(Chaetodon striatus):* Delicate, aggressive.

Copper-band butterfly fish *(Chelmon rostratus):* Delicate, finicky eater; requires very high water quality.

Four-eyed butterfly fish *(Chaetodon capistratus):* Delicate.

Red-headed butterfly fish *(Chaetodon larvatus):* Delicate.

Chevron butterfly fish *(Chaetodon trifascialis):* Delicate.

DAMSELFISH
Blue devil *(Pomacentrus coeruleus):* Aggressive.

DOTTYBACKS
False gramma *(Pseudochromis paccagnellae):* Aggressive.

FAIRY BASSLETS
Black-cap gramma *(Gramma melacara):* Highly territorial.

Royal gramma *(Gramma loreto):* Highly territorial.

FILEFISH
Long-nosed filefish *(Oxymonocanthus longirostris):* Delicate.

LIONFISH
Turkeyfish *(Dendrochirus brachypterus):* Predatory.

Lionfish *(Pterois* species): Predatory.

MORAY EELS
Snowflake Moray *(Echidna nebulosa):* Large, predatory

Reticulated Moray *(Gymnothorax tesselatus):* Large, predatory.

PORCUPINE FISH
Spiny box fish *(Chilomycterus schoepfi):* Large, predatory.

Long-spined porcupine fish *(Diodon holacanthus):* Large, predatory.

Common porcupine fish *(Diodon hystrix):* Large, fouls water during eating.

PUFFER FISH
Spotted puffer *(Arothron meleagris):* Large, fouls water during eating.

SEA BASSES
Marine Betta *(Calloplesiops altivelis):* Predatory.

Coral Trout *(Cephalopholis miniatus):* Large, predatory.

Golden-stripe grouper *(Grammistes sexlineatus):* Large, predatory.

SEA HORSES/PIPEFISH
Banded pipefish *(Dunkerocampus dactyliophorus):* Delicate.

Florida Sea horse *(Hippocampus erectus):* Delicate

Yellow Sea horse *(Hippocampus kuda):* Delicate.

SNAPPERS
Emperor snapper *(Lutjanus sebae):* Grows too large.

SQUIRREL FISH
Common squirrel fish *(Holocentrus diadema):* Predatory, boisterous.

SURGEONS AND TANGS
Achilles tang *(Acanthurus achilles):* Delicate, aggressive.

Blue tang *(Acanthurus coeruleus):* Aggressive as juveniles.

Yellow tang *(Zebrasoma flavescens):* Highly territorial.

TRIGGERFISH
Undulate triggerfish *(Balistapus undulatus):* Large, very aggressive.

White-lined triggerfish *(Balistes bursa):* Aggressive.

Queen triggerfish *(Balistes vetula):* Large predator.

Clown triggerfish *(Balistoides conspicillum):* Large predator.

WRASSES
Dwarf parrot wrasse *(Cirrhilabrus rubriventralis):* Delicate.

Twin-spot wrasse *(Coris angulata):* Grows too large.

Birdmouth wrasse *(Gomphosus caeruleus):* Boisterous.

Harlequin tuskfish *(Lienardella fasciata):* Large, predatory.

Moon wrasse *(Thalassoma lunare):* Boisterous, large, aggressive.

Once you've been able to establish and maintain a community saltwater tank, expanding your knowledge and abilities, then and only then will you be prepared to keep some of the more delicate species. Once you've attained the knowledge, then watch out. You will, in fact, be the Jacques Cousteau of the aquarium world, and you will be able to establish an aquarium of almost any species. Maybe you'll establish a species-only tank, or a mixed grouping of aggressive species. But that's a little ways off. Right now you're at the guppy level. For now, let's just learn how to maintain water quality with a few peaceful and hardy fish, and see if we can keep them alive.

Experts Only—No Rookies Allowed!

Some fish are all difficult to keep, and they are the fish you will most readily see available in pet stores. To keep these fish you need to have more solid information per species than there is room for in this book. However, we have identified them and have identified some of their difficulties. We cannot stress enough how much more you should investigate these species before keeping them. In fact, if you are already an experienced saltwater aquarist, you probably have established relationships with a few shopkeepers and pet store professionals you trust.

Some of the species listed here are usually available only through mail order or direct sales situations. Some of these incompatible fish can live with each other, just as some incompatible freshwater fish can. And, just like in the freshwater world, some can only live alone or with those of their own kind. Find out as much as you can about these fish. Talk to everyone you can before you spend countless hours and money. Then have fun. Yes, fun. Setting up a species tank is very involved. Many who spend time setting up species tanks try to recreate the many areas these fish come from, down to minute details. The more you try to emulate their wild environs, the more chance you have of creating a unique and exciting habitat for your fish and for yourself.

Maintaining Your Saltwater Aquarium

Maintaining a freshwater and a saltwater aquarium are very much the same, with several variations. Many of the things covered here are substantially the same as in the first section. In some cases we will repeat material where it seems best to do so. However, you should read Section 1 in order to understand many of the concepts and routines necessary to establish and maintain a healthy marine community tank.

Feeding

Is there any difference in feeding saltwater versus freshwater fish. No, not really. Both categories have herbivores, carnivores, and omnivores. The variety of foods and how to prepare them are indeed the same.

The dietary needs of some of the saltwater fish are unique. Then again those needs also exist in the freshwater world as well. Many have been covered in the preceding section. As far as what foods to feed them, you can read about them in Section 1, under feeding. All the main foods for fish are covered therein. You can feed your marine fish all of the same kinds of foods that freshwater fish eat. However, make sure the flake food and pellet food you purchase is formulated for marine fishes.

Maintaining Your Aquarium

As in freshwater aquarium maintenance, saltwater maintenance requires the same vigilance. Your tank's maintenance includes everything from turning the hood light on and off every day, to maintaining a feeding schedule, to making time to observe the fish. The last of these tasks should be the most satisfying and interesting. You need to get to know your fish. You need to understand how they interact. If you do, this will help you key into any unusual behavior much more quickly and effectively. You should always carefully check your fish for the slightest signs of stress or illness. Are their bodies marked or marred in any way?

Be Cautious!

An ounce of prevention is worth a pound of cure in the saltwater community tank. Make sure to do the little things, and you won't have to worry about the big ones.

In a saltwater aquarium, you especially need to maintain water quality and salinity. You need to make sure your filter is operating effectively, that the water temperature is constant, and that all your other equipment is functioning at optimum levels. The less change in your aquarium, the less likely you are to cause stress to your fish.

Always maintain the water level and specific gravity. The water level should always be topped off, but remember to use aged freshwater! Inspect the air pump and airstones. Be sure to empty the protein skimmer cup. You need to check these things daily. Don't be lazy. They'll only take a few minutes and will add count-less hours of fun and excitement if you take care of them on a constant basis. A lot of these things can be checked if you just take a few minutes before you feed your fish.

Test the Water

You'll remember that when you were setting up your aquarium, you tested the water every couple of days. Constantly checking the water quality is critical to maintaining a healthy and thriving salt-water community aquarium. Your job doesn't end after you've added your fish. It gets harder! The presence of the fish may influence the water chemistry at any given time, especially in the first two to four months after all the fish have been added. You should check the water twice a week in the first four months. After that, you can slow down to once every two weeks.

Be aware, though. Any sudden changes in behavior, possible sign of illness or stress, loss of appetite, excessive algal growth, or even death should be immediately followed up with a water test. Smelly water or cloudy water are obvious signs of problems that are looming. At this point, you're late, but you should not fail to act immediately.

Water Changes

As with freshwater aquariums, water changes are an integral part of saltwater aquarium maintenance. As covered in Section 1, this is when you literally exchange approximately 20 percent of the tank water for 20 percent new water. Now that we are dealing with

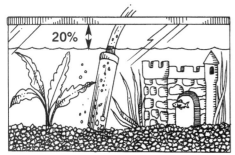

20%

a water change in a saltwater aquarium, you must add 20 percent new salt water. This should be *properly balanced* salt water with the correct pH levels. You should prepare a 5-gallon bucket several days or a week before you'll need to add it.

Some experts think a 10 percent water change every two weeks is the right way to go, while other experts feel it should be 20 percent. In the beginning you should start with a water change of 20 percent every two weeks. You may want to lessen it if your water quality is holding pretty well. Of course, if your water quality isn't holding, you may want to increase the frequency. If this happens too often, your filter may not be powerful enough to support the population of your tank. However, even in good scenarios, you should do this no less than once a month.

Why are these water changes so important? We work so hard to maintain the right water balance, and then we fool around with it. What's up with that? Lest you forget, in nature the flow of water washes away many nitrites and nitrates that are harmful to fish. In the aquarium, there's no fresh flow of water. So you have to supply one. Your water changes will go a long way in maintaining good water quality. You will dilute the number of nitrogenous compounds and harmful gases, as well as other toxic things, and you'll make the water more livable. You'll also add trace elements and nutrients in the water that were exhausted in the water you took out.

To do a water change, you should see the water change and siphoning instructions as outlined in Section 1.

Yearly Maintenance of the Saltwater Aquarium

In Section 1, when we were discussing the freshwater aquarium, you were advised to do a complete aquarium breakdown once a year. A complete breakdown meant that you took apart the aquarium and started all over again. You don't have to do this with a marine aquarium. A well-established biological filter will last for years without having to break everything down. Over a long period of time, however, your under-gravel filter may become clogged by detritus or other deteriorating matter. Gravel itself has been known

Water Changes vs. Changing Water Levels

This is incredibly important! When you add water because of evaporation you add fresh water, because the salt is still in the tank; it's the water that's evaporated.

When you make a water change, you are taking out saltwater, so you must replace it with saltwater. Not remembering this very important fact may cause problems down the line.

to break down over time. Some experts begin to combat this by replacing small amounts of gravel one section at a time over the space of a few months. That way you never fully destroy your biological substrate but can begin to replace deteriorating gravel. Don't try to do this in one step, because you'll have to start all over again, sacrificing the health and well-being of your fish.

Sick Bay—Marine Fish Diseases

If you are going through all the trouble of establishing a successful saltwater tank, it can safely be assumed that you are going to be a saltwater aquarist for some time. That's great news. Now the bad news. The odds will eventually catch up with you. You will have fish that will succumb to illness. Whether through the buildup of stress and the wearing down of the immune system, or through the introduction into the tank of a disease, something will affect your tank.

Freshwater and saltwater fish share some diseases and not others. While the agents and methods may be the same or different, you need not look elsewhere in this book regarding the illnesses and cures of saltwater fish. They are all right here.

Saltwater fishes are prone to many kinds of illnesses. Many kinds of organisms, including parasites, bacteria, viruses, and fungi, are always present. Most illnesses are introduced to your tank by the addition of new fish. Many are very contagious. One of the great things about maintaining high water quality is that it helps keep your fish healthy and less prone to these maladies. Conversely, chronic stress caused by poor water quality will break down your fishes' immune system, weakening their resistance. And that's when the disease most often strikes.

When this happens don't despair. This even happens to the best of experts.

As we discussed in maintenance, observing your fish and checking for signs of illness, stress, or marks is the first line of defense against disease. Once you get to know your fish, you'll be able to pick up on maladies all the sooner. These are some of the signs you need to look out for that indicate problems:

- loss of appetite
- hyperventilation of the gills
- gasping for air near the surface
- odd swimming patterns or behavior
- sudden lack of energy or lack of movement
- rubbing of body or fins
- constant twitching of fins

You should also watch for external signs as well. Places on the body to check include:

- abnormalities of the head
- odd swelling or inflammations of the body
- abnormalities of the fins
- inflamed gills
- irritated or scarred scales
- inflamed or bloated anus

Commercial Remedies

Let's leave the homeopathy alone, at least for now. Especially for beginners, it's recommended that you use the commercial remedies available on the market today. There's nothing wrong with homemade remedies, but you really should leave those to the experts. Buy the name brand, and be safe. Some experts will recommend treats that include things like malachite green or other chemicals. These chemicals must be handled by people who know what they are doing. In the exact dosages, these chemicals are possible cures for what ails your fish. But use too much and they are deadly—usually more so than the disease itself.

At times like this make good use of your pet store professional. They'll usually be able to tell you exactly what it is you should use. Remember, if you don't feel good about your local pet professional's prognosis, then you can always call your local veterinarian. If your local vet doesn't treat fish, he or she can usually refer you to one who does.

Whatever you do, when you apply the remedy, make sure you follow the instructions exactly. Some of these medicinal baths are

quite powerful and over-treatment can be just as deadly as the disease.

Treatment Methods

Now, remember, even the folks on *Chicago Hope* and *ER* lose a few patients. And, unfortunately, so will you. Even though you've put all your energy into saving a fish, and followed all the instructions, sometimes the fish still die.

Basically there are four methods for treating illnesses in saltwater fish:

- directly treating your tank with medicinal treatments
- using a hospital tank
- using the dip method
- administering internal medication

Directly Treating Your Tank

Basically, this means adding the commercial therapies directly to your saltwater aquarium. Some experts call this the long bath. It is effective in many cases, but is not always successful. In some cases, these commercial remedies are absorbed by the aquarium decorations or can be trapped in the filter media. Sometimes they kill the filter bacteria! If this is the case, you are better off singling out the infected fish and using the hospital tank method.

Using a Hospital Tank

Some experts often establish a hospital tank for emergency use. These are usually much smaller than the regular tank, and are usually meant to accommodate one fish. The idea is to place the suffering fish in this isolated chamber to help stop the spread of the disease and to effect the cure, without affecting the other, presumably healthy fish. Also, fish suffering from illness often fall prey to the more aggressive fish. It's one of the realities in the animal world—weakness is a curse. The hospital tank gives the fish a chance to escape its tormentors. At the very least, the hospital tank makes it easier to keep a close eye on the ailing fish.

A 10-gallon tank will make a fine hospital tank. Some experts keep smaller ones, depending on the size of their fish. As with a freshwater hospital tank, in a saltwater hospital tank there are no decorations or gravel. It is kept as bare as possible to lower the risk of infections. You can include a flower pot or rock, but you must throw it away or put it to another use after the treatment is over. Under no circumstances are you to put it into your main aquarium! The hospital tank must have it own filtration system and should not share any waters with the main tank in any way, shape, or form.

Using the Dip Method

While it may seem like a harkening back to the days when doctors were also barbers, the dip method is as stressful to the fish as to the disease. There are different kinds of dips. In effect, you are taking the fish from the aquarium and dipping it into a solution bath of some kind or sometimes just fresh water. Usually the dip isn't too long. This will cause your fish some discomfort, but is enough of a cure to kill some of the bacteria plaguing your fish. One negative aspect about this treatment is that it treats the fish, not your tank, which is also presumably infected as well.

While the saltwater bath has been an invaluable part of the freshwater aquarist's therapeutic methods, the freshwater bath has in fact become one of the most popular cures for certain illnesses. The procedure calls for the dipping of the infected fish into a freshwater bath for three to ten minutes. It is understood that the osmotic differences between the salt water tank and the freshwater treatment bath are enough to quickly destroy certain pathogens. To prepare the bath, fill a 2-gallon container with fresh, aged water. Try to match the temperature and pH of your main aquarium. A trick to elevating the pH is by adding sodium bicarbonate to the freshwater. You should add a quart of saltwater to the bath as an attempt to lessen the osmotic shock to the infected fish. You net the fish in its tank, and then place it in the prepared container. It may lose its bearings at first or act uncontrollably. It should regain itself in a few minutes. If it does not right itself in a few minutes, take the fish out and place it back in the tank.

Administering Internal Medication

Odd as it may sound, sometimes your ill fish needs medicine that can only be administered internally. Owners sometimes administer the medicine with a syringe (no needle) or with an eyedropper. Internal medicines don't always necessitate the handling of the fish. Sometimes the fish can be given its medicine by including it in the fish's food. This isn't always as easy as it sounds. Sometimes it's hard to estimate the correct dosage in these instances, and you can't always insure that the right fish is eating it. It's not a thoroughly successful treatment, and so should be generally avoided by the beginner.

Some Common Disease Treatments

The number of treatments offered to the freshwater aquarist vary greatly. However, the saltwater aquarist is not so lucky. In fact, the number is quite small. And they are not always successful even in cases where they are known to be a cure. Truth be known, they are successful only some of the time.

Copper or antibiotics are the cod-liver oil and Pepto Bismol of the saltwater aquarist's world.

Copper

In the open ocean, copper is thought of as a pollutant. However, many experts believe it can produce cures by killing parasites. However, like any other treatment, copper is known to not have a good effect on fish. Some experts, on the other hand, believe it serves no purpose and is basically a torture to the fish. There is no clear answer. In the end, it continues to be a popular treatment offered in the pet trade. Generally speaking, it is recommended you stay away from the use of copper treatments. Use them only if no other treatments are available, and only as a last-ditch effort. Always use copper treatments in an isolated setting, such as a hospital tank, or unless otherwise instructed. Also, copper is deadly to invertebrates! So be careful!

Antibiotics

Most antibiotics are chemotherapeutic agents that are used to treat many saltwater diseases. If you are going to use antibiotics, you must use them in conjunction with a hospital tank. You don't want to adversely affect your main aquarium. While many consider antibiotics cure-alls, this is not the case. While they have sometimes proven to be effective, they have not been proven to be what some claim they are. In short, they don't always work.

Get Well Soon— Common Aquarium Diseases

The illnesses that can afflict saltwater fish are innumerable. While some are peculiar to specific fishes, others are easily passed between species. Not all are common in the average home aquarium. Bacteria, viruses, fungi, or parasites are the four major causes of illness.

The listing that follows will give the saltwater aquarist a solid overview of the diseases you will most likely encounter in your saltwater community aquarium. It is arranged by grouping, so that it is easier to follow. Certainly, there are more intense books on fish illnesses available. They can be found in pet stores, libraries, or purchased through the Internet.

Bacterial Diseases

Bacteria are microscopic organisms, usually single-celled, that are able to reproduce quickly. Bacteria exist in countless living spaces, and there are thousands of different types. Some bacteria, as we already know, are beneficial. The under-gravel filter is proof of that. But some will obviously cause infection, too.

Fin Rot

Symptoms: Fin rot is an external bacterial infection. It displays itself by eroding or rotting the fins and fin rays of the fish. The fin base often reddens due to irritation, too. If the disease goes untreated for too long, the illness will spread to the skin. It will cause ulcers in the skin and bleeding, and will affect the lungs in the same way.

Emergency Cleaning

This takes place when the tank has been heavily infected.

As with an emergency cleaning for a freshwater tank, the tank is emptied. Everything is sterilized. The aquarium water is dumped. Save nothing! A new tank must be immediately established. All tank decorations must be boiled or discarded. Wood is discarded. Plastic plants should be replaced as a precaution. Nothing from the old tank gets placed in the "new" tank without being scoured or sterilized in some way. The fish should be netted. No gravel or bacteria from the old tanks should be saved.

Treatment: The appearance of this disease is often attributed to deteriorating water quality. Steps must be taken immediately. You must improve the water quality. Quickly prepare for a partial water change, vacuum as much detritus off the gravel as possible, and change the activated carbon in your filter. The antibiotics Furanace, Augmentin, and Ciprofloxin are recommended. They are sometimes proven to be effective.

Fish Tuberculosis, Wasting Disease

Symptoms: It is difficult to spot this disease since it is internal. The infected fish many appear fine externally. Infected fish may survive up to a year, maybe more at most. Lesions on the skin, emaciation, labored breathing, scale loss, frayed fins, and loss of appetite are all external signs that the fish is diseased. However, by the time you notice these symptoms, it is often too late.

Treatment: This disease is passed on orally from fish to fish. This happens through raw infected fish flesh, detritus, and the feces of infected fish. Skin wounds and lesions can easily be infected by these bacteria. Sad to say, the best cure is prevention. If you are feeding raw fish or shellfish to your fish, you should stop for a while. Antibiotics are recommended. These include kanamycin, erythromycin, and streptomycin. All of these have exhibited some success in fighting these bacteria.

The aquarium may be extremely infected. The only possible treatment at this point is an emergency cleaning.

Vibriosis, Ulcer Disease

Symptoms: Lethargy, darkening of color, anemia, ulcers on the skin and lower jaw, bleeding of the gills, skin, and intestinal tract, clouded eyes, loose scales, pale gills, and sudden death.

Treatment: In this disease, bacteria usually establish themselves in the intestinal tracts of healthy fish. They become active, and of course, thrive, when the fish become stressed. Thus, stress equals infection. Poor water quality, crowding, excessive handling, and copper treatments are common causes of stress in aquarium fish. Using the dip method with antibiotic compounds, including Furanace, erythromycin, halquinol, and nitrofurazone, have sometimes shown signs of success.

Viral Disease

Viruses are simple microscopic organisms. However, they thrive and survive by inserting themselves into the cells of their victim. Many times, unfortunately, viral diseases are not treatable.

Cauliflower Disease, Lymphocystis

Symptoms: fin and body lesions that are raised, whitish, warty, and have a lumpy texture like cauliflower. These lesions may take three to four weeks to reach their full size. Despite displaying these symptoms, the diseased fish usually show little distress. In fact, they often continue to feed and behave normally. This infection is usually not deadly; however, it is contagious.

Treatment: The best treatment is the hospital tank. Isolation is the best possible thing, as the fish needs time to let its immune system deal with the illness. This may taken two to three months. Other than that, there really is no cure.

Fungal Diseases

Fungi are plant-like organisms. They tend to be parasitic in nature. They need to feed off of living things—especially fishes. They can sometimes cause illness.

Ichthyophonus Disease, Whirling Disease

Symptoms: In this disease, fungi invade the internal organs of a fish. They infect the kidney, heart, spleen, and liver. Symptoms include emaciation, spinal curvature, darkening or paling of the skin, roughening of the skin, fin erosion, and skin ulcers. Erratic swimming may also be a sign of this disease. This fungus is like something out of the movie *Alien*. A parasitic organism or fungal cyst is usually ingested by the fish. Once inside the fish, the organism bursts and enters the bloodstream. Once in the bloodstream, they infect the internal organs.

Treatment: Usually, infected fish die in as little as two months. Treatment is very difficult, because the illness doesn't expose itself until it's too late to save the fish. The affected fish must be removed from the tank immediately. This disease can be contagious.

Exophiala Disease

Symptoms: Lethargy, disorientation, and abnormal swimming are signs of this fungal infection.

Treatment: Not much is known about this fungus. No successful treatment is known. You should isolate the infected fish, perhaps using a hospital tank, in order to prevent other cohabitants from contracting the disease.

Parasitic Diseases

Parasites

There are a wide range of parasites that are small one-celled organisms. Protozoa, crustaceans, and worms are just a few. The parasite is not usually the direct cause of death. It desires to feed off the host, indefinitely if it can. However, the parasite leaves wounds on the skin, which leaves the fish vulnerable to other bacteria. Parasites can occur both internally and externally. Internal parasites are more difficult to detect, while exterior ones are often easy to spot.

Marine Velvet Disease (aka rust disease)

Symptoms: The gills are the first to show signs of infection. It then spreads to the skin, which becomes dull, patchy, and velvet-like; white spots are visible on sections of intact skin. As the disease takes hold, the fish may exhibit loss of appetite, gasping, scratching against objects, and sluggishness. The lesions may lead to secondary bacterial infection.

Treatment: There is no surefire cure. Some antibiotics have shown some success in combating this illness. Some of those that have exhibited success include malachite green, nitrofurazone, and acriflavin. The freshwater dip sometimes dislodges these parasites from the host. However, these parasites do not die in freshwater. Treatments can sometimes take a long time. If there are sign of aquarium infection, that being more than one case of it, then the tank will require an emergency cleaning. It's the only sure way to know you've eradicated the disease in your aquarium.

Marine White Spot, Cryptocaryoniasis, Marine Ich

Symptoms: Early signs include loss of appetite, cloudy eyes, troubled breathing, excess skin mucus, and pale skin. Later, white spots appear on the skin, gills, and eyes. Death follows within a few days after these later symptoms appear, most likely due to gill damage.

CONCLUSION

As stated above, your pet store and your pet store professional will have a lot of information on the latest and most effective commercial remedies. Make sure always to follow the directions carefully and not to over expose the fish to any of these. Sometimes they are more deadly than the disease your fish is fighting. You don't want your fish to die from the cure, you want it to survive the cure.

In the end, one of the best ways to cure all illnesses is to maintain a healthy, vibrant tank. What's that little ditty? An ounce of prevention is worth a pound of cure. If stress is the major reason any fish gets sick, it's important to remove the possibility of stress right from the start.

Remember, many diseases exist all around fish, everyday. Just like they do humans. The healthier your fish, the less likely they will be to fall victim to these predators. Proper maintenance and feeding will keep your fish healthy and disease resistant.

Treatment: Much like marine velvet, this parasite is resistant to most treatments. Worse yet, it remains imbedded in the gravel of your aquarium! While the freshwater dip can sometimes be effective in destroying the parasites on the fish, it does nothing to treat the tank. The best thing to do is treat the entire tank. The antibiotic chloramin T has been used somewhat effectively to confront this illness.

Uronema

Symptoms: External ulcers, muscle and skin bleeding, lethargic behavior, sloughing of the skin, and internal infection are signs of this disease. Death can occur quickly because the circulation in the gills is impaired.

Treatment: Not much is known about this parasite. Formalin and malachite green are recommended. Treat the infected fish separately in a hospital tank.

Tang Turbellarian Disease, Black Spot

Symptoms: While the appellation implies that only tangs may be afflicted, this is not the case. Many varieties of fish may be infected. In the parasitic phase these organisms look like numerous dark spots distributed unevenly over the fins, gills, and body. Other signs include fasting, listlessness, paling or whitish skin, and scratching against objects. Secondary bacterial infections are known to occur as well.

Treatment: As with most parasitic infestations, the more crowded your tank, the faster these things will spread from fish to fish. The freshwater dip, trochlorfon, or praziquantel immersion have all proven to be successful.

Trematode Infestations

Symptoms: These tiny worms are too small to view without a microscope. They normally infect the gills, eyes, skin, mouth, and anal opening. Infected fishes usually rub themselves against objects in the aquarium. The fish are obviously trying to dislodge these parasites. Unfortunately, they are increasing their risk of furthering this illness. The rubbing usually causes more damage. This further damage leads to secondary bacterial infections.

Treatment: These infestations are somewhat difficult to eradicate. Immersion in freshwater, mebendazole, praziquantel, or trichlorfon have all showed promise against this illness.

Crustacean Infestations

Symptoms: Many of these tiny crab-like organisms are visible to the naked eye. Copepods will remain fixed in the same position while argulids will move over the surface of the host. Both groups feed by piercing the host, causing tissue damage. Fishes with heavy infestations swim erratically, rub against objects, and jump. The lesions will eventually be infected by bacteria.

Treatment: Remove the infested fish immediately! You must also quickly remove all the aquarium decorations. Either dry them to kill egg masses or immerse them in 2 percent Clorox solution for two hours. Treat infested fishes by immersing them in trichlorfon or malathion baths in a hospital tank.

Other Health Problems

Head and Lateral Line Erosion

Symptoms: As in the freshwater disease, hole-in-the-head, holes develop and enlarge in the sensory pits of the head. The disease also moves on down the lateral line on the body. The disease will progress slowly. For a while the fish does not seem to be affected. Advanced stages can lead to secondary bacterial infection, and later to death.

Treatment: There are no specific treatments for this disease although some recommend the use of the freshwater antibiotic Flagyl. Check your water quality and make necessary adjustments. You should also make sure that you are meeting the nutritional needs of your fish. Diversify their diet and add vitamin supplements to their food.

Poisoning

Symptoms: Low levels of toxins in the aquarium will stress fish, thereby lowering their resistance to other diseases. Higher levels will cause abnormal behavior including darting movements, jumping, and gasping at the surface.

Treatment: Make sure that activated carbon is being used to remove toxins and conduct a 20 percent to 40 percent water change. If pollutant levels are high, move the fish to the hospital tank until the main aquarium water problems are corrected.

CHAPTER EIGHT

Resources

Magazines, Web Sites, and Bibliography

Magazines

There are several major aquarist magazines on the market. They are excellent resources that include articles on the latest fish and aquarium information and technologies. They are very widely distributed and contain a great wealth of information and resources for the interested aquarist. Aquarium Fish Magazine

Fancy Publications
P.O. Box 5331
Boulder, CO 80322

Tropical Fish Hobbyist
TFH Publications
One TFH Plaza
Neptune City, NJ 07753

Freshwater and Marine Aquarium
R/C Modeler Corp
P.O. Box 487
Sierre Madre, CA 91025

Practical Fishkeeping
Motorsport
550 Honey Locust Road
Jonesburg, MO 63351

Marine Fish Monthly
Publishing Concepts Corp.
3243 Highway 61
East Luttrell, TN 37779

Koi USA
P.O. Box 1
Midway City, CA 93655

Mid-Atlantic Koi
3290 Shaker Ct.
Montclair, NJ 22026
Pondkeeper Magazine

Garden Pond Promotions, Inc.
1000 Whitetail Ct.
Duncansville, PA 16635

Watergardening
49 Boonevillage
Zionsville, IN 46077

Web Sites

General Pet Sites
Petopia
www.petopia.com

Pets.com
pets.com

ACME Pet
www.acmepet.com

Tropical Fish Sites
Badman's Tropical Fish
www.geocities.com/Heartland/Plains/8115/index.html

Conway Tropical Fish
www.pbsco.com/conwayfish/index.html

Dragon Fish Industry
dragonfish.com/

Fish
pages.prodigy.com/aqua/home.htm

Freshwater Tropical Fish
*www.geocities.com/Heartland/Plains/8115/
index.html*

Jeff's Exotic Fish
www.exoticfish.com/

The Krib
www.thekrib.com/index.html

Tom's Caribbean Tropicals
www.divertom.com/

Tropical Fish Food
www.mreed.com/

Tropical Fish Central
www.geocities.com/HotSprings/3689/

Tropical Fish Centre
www.radtropical.force9.co.uk/

Tropical Fish Page
imagine-hawaii.com/tropical.html

Tropical Fish Online Store
www.fishsupply.com/

Angelfish Sites
AngelsPlus Home Page
www.angelsplus.com/

Goldfish Sites
A & P Trading Company
www.ap-goldfish.com/

The Goldfish Sanctuary
www.petlibrary.com/goldfish/goldfish.html

RWT's Goldfish Information Page
www.geocities.com/Tokyo/4468/

Goldfish Society of America
www.geocities.com/Heartland/Plains/8894/

My Pet Site! Goldfish Chat!
*www.geocities.com/Heartland/Hills/5086/
chat.htm*

Nippon Goldfish Company
www.nippongoldfish.com/

Koi Sites
Utah Koi
home.att.net/~utahkoi/

Oscar Sites
Oscarfish.com
www.oscarfish.com/

Suppliers
All Glass Aquarium
www.all-glass.com/

Aqualog Books
www.aqlog.com/

Aquarium Pharmaceuticals
www.aquariumpharm.com/

Aquarium World
www.aqworld.net/

Mail Order Pet Supplies
www.mops.on.ca/

San Francisco Bay Brand
www.sfbb.com/

Singapore Supreme Aquarium
www.supremefish.com.sg/

Waterwerks Aquariums
www.waterwerks.net/

Bibliography

Andrew, Dr. Chris. *Fancy Goldfishes.* Morris Plains: Tetra Press, 1987.

Axelrod, H. R. *Encyclopedia of Tropical Fishes: With Special Emphasis on Techniques of Breeding.* Neptune City: TFH Publications, 1986.

Axelrod, H. R. *Tropical Fish as a New Pet.* Neptune City: TFH Publications, 1991.

Axelrod, Dr. Herbert R., and Dr. Leonard P. Schultz. *Handbook of Tropical Aquarium Fishes.* Neptune: TFH., 1955, 1990 ed.

Axelrod, Dr. Herbert R., and William Vanderwinkler. *Goldfish and Koi in Your Home.* Neptune: TFH, revised edition 1984.

Bailey, M., and G. Sandford. *The Ultimate Aquarium.* New York: Smithmark Publishers, 1995.

Barrie, Anmarie. *Goldfish as a New Pet.* Neptune: TFH, 1990.

Barrie, Anmarie. *The Professional's Book of Koi.* Neptune: TFH Publications, Inc., 1992.

Blasiola, G. *Koi.* Hauppauge: Barron's Educational Series, Inc., 1995.

Bower, C. E. *The Basic Marine Aquarium.* Springfield: Charles C. Thomas Publishing, 1983.

Burgess, W. E. *Marine Aquariums: A Complete Introduction.* Neptune City: TFH Publications, 1989.

Burgess, W. E., H.R. Axelrod, and R.E. Hunziker III. *Atlas of Marine Aquarium Fishes.* Neptune City: TFH Publications, 1990.

Coborn, John. *Howell Beginner's Guide to Goldfish.* New York: Howell Book House, 1985.

Conrad, R. *An Owner's Guide to the Garden Pond.* New York: Howell Book House, 1998.

Dakin, N. *The Macmillan Book of the Marine Aquarium.* New York: Macmillan Publishing Co., 1992.

DeVito, C. and G. Skomal. *The Goldfish: An Owner's Guide to a Happy Healthy Pet.* New York: Howell Book House, 1996.

Emmens, C. W. *Tropical Fish: A Complete Introduction.* Neptune City: TFH Publications Inc., 1987.

Eschmeyer, W. M. *Catalogue of the Genera of Recent Fishes.* San Francisco: California Academy of Sciences, 1990.

Freise, U. E. *Aquarium Fish.* Neptune City: TFH Publications Inc., 1989.

Geran, James. *The Proper Care of Goldfish.* Neptune: TFH, 1992.

Goldfish Society of America. *The Official Guide to Goldfish.* Neptune: TFH, 1991.

Grzimek, Dr. Bernhard, and W. Ladiges. *Grzimek's Animal Life Encyclopedia.* New York: Van Nostrand Reinhold Company, 1973.

Halstead, B. W., and B. L. Landa. *Tropical Fish.* New York: Golden Press, 1975, 1985.

Hervey, George F., and Jack Hems. *The Goldfish.* London: Faber And Faber, 1968 edition.

James, B. *A Fishkeeper's Guide to Aquarium Plants.* London: Salamander Books, 1986.

Kay, G. *The Tropical Marine Fish Survival Manual.* London: Quarto Inc., 1995.

Lundegaard, G. *Keeping Marine Fish: An Aquarium Guide.* New York: Sterling Publishing Co., 1991.

Melzak, M. *The Marine Aquarium Manual.* New York: Arco Publishing Inc., 1984.

Mills, D. *Aquarium Fish.* New York: Dorling Kindersley Publishing, 1993.

Moyle, P. B., and J. J. Cech, Jr. *Fishes: An Introduction to Ichthyology.* Englewood Cliffs: Prentice-Hall Inc., 1982.

Ostrow, Marshall. *Goldfish.* Hauppauge: Barron's, 1985.

Paradise, Paul. *Goldfish.* Neptune: T.F.H., 1992.

Penes, B., and I. Tolg. *Goldfish and Ornamental Carp.* Hauppauge: Barron's, 1986.

Piers, Helen. *Taking Care of Your Goldfish.* Hauppauge: Barron's, 1993.

Rothbard, S. *Koi Breeding.* Neptune: TFH Publications, Inc., 1997.

Sandford, G. *An Illustrated Encyclopedia of Aquarium Fish.* New York: Howell Book House, 1995.

Scheurmann, I. *The New Aquarium Handbook.* Hauppauge: Barron's, 1986.

Scheurmann, I. *Water Plants in the Aquarium.* Hauppauge, Barron's, 1987.

Schnieder, Earl. *All About Aquariums.* Neptune: TFH, 1966, 1982 ed.

Scott, P. W. *The Complete Aquarium.* New York: Dorling Kindersley Publishing, 1995.

Seto, Zenji. *Goldfish and Fish-Pathology and Its Treatment.* New York: Museum of Naural History Archives, 1934.

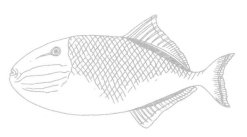

Skomal, Gregory. *The Koi: An Owner's Guide to a Happy Healthy Pet.* New York: Howell Book House, 1999.

Skomal, Gregory. *Starting a Freshwater Aquarium: An Owner's Guide to a Happy Healthy Pet.* New York: Howell Book House, 1997.

Skomal, Gregory. *Starting A Saltwater Aquarium: An Owner's Guide to a Happy Healthy Pet.* New York: Howell Book House, 1998.

Spotte, S. *Captive Seawater Fishes: Science and Technology.* New York: John Wiley and Sons, 1992.

Spotte, S. *Seawater Aquariums.* New York: John Wiley and Sons, 1979.

Stadelmann, P. *Tropical Fish: A Complete Pet Owner's Manual.* Hauppauge: Barron's, 1991.

Stoskopf, M. K. *Fish Medicine.* Philadelphia: W. B. Saunders Co., 1993.

Teitler, Neal. *The ABCs of Goldfish.* Neptune: TFH, 1986.

Waddington, P. *Koi Kichi.* Cheshire: Peter Waddington Ltd., 1997.

Wardley Coporation. *Fin Facts Aquarium Handbook.* Secaucus: Wardley Corporation, 1992.

Wisner, S. C., and F. A. Simon. *Keeping Koi.* New York: Sterling Publishing Co., Inc., 1996.

Index

We Have EVERYTHING!

Everything® **After College Book**
$12.95, 1-55850-847-3

Everything® **American History Book**
$12.95, 1-58062-531-2

Everything® **Angels Book**
$12.95, 1-58062-398-0

Everything® **Anti-Aging Book**
$12.95, 1-58062-565-7

Everything® **Astrology Book**
$12.95, 1-58062-062-0

Everything® **Baby Names Book**
$12.95, 1-55850-655-1

Everything® **Baby Shower Book**
$12.95, 1-58062-305-0

Everything® **Baby's First Food Book**
$12.95, 1-58062-512-6

Everything® **Baby's First Year Book**
$12.95, 1-58062-581-9

Everything® **Barbeque Cookbook**
$12.95, 1-58062-316-6

Everything® **Bartender's Book**
$9.95, 1-55850-536-9

Everything® **Bedtime Story Book**
$12.95, 1-58062-147-3

Everything® **Bicycle Book**
$12.00, 1-55850-706-X

Everything® **Build Your Own Home Page**
$12.95, 1-58062-339-5

Everything® **Business Planning Book**
$12.95, 1-58062-491-X

Everything® **Casino Gambling Book**
$12.95, 1-55850-762-0

Everything® **Cat Book**
$12.95, 1-55850-710-8

Everything® **Chocolate Cookbook**
$12.95, 1-58062-405-7

Everything® **Christmas Book**
$15.00, 1-55850-697-7

Everything® **Civil War Book**
$12.95, 1-58062-366-2

Everything® **College Survival Book**
$12.95, 1-55850-720-5

Everything® **Computer Book**
$12.95, 1-58062-401-4

Everything® **Cookbook**
$14.95, 1-58062-400-6

Everything® **Cover Letter Book**
$12.95, 1-58062-312-3

Everything® **Crossword and Puzzle Book**
$12.95, 1-55850-764-7

Everything® **Dating Book**
$12.95, 1-58062-185-6

Everything® **Dessert Book**
$12.95, 1-55850-717-5

Everything® **Digital Photography Book**
$12.95, 1-58062-574-6

Everything® **Dog Book**
$12.95, 1-58062-144-9

Everything® **Dreams Book**
$12.95, 1-55850-806-6

Everything® **Etiquette Book**
$12.95, 1-55850-807-4

Everything® **Fairy Tales Book**
$12.95, 1-58062-546-0

Everything® **Family Tree Book**
$12.95, 1-55850-763-9

Everything® **Fly-Fishing Book**
$12.95, 1-58062-148-1

Everything® **Games Book**
$12.95, 1-55850-643-8

Everything® **Get-A-Job Book**
$12.95, 1-58062-223-2

Everything® **Get Published Book**
$12.95, 1-58062-315-8

Everything® **Get Ready for Baby Book**
$12.95, 1-55850-844-9

Everything® **Ghost Book**
$12.95, 1-58062-533-9

Everything® **Golf Book**
$12.95, 1-55850-814-7

Everything® **Grammar and Style Book**
$12.95, 1-58062-573-8

Everything® **Guide to Las Vegas**
$12.95, 1-58062-438-3

Everything® **Guide to New York City**
$12.95, 1-58062-314-X

Everything® **Guide to Walt Disney World®, Universal Studios®, and Greater Orlando, 2nd Edition**
$12.95, 1-58062-404-9

Everything® **Guide to Washington D.C.**
$12.95, 1-58062-313-1

Everything® **Guitar Book**
$12.95, 1-58062-555-X

Everything® **Herbal Remedies Book**
$12.95, 1-58062-331-X

Everything® **Home-Based Business Book**
$12.95, 1-58062-364-6

Everything® **Homebuying Book**
$12.95, 1-58062-074-4

Everything® **Homeselling Book**
$12.95, 1-58062-304-2

For more information, or to order, call 800-872-5627
or visit everything.com
Adams Media Corporation, 57 Littlefield Street, Avon, MA 02322

Visit us at everything.com

Everything® **Home Improvement Book**
$12.95, 1-55850-718-3

Everything® **Horse Book**
$12.95, 1-58062-564-9

Everything® **Hot Careers Book**
$12.95, 1-58062-486-3

Everything® **Internet Book**
$12.95, 1-58062-073-6

Everything® **Investing Book**
$12.95, 1-58062-149-X

Everything® **Jewish Wedding Book**
$12.95, 1-55850-801-5

Everything® **Job Interviews Book**
$12.95, 1-58062-493-6

Everything® **Lawn Care Book**
$12.95, 1-58062-487-1

Everything® **Leadership Book**
$12.95, 1-58062-513-4

Everything® **Learning Spanish Book**
$12.95, 1-58062-575-4

Everything® **Low-Fat High-Flavor Cookbook**
$12.95, 1-55850-802-3

Everything® **Magic Book**
$12.95, 1-58062-418-9

Everything® **Managing People Book**
$12.95, 1-58062-577-0

Everything® **Microsoft® Word 2000 Book**
$12.95, 1-58062-306-9

Everything® **Money Book**
$12.95, 1-58062-145-7

Everything® **Mother Goose Book**
$12.95, 1-58062-490-1

Everything® **Mutual Funds Book**
$12.95, 1-58062-419-7

Everything® **One-Pot Cookbook**
$12.95, 1-58062-186-4

Everything® **Online Business Book**
$12.95, 1-58062-320-4

Everything® **Online Genealogy Book**
$12.95, 1-58062-402-2

Everything® **Online Investing Book**
$12.95, 1-58062-338-7

Everything® **Online Job Search Book**
$12.95, 1-58062-365-4

Everything® **Pasta Book**
$12.95, 1-55850-719-1

Everything® **Pregnancy Book**
$12.95, 1-58062-146-5

Everything® **Pregnancy Organizer**
$15.00, 1-58062-336-0

Everything® **Project Management Book**
$12.95, 1-58062-583-5

Everything® **Puppy Book**
$12.95, 1-58062-576-2

Everything® **Quick Meals Cookbook**
$12.95, 1-58062-488-X

Everything® **Resume Book**
$12.95, 1-58062-311-5

Everything® **Romance Book**
$12.95, 1-58062-566-5

Everything® **Sailing Book**
$12.95, 1-58062-187-2

Everything® **Saints Book**
$12.95, 1-58062-534-7

Everything® **Selling Book**
$12.95, 1-58062-319-0

Everything® **Spells and Charms Book**
$12.95, 1-58062-532-0

Everything® **Stress Management Book**
$12.95, 1-58062-578-9

Everything® **Study Book**
$12.95, 1-55850-615-2

Everything® **Tall Tales, Legends, and Outrageous Lies Book**
$12.95, 1-58062-514-2

Everything® **Tarot Book**
$12.95, 1-58062-191-0

Everything® **Time Management Book**
$12.95, 1-58062-492-8

Everything® **Toasts Book**
$12.95, 1-58062-189-9

Everything® **Total Fitness Book**
$12.95, 1-58062-318-2

Everything® **Trivia Book**
$12.95, 1-58062-143-0

Everything® **Tropical Fish Book**
$12.95, 1-58062-343-3

Everything® **Vitamins, Minerals, and Nutritional Supplements Book**
$12.95, 1-58062-496-0

Everything® **Wedding Book, 2nd Edition**
$12.95, 1-58062-190-2

Everything® **Wedding Checklist**
$7.95, 1-58062-456-1

Everything® **Wedding Etiquette Book**
$7.95, 1-58062-454-5

Everything® **Wedding Organizer**
$15.00, 1-55850-828-7

Everything® **Wedding Shower Book**
$7.95, 1-58062-188-0

Everything® **Wedding Vows Book**
$7.95, 1-58062-455-3

Everything® **Wine Book**
$12.95, 1-55850-808-2

Everything® **World War II Book**
$12.95, 1-58062-572-X

Everything® is a registered trademark of Adams Media Corporation.

**For more information, or to order, call 800-872-5627
or visit everything.com**
Adams Media Corporation, 57 Littlefield Street, Avon, MA 02322

We Have

EVERYTHING KIDS'®

Everything® Kids' Baseball Book
$6.95, 1-58062-688-2

Everything® Kids' Joke Book
$6.95, 1-58062-686-6

Everything® Kids' Mazes Book
$6.95, 1-58062-558-4

Everything® Kids' Money Book
$6.95, 1-58062-685-8

Everything® Kids' Nature Book
$6.95, 1-58062-684-X

Everything® Kids' Online Book
$9.95, 1-58062-394-8

Everything® Kids' Puzzle Book
$6.95, 1-58062-687-4

Everything® Kids' Science Experiments Book
$6.95, 1-58062-557-6

Everything® Kids' Space Book
$9.95, 1-58062-395-6

Everything® Kids' Witches and Wizards Book
$9.95, 1-58062-396-4

Available wherever books are sold!

For more information, or to order,
call 800-872-5627 or visit everything.com

Adams Media Corporation, 57 Littlefield Street, Avon, MA 02322